Davies Aeschylus, John Fletcher

The Agamemnon of Aeschylus

Davies Aeschylus, John Fletcher

The Agamemnon of Aeschylus

ISBN/EAN: 9783744723060

Printed in Europe, USA, Canada, Australia, Japan

Cover: Foto ©Andreas Hilbeck / pixelio.de

More available books at **www.hansebooks.com**

THE

AGAMEMNON OF ÆSCHYLUS

REVISED AND TRANSLATED

BY

JOHN FLETCHER DAVIES, B.A.,

FIRST CLASSICAL MASTER IN KINGSTOWN SCHOOL, IRELAND.

WILLIAMS AND NORGATE,

14, HENRIETTA STREET, COVENT GARDEN, LONDON
AND 20, SOUTH FREDERICK STREET, EDINBURGH.

KEMINK AND SON,
UTRECHT.

—

1868.

"Farthermore there were lefte out in diuers places of the warke lines and columes, ye and sometyme holle padges, whiche caused, that this moste pleasant auctour coude not well be perceiued: for that, and chaungeyng of wordes, and misordrynge of sentences, wold haue mased his mynde in redyng, that had ben very well lerned: and what can be a greatter blemisshe vnto a noble auctour? And for to preise worthily vnto you the great lernyng of this auctour, I know my selfe right muche vnable, ye shal your selfe now deme, whan ye shal see hym (as nere as I can) set forth in his owne shappe and likenes." Preface to Gower's Poems.

PREFACE.

.

The principal features of this Edition are:

(1) an attempt to reproduce the metres of the Greek Text in a literal line-for-line Translation,

(2) the correction of the Text by the aid of the most recent Æschylean literature,

(3) the arrangement of the lines of the choral odes according to the principles laid down by Boeckh,

(4) the explanation of the Text in an entirely new Commentary,

(5) a statement of the rhythm of each verse in the play.

(1) The deviations from an exact representation of the Greek metres are the substitution of the English decasyllabic for the Greek iambic trimeter and the contraction of resolved syllables in pæons, cretics, and dochmiacs. The anapæstic lines, also, correspond only as consisting of anapæstic feet, i. e., anapæsts, dactyls, and spondees. The correspondence, therefore, consists in the facts that the Greek arsis is represented by the English accent, and that the Greek and English lines have the same number of moræ.

A work of so much difficulty partakes largely of the nature

of a first experiment which is soon superseded by something better
from a more skilful hand; and the Editor naturally hopes for
some indulgence from the reader.

By a 'literal' Translation the Editor means one which follows
the construction of the Greek. With the exception of minor
points, such as 'σιγῶ hush!' and the passages which could not
be literally rendered in any idiomatic prose version, this professes
to be a literal translation. Of course the ordinary and well-
known deviations from the Greek to the English idiom are
systematically made. A peculiarity of the English language is
its neglect of connecting particles between the periods. The
logical connexion is always defined in Greek by the proper particles; in English the reader is nearly always left to discover it
without assistance. The participle and finite verb usually become
two finite verbs. The aorist participle is most frequently rendered
by the English present. The present and imperfect tenses with
a word of time must be translated by the perfect and pluperfect
with 'been', thus: 'I have been asking'. The force of γὰρ in
a monostichia may be given by other words besides 'for'. The
gnomic aorist, as it is called, should always be turned into the
present. Sometimes the Greek idiom prefers the singular number,
while the English demands the plural; and vice versa. In the
use of 'you' and 'thou' the translator must be guided by the
tone of the passage, and the earnestness of the speaker; but,
in general, the former is to be preferred. And so on. Without
the observance of these and other idioms the Translation could
not have passed even for English prose with poetic licenses.
Where words are supplied for the sake of the metre they are
written in italics, and care has been taken to use such words
as would merely help to put the idea more clearly without adding
to or subtracting from the sense or colouring of the sentence.
Such words as are implied in the Greek but not expressed are
not distinguished by italics.

The transcription of Greek proper names is made as nearly as possible like the Greek: thus, Casandra, Ægæan; the Greek names of divinities should, undoubtedly, be retained, but the Editor has once or twice availed himself of 'Jove', 'Mars', and 'Furies' for the sake of the metre. He has always written 'Erinnys' where the Greek name is retained, in order that the proper pronunciation may be evident from the form of the word.

(2)   The Text has been corrected with the aid of the Editions of Professor Karsten 1855, Professor Weil 1858, (whose Eumenides, 1861, contains an appendix to his Agamemnon, and his Persæ, 1867, another appendix) Heimsoeth 1861 and 1862, and Enger 1863. These authors have given an account of the critical discoveries of Schneidewin, Ahrens, and many others. Professor Weil's appendix to his Persæ brings us up to the year 1867. The Editor's own corrections are the result of nearly seven years' special and constant study of this one Text. As a test of his vigilance in retaining or rejecting a vulgate reading the following examples, in which he dissents from the latest Editors, are such as he can most readily call to mind:

Eur. Phœn. 784—793 is sound throughout: the following annotations alone are necessary for the explanation of this exceptionally fine passage. κατέχει 'inspired with a spirit of bloodshed and death' κάτοχος εἶ. οὐκ ἐπὶ καλλιχόροις etc. 'thou dost not, (like Bacchus) to win the prize of the elegant chorus (i. e. in dramatic contests) let loose the curl of youthful loveliness (νεάνιδες ὥρας) and modulate to the breathings of the flute a strain in which are the charms that move the dance'. ἐπὶ with the dat., as in the phrase ἐπὶ τινὶ ἀθλεύειν, ἐπὶ δώρῳ, ἐπὶ μισθῷ, ἐπὶ σοφίᾳ. ἐπιπνεύσας αἵματι Θήβας is a similar use of ἐπὶ 'inspired (trans.) with a desire to win the blood of Thebe'. οὐδ' ὑπὸ θυρσομανεῖ etc. 'nor to the music of the maddened thyrsus-bearer dost thou career with fawn-skins, but thou makest the solid-hoofed colt curvet to the rattle of chariots and quartets of trappings'. ὑπὸ with dat. as in the phrase ὑπ' αὐλητῆρι ἔκιον, ὑπ' αὐλῷ, ὑπὸ κήρυκι, and for the idea compare Hom. Il. 7. 240 δηίῳ μέλπεσθαι Ἄρηϊ 'to dance to the discord of the destroyer Ares'. δινεύειν is both trans., and intrans., in Homer. The difficulty arose from overlooking the carefully arranged antithesis and the meanings of ἐπὶ and ὑπό.

It is shown in the Commentary that Hom. Il. 3. 224 is not spurious.

τεθραμμέναι Æsch. Sept. 792 is undoubtedly sound, and Hermann's corrrection τεθρυμμέναι is absurd. παῖδες ὑπὸ μητέρων τεθραμμέναι is a periphrasis for κόραι.

καταχράσμων Theocr. 4. 22 is sound, and rightly explained by the scholiast κακὸς εἰς τὸ χρῆσθαι αὐτῷ τινα 'for the townspeople drive hard bargains'. Battus is speaking of a bullock for sacrifice; and Virgil knew what he meant, for he says in his imitation Ecl. 1. 35 'quamvis multa meis exiret *victima* septis, pinguis et *ingratæ* premeretur caseus *urbi*': i. e. 'sold many a victim for sacrifice, and many a cheese to the townspeople who showed little gratitude in the price they gave'.

πλάνης τις ὡς Soph. Phil. 758 is sound, whether you take πλάνης to mean 'a planet' or 'an epidemic disease', or to contain an allusion to both.

In Demosthenes' speech against Meidias p. 179. (C. Tauchnitz) p. 525 Reiske, πότερα μὴ δῷ διὰ τοῦτο δίκην, ἢ μείζω δοίη δικαίως; is sound and does not require the κὰν which Bekker, Schafer, and Buttmann wish to introduce. Translate: 'whether *shall we say* 'let him, on this account, not be punished'; or 'would that he might suffer greater punishment, as he deserves'? In the same speech p. 190 (538) καὶ τοῦ πράγματος τῷ πάσχοντι the καὶ has got out of place; it should come after πράγματος.

On the other hand there are some which he rejects although they have never been suspected.

Eur. Med. 240 is corrupt and untranslatable. The lady has

had her husband chosen for her; the question is how to accommodate her disposition and habits to his. We must read ὅπως for ὅτῳ and translate 'and coming into contact with a person of strange habits and rules of conduct, one must be a diviner, since we cannot bring the knowledge from home, how one should treat a husband'.

In the same play, v. 710, χθόνα must be changed to χθονί i. e. Corinth.

In Soph. Ant. 585 γενεᾶς must be changed to γενεᾶν. At v. 596 γενεᾶν must be changed to γενεά.

In the same play v. 990 the vulgate, and Dindorf's, αὕτη is absurd. Read αὐτή, and you have sense.

The Manuscripts of the Agamemnon are:

M. Codex Mediceus, preserved at Florence. It was written about the 10 th. century A.D., and has been collated by Niebuhr, Bekker and C. F. Weber for Hermann, and by John Franz. It is of parchment. A whole quaternio is lost after v. 295. A quaternio is four sheets of parchment (written on both sides) laid on one another and folded once; and so answering to a printer's sheet folded to octavo size and cut, except that these parchments were twice as long as broad, so that, after folding, the leaf is square. Of the next quaternio there is only the first leaf and its fellow the last; the intermediate six leaves are lost. That first leaf contains vv. 1026—1118. The fellow-leaf goes on at the top with Choëph. v. 10 τί χῆμα λεύσσω; The average number of lines on a leaf is $91\frac{1}{4}$. Thus: 1026—295 = 731 which divided by 8 gives $91\frac{3}{8}$: and 1118—1026 = 92: there are 45 lines on the fac-simile page exhibited by Dindorf Æsch. Scholia p. 140. Then for the six lost leaves we get 549 lines, which added to 1118 gives 1667. Subtract 1644, the number of lines in the Agamemnon according to the Fl. Ms., a copy of M., (and also in the editions of Hermann, Enger etc.) and we have remaining 23 lines. Now the Argument of the Eume-

nides is only about four lines. Allow as many for that of
the Choephoræ, and 7, the exact number required for the
Title and Dramatis Personæ, and we have a remainder of
12 as the number of lines lost in the prologue of the Choephoræ. But, by applying Professor Weil's theory, we find
that the latter part of the prologue consists of 6. 4. 2 = 12
lines; therefore the preceding part which is lost was probably
6. 4. 2 = 12, of which 7 lines and parts of two have been
recovered. Therefore the lacunas still existing in the Prologue of the Choephoræ amount to 3 lines and parts of 2.

This calculation and the interpretation of the word quaternio,
which the Ed. has made out from some data furnished in the
editions of Hermann and Enger, require to be verified by inspec-
tion of the Ms. It is assumed that the names of the Dramatis
Personæ occupied each a line.

G.   Codex Guelpherbytanus, of the 15 th. century. A copy
of M. after the losses mentioned above.

Fl.   Codex Florentinus, of the 14 th. century. It contains
the Agamemnon entire, and was copied from M. before
the leaves were lost. It does not contain the Choephoræ.

F.   Codex Farnesianus, copied by Dem. Triclinius at the
end of the 14 th. century from Fl.

Ven.   Codex Venetus, of the 13 th. century. It contains the
same plays as Fl., but has a lacuna in the Agamemnon
from v. 45 to v. 1054. It was copied from M. before
the loss.

Bess.   Bessarionis codex, probably of the 13 th. century. It
contains the first 333 verses of the Agamemnon, copied
from M. when entire.

The early editions quoted are:

A.   The Aldine, printed from G. in February, 1518 A. D.,
at Venice.

R.   Robortelli's edition, from M.; Venice, 1552 A. D.

T.   The edition of Turnebus, printed at Paris shortly
after R. in the same year.

V. or Vict. Edited by Peter Victorius and printed by H. Stephens
at Paris in 1557 A. D. This is the first edition which
contained the Agamemnon entire. Victorius used M.,
Fl., and F.

Canter's Edition was published at Antwerp in 1580 A. D.;
Stanley's in London, 1663 A. D.

"Hermann procured the conjectural emendations of John
Auratus and Joseph Scaliger from a manuscript of Spanhemius
in the Royal Library at Berlin. Ezechiel Spanhemius had tran-
scribed them from (notes written in) copies of the edition of
Victorius which belonged to Isaac Voss. These copies are now
in the Library of Leyden." Haupt's Preface to Hermann's Edition.

(3) The text also differs from the text of previous editions in
the arrangement of many lines in the choral odes. Even Enger
(1863) did not venture to make any change. But when the principles of Greek Metres had been so clearly explained by Boeckh
in his three books 'de metris Pindari' there could be no reason
why the change should not be made. In the choruses, then,
as here arranged, the verses always begin *out*, the rhythmical
orders, of which the verses are composed, begin *in*. The
verses are divided at the points most convenient for scanning and
printing; for this is a matter which has to do with the breadth
of the page. Boeckh's Pindar is in quarto, but even so there
is not room for the longer verses to be written in one line. In
the anapæstic systems the first line begins *out* and the rest,
down to the parœmiac, begin *in*. This arrangement is justified
by the synapheia, and it seems to be a convenient arrangement.
Since editors have often divided the verses capriciously, it, seems
necessary to inform the reader that there is only one right way
in this, as in every thing else; and that the most convenient
division of verses which leaves the orders and the feet undivided

is the right one to adopt for the lines. For the information of junior students it may be added that the verses are determined by hiatus, the syllable of doubtful quantity 'anceps', the nature of the clausula and catalexis, or by the anacrusis and base which commonly announce the commencement of a new verse. A correct ear, well practised in Greek rhythms, is also necessary to the discovery of the verses.

(4) Besides these innovations in the form of the Translation, in the text, and in the arrangement of the lines, a Commentary is added which is almost entirely new, and in which nothing is inserted but what seemed quite necessary to a right under-standing of the play. One principal feature is the frequency of quotations from Hesiod and the Gnomic poets. The Editor had often read the Hesiod before he discovered that the phrase and thoughts of Æschylus in this play were to so great an extent the reflection of those of Hesiod. In the Choëphoræ he was constantly reminded of the Odyssey; but very much more of the works of Hesiod in his minute study of the Agamemnon. This is a discovery which has a twofold relation: we can interpret the play from Hesiod, and we ascertain that the Theogony and The Shield of Hercules were read by Æschylus as part of Hesiod's poems. There are some sins of omission in the Commentary. For instance; it should be said respecting v. 227 that ἀρωγὰν is in apposition with θυσίαν implied in θυτὴρ γενέσθαι = θυσίαν ποιεῖσθαι, and that οὖν in v. 34 refers back to v. 11, the Watch-man's statement of Clytemnestra's confident assurance that Aga-memnon would return. οὖν in v. 473 refers to a conclusion which might have been inferred from the line above. So in Soph. Ant. 722 οὖν signifies "if not, *as you might infer from my saying* πρεσβεύειν". On κτήνη, v. 129, it should be said that it is directly taken from Hom. Il. 18. 512 κτῆσιν ὅσην πτολίεθρον ἐπήρατον ἐντὸς ἐέργει, a line which finally determines the genu-ineness of the word κτήνη.

(5) Finally, this is the first of English editions to give an explanation of the rhythm and metre of each line in the play. And here it may be added for the further information of junior students that rhythm is the regular succession of arsis and thesis in a verse; metre, the regular succession of long and short syllables arranged for the expression of rhythm.

. It was part of the Editor's ambition to dedicate this Essay in Translation and Criticism to his University, Trinity College, Dublin, and so give some expression to his gratitude for inestimable benefits: but neither now, nor on a former occasion, could he bring himself to think that the offering was worthy of formal presentation; and he can only add that what is good in his book is the offspring of studies in which he willingly engaged at the dictation and with the indispensable aid of his Alma Mater.

PRÆFATIO ADNOTATIONIS CRITICÆ.

En vobis, lectores eruditi, ea tradenda curavi quæ amore atque labore ducibus, omnium illis rerum victoribus, ad hanc fabulam emendandam reperire potui. Nam quum versio Anglica in hujus operis consilio primas partes teneret, et Commentarium versioni explicandæ inserviret, non absurde, ut mihi videtur, linguam Anglicam in Commentario quoque adhibui. Præfatio autem prior versionem meam maxime spectat talesque res quales intellexisse popularium meorum potissimum intererat. Itaque factum est ut notas criticas tantum Latine scripserim: id quod quam brevissime feci et fortasse non ita ut jejunitatis crimen evitem. Sed vos ii estis coram quibus si quis oculum modo, ut aiunt, conniveat, plura intelligatis, quam vulgus hominum profanorum si quis aliquid inculcando in ævum perstet.

Usus sum Karsteni, Engeri, Weilii editionibus; præsto erant et libri duo quibus editis de nobis optime meritus est Heimsoethius. His dictis, vix est cur addam me duro tirocinio imbutum esse in Wellaueri, Bothii, Blomfieldii, Hermanni, E. Ahrentis, Paleii, Coningtoni, Dindorfii editionibus perlegendis. Sed nondum aderat, etiamnunc abest, Dindorfii editio quinta Poetarum Scenicorum Græcorum; eam partem dico in qua Dindorfius Æschyli relliquias tractabit.

Quod ad rem metricam pertinet rationes secutus sum Boeckhii, supra quod enarrari potest, viri clarissimi.

Restabat solum ut vobis congratularer quod hæc fabula in eo est ut et facilior intellectu et mendarum purior evadat quam ulla alia fabula Græca. Tantum valuit indomitus virorum doctorum labor et ingenitus nudæ veritatis amor.

Dabam Kingstownii apud Dublinium,
a. d. VI Id. Maias, MDCCCLXVIII.

ERRATA.

In the Argument. *Page* 5, *last line* murder.

In the Text. *P.* 8, *l.* 1. ΦΥΛΑΞ. *V.* 276 ἐπίανέν. *V.* 584 εὖ. *V.* 1078 τὸν. *V.* 1238 ἐδόκει. *V.* 1245 ἀλλ'. *V.* 1292 ἐπεύχομαι. *V.* 1457 ὑπὸ. *V.* 1492 ὑφάσματι.

In the Translation. *V.* 111 soldiers'. *V.* 121 victor. *Vv.* 203, 4 *should begin in. V.* 205 *for* thus *read* then. *Vv.* 245, 256 *should begin out. Vv.* 355, 433 *place commas after* beloved *and* remembers. *Vv.* 545, 604, 650 *for* host. war. Greeks: *read* host? war? Greeks? *V.* 515 heralds'. *V.* 572 *for* wish *read* bid. *V.* 689 *for* knell-like to *read* death-knell of. *V.* 750 pronounced. *V.* 794 *for* gladness *read* mirth. *V.* 795 *should begin out. V.* 825 *place a comma at* town. *V.* 826, 7 *read* set: and. *V.* 1090 *for* god-hating *read* god-hated. *V.* 1114 *for* view *read* view? *V.* 1133 *for* men: *read* men? *V.* 1342 *should begin in. V.* 1371 *for* see *read* know. *V.* 1535 '*the*, *Right*' *read* the, Right.

In notis criticis. *V.* 30 Sic Vict. *V.* 102 Sic Fl. *V.* 304 πῃ (*ubi legitur* πῇ.) *V.* 345 poena. *V.* 373 *dele* τι. *V.* 585 (libri ἐμέ). *V.* 557 πραπίδων subaud. μέρος. *V.* 562 τρίχα. *V.* 817 gravidam. *V.* 1017 adscripta. *V.* 1041 (*ubi legitur* 421) nullo. *V.* 1092 audieris. *V.* 1251 libri. *V.* 1354 ὁρᾶν. *V.* 1590 'Ατρεύς·

In the Commentary. *V.* 2 explained. *V.* 17 ἀπότομος. *V.* 105 also. *Page* 181, *line* 4 that. *line* 33 (none in. *V.* 123 learn. *V.* 246 perform-ing. *V.* 612 follow-ing. *V.* 829 substituted.

ΑΙΣΧΥΛΟΤ ΑΓΑΜΕΜΝΩΝ.

THE AGAMEMNON OF ÆSCHYLUS.

ΤΑ ΤΟΥ ΔΡΑΜΑΤΟΣ ΠΡΟΣΩΠΑ.

———

ΦΥΛΑΞ.

ΧΟΡΟΣ.

ΚΛΥΤΑΙΜΝΗΣΤΡΑ.

ΚΗΡΥΞ.

ΑΓΑΜΕΜΝΩΝ.

ΚΑΣΑΝΔΡΑ.

ΑΙΓΙΣΘΟΣ.

M. non habet personarum indicem.

Ταλθύβιος κῆρυξ libri. Ego Talthybium ejeci quia, me judice, Medicei codicis archetypus eum non habuit. Hæc M. post nomen fabulæ: θεράπων Ἀγαμέμνονος ὁ προλογιζόμενος, οὐχὶ ὁ ὑπὸ Αἰγίσθου ταχθείς. Qui ea scripsit lectores admonendos curavit Æschyleam narrationem ab Homerica illa (Od. 4. 524) discrepare. Is igitur Arg. non scripsit. Porro autem M. habet Arg. sec. Dind., non habet sec. Franz. Hic ideo mihi fidem facit quod Arg. habet Talthybium.

———

PERSONS REPRESENTED.

A WATCHMAN: acted by the Deuteragonist, who speaks about 490 lines altogether.

CHORUS.

CLYTEMNESTRA: acted by the Protagonist: about 340 lines.

A HERALD: ⎫
AGAMEMNON: ⎪
              ⎬ Deuteragonist.
CASANDRA: ⎪
ÆGISTHUS: ⎭

THE MUTE ACTORS ARE:

Attendants of Clytemnestra vv. 92, 595.

Personator of Casandra v. 950: his place is taken by the Deuteragonist after v. 974, by stage-contrivance.

Attendants of Agamemnon v. 944.

Personators of Agamemnon and Casandra lying dead vv. 1404, 1440.

Attendants of Ægisthus v. 1650.

ΤΠΟΘΕΣΙΣ.

'Αγαμέμνων εἰς "Ιλιον ἀπιὼν τῇ Κλυταιμνήστρᾳ, εἰ πορθήσοι
τὸ "Ιλιον, ὑπέσχετο τῆς αὐτῆς ἡμέρας σημαίνειν διὰ τοῦ πυρσοῦ.
ὅθεν σκοπὸν ἐκάθισεν ἐπὶ μισθῷ Κλυταιμνήστρᾳ, ἵνα τηροίη
τὸν πυρσόν. καὶ ὁ μέν ἰδὼν ἀπήγγειλεν· αὐτὴ δὲ τὸν τῶν
πρεσβυτῶν ὄχλον μεταπέμπεται περὶ τοῦ πυρσοῦ ἐροῦσα· ἐξ   5
ὧν καὶ ὁ χορὸς συνίσταται· οἵτινες ἀκούσαντες παιανίζουσι.
μετ' οὐ πολὺ δὲ καὶ Ταλθύβιος παραγίνεται καὶ τὰ περὶ
τὸν πλοῦν διηγεῖται. 'Αγαμέμνων δ' ἐπὶ ἀπήνης ἔρχεται·
εἵπετο δὲ αὐτῷ ἑτέρα ἀπήνη, ἔνθα ἦν τὰ λάφυρα καὶ ἡ
Κασάνδρα. αὐτὸς μὲν οὖν προεισέρχεται εἰς τὸν οἶκον σὺν τῇ   10
Κλυταιμνήστρᾳ. Κασάνδρα δὲ προμαντεύεται, πρὶν εἰς τὰ
βασίλεια εἰσελθεῖν, τὸν ἑαυτῆς καὶ τοῦ 'Αγαμέμνονος θάνατον
καὶ τὴν ἐξ 'Ορέστου μητροκτονίαν, καὶ εἰσπηδᾷ ὡς θανουμένη,
ῥίψασα τὰ στέμματα. τοῦτο δὲ τὸ μέρος τοῦ δράματος
θαυμάζεται ὡς ἔκπληξιν ἔχον καὶ οἶκτον ἱκανόν. ἰδίως δὲ   15
Αἰσχύλος τὸν 'Αγαμέμνονα ἐπὶ σκηνῆς ἀναιρεῖσθαι ποιεῖ,
τὸν δὲ Κασάνδρας σιωπήσας θάνατον νεκρὰν αὐτὴν ὑπέ-
δειξεν, πεποίηκέ τε Αἴγισθον καὶ Κλυταιμνήστραν ἑκάτερον
διισχυριζόμενον περὶ τῆς ἀναιρέσεως ἐνὶ κεφαλαίῳ, τὴν μὲν

ARGUMENT.

Agamemnon on his setting out for Ilion promised Clytemnestra, if he sacked Ilion, to send the intelligence the same day by a fire-signal. So Clytemnestra set a paid watchman to look out for the fire-signal; and when he saw it he brought word. Then she sends for a number of elders to tell them about the fire-signal, and of these the Chorus is composed. On hearing the news they sing a thanksgiving hymn. Not long after Talthybius arrives and gives an account of the voyage. Next, Agamemnon comes on a mule-car: another car was following, in which were the spoils of war and Casandra. He himself goes on before into the house with Clytemnestra; Casandra, before going into the palace, predicts the death of herself and Agamemnon, and the matricidal deed of Orestes; then, throwing off her diviner's badge, hurries in to die. This part of the drama is admired for its power to inspire horror and pity. In a peculiar manner Aeschylus represents Agamemnon as being killed on the stage, and exhibited the corpse of Casandra though he said nothing about her death, and has made Aegisthus and Clytemnestra justify the murder each on one plea; the latter by the murder of Iphigenia, the

τῇ ἀναιρέσει Ἰφιγενείας, τὸν δὲ ταῖς τοῦ πατρὸς Θυέστου 20
ἐξ Ἀτρέως συμφοραῖς.

Ἐδιδάχθη τὸ δρᾶμα ἐπὶ ἄρχοντος Φιλοκλέους, Ὀλυμπιάδι
ὀγδοηκοστῇ, ἔτει δευτέρῳ. πρῶτος Αἰσχύλος Ἀγαμέμνονι,
Χοηφόροις, Εὐμενίσι, Πρωτεῖ σατυρικῷ. ἐχορήγει Ξενοκλῆς
Ἀφιδνεύς.   25

Προλογίζει δὲ ὁ φύλαξ, θεράπων Ἀγαμέμνονος.

---

l. 16. ἐπὶ σκηνῆς. I. e. tam prope a scena ut ejus clamores a specta-
toribus exaudiri possent.

former, by the misfortunes brought upon his father Thyestes by Atreus.

The drama. was exhibited in the archonship of Philoclês, in the second year of the eightieth Olympiad. Aeschylus was first with the tragedies, Agamemnon, Choëphoroe, Eumcnides, and the satyric drama, Proteus. Xenoclês of Aphidnae was choregus.

The watchman, a servant of Agamemnon, speaks the prologue.

Θεοὺς μὲν αἰτῶ τῶνδ' ἀπαλλαγὴν πόνων
Φρουρᾶς ἐτείας μῆκος, ἣν κοιμώμενος
στέγης Ἀτρειδῶν ἄγκαθεν, κυνὸς δίκην,
ἄστρων κάτοιδα νυκτέρων ὁμήγυριν,
καὶ τοὺς φέροντας χεῖμα καὶ θέρος βροτοῖς   5
λαμπροὺς δυνάστας, ἐμπρέποντας αἰθέρι.
Καὶ νῦν φυλάσσω λαμπάδος τὸ σύμβολον,
αὐγὴν πυρὸς φέρουσαν ἐκ Τροίας φάτιν
ἁλώσιμόν τε βάξιν· ὧδε γὰρ κρατεῖ   10
γυναικὸς ἀνδρόβουλον ἐλπίζον κέαρ.
Εὖτ' ἂν δὲ νυκτίπλαγκτον ἔνδροσόν τ' ἔχω
εὐνὴν ὀνείροις οὐκ ἐπισκοπουμένην
ἐμήν, φόβος γὰρ ἀνθ' ὕπνου παραστατεῖ
τὸ μὴ βεβαίως βλέφαρα συμβαλεῖν ὕπνῳ,   15
ὅταν δ' ἀείδειν ἢ μινύρεσθαι δοκῶ,
ὕπνου τόδ' ἀντίμολπον ἐντέμνων ἄκος,

2. ἐτείας· μῆκος δ' ἦν M. μῆκος, ἣν Fl. cet. Edd. inde a Victorio.
3. στέγαις libri. στέγης Schueidew. ἄγκαθεν libri. Fortasse ἀνέκαθεν legendum, monente Engero; idque invitis Schol. et Gramm. Herm. sibi ipse imposuit, nimirum et aliis, ratiunculis suis de hujus voc. sign.; quod non fecisset, si ἐπ' ἀγκῶνος recte vertisset 'cubito presso'. At ille 'in ulnis', ambigue.

Post v. 6. sequitur v. ἀστέρας,

I have been asking of the gods relief
from these *my* toils a year-long sentry's space;
in which couched dog-like on the Atreids' roof
I've learned the host of nightly grouping-stars,
5   the bearers both of cold and heat to men,
bright rulers who in æther keep their state.
And still I'm watching for the beacon's sign,
the flare of fire which bears report from Troy,
10   news of its capture; so our lady's wit,
hopeful, with manlike reasoning, proves 't will be.
And whensoe'er I take my dewy rest
broke by night wanderings, not o'erlooked by dreams —
for fear 's my comrade in sleep's stead, and so
15   my eyelids have no firm set-to with sleep —
and when I have a mind to sing or hum,
plying that knife of song to cure my sleep,

ὅταν φθίνωσιν, ἀντολάς τε τῶν, aperte
spurius.
    14. ἐμήν. Sic et Eum. 578, Suppl.
366 in hac sede cum interpunctione.
    17. Sic libri. Malim ἀντίμηλον

'specilli loco'; nam vulg. corruptum
esse vel infanda vertendi difficultas
ostendit: neque vero ineptum est
militem quondam vulneratum hoc
dicere.

κλαίω τότ' οἴκου τοῦδε συμφορὰν στένων,
οὐχ ὡς τὰ πρόσθ' ἄριστα δεσποτουμένου.
Νῦν δ' εὐτυχὴς γένοιτ' ἀπαλλαγὴ πόνων,   20
εὐαγγέλου φανέντος ὀρφναίου πυρός.
Ὦ χαῖρε λαμπτὴρ νυκτός, ἡμερήσιον
φάος πιφαύσκων καὶ χορῶν κατάστασιν
πολλῶν ἐν Ἄργει τῆςδε συμφορᾶς χάριν.
Ἰοῦ ἰοῦ.   25
Ἀγαμέμνονος γυναικὶ σημανῶ τορῶς
εὐνῆς ἐπαντείλασαν ὡς τάχος δόμοις
ὀλολυγμὸν εὐφημοῦντα τῇδε λαμπάδι
ἐπορθιάζειν, εἴπερ Ἰλίου πόλις
ἑάλωκεν, ὡς ὁ φρυκτὸς ἀγγέλλων πρέπει.   30
αὐτός τ' ἔγωγε φροίμιον χορεύσομαι.
Τὰ δεσποτῶν γὰρ εὖ πεσόντα θήσομαι,
τρὶς ἓξ βαλούσης τῆςδέ μοι φρυκτωρίας.
Γένοιτο δ' οὖν μολόντος εὐφιλῆ χέρα
ἄνακτος οἴκων τῇδε βαστάσαι χερί.   35
Τὰ δ' ἄλλα σιγῶ· βοῦς ἐπὶ γλώσσῃ μέγας
βέβηκεν· οἶκος δ' αὐτός, εἰ φθογγὴν λάβοι,
σαφέστατ' ἂν λέξειεν· ὡς ἑκὼν ἐγὼ
μαθοῦσιν αὐδῶ, κοὺ μαθοῦσι λήθομαι.

ΧΟΡΟΣ.

Δέκατον μὲν ἔτος τόδ' ἐπεὶ Πριάμου   40
    μέγας ἀντίδικος,
    Μενέλαος ἄναξ ἠδ' Ἀγαμέμνων,

---

19. διαπονουμένου libri. Corr. Eng.,   25. ἰοὺ ἰοὺ libri. Corr. Herm.
Dubner, Schmidt, ego olim.   26. σημαίνω M. Corr. in Fl.

then, sighing, I deplore this household's lot,
which is not as before most fairly ruled.

20 Now may there be a blest release from toil
by advent of the evangel gloom-wrapt ray.
Welcome, thou lamp of night! revealing beams
like daylight, and in Argos many a choir's
glad marshalling because of this event.

25 Io! Io!
I 'll plainly signal Agamemnon's dame
to rise with haste from bed and in the house
to high notes tune a jovial salute
for yonder flame: of course; since Ilion's town

30 is taken, as the beacon beams report.
I'll dance a prelude too all by myself.
I'll wager on the masters's lucky throws
for this fire-signal throws me triple-sice.
Heaven send he may return, that in this hand

35 I may hold clasped the palace-lord's dear hand.
For the rest, hush! a great ox on my tongue
treads; and the house itself if it got speech
would tell the truest tale; since freely I
tell those who know, to those who dont, forget.

CHORUS.

40 This year is the tenth since *that* when the great
foeman of Priam,
king Menelaus and king Agamemnon,

30. Sic. Vict. ἀγγέλων Fl. M.   42. Et hic suspectus Boissonadio,
32. Versus suspectus; non mihi.   Karst., Eug.

διθρόνου Διόθεν καὶ δισκήπτρου
τιμῆς, ὀχυρὸν ζεῦγος Ἀτρειδᾶν,
στόλον Ἀργείων χιλιοναύτην   45
τῆςδ' ἀπὸ χώρας
ᾖραν στρατιῶτιν ἀρωγήν·
μέγαν ἐκ θυμοῦ κλάζοντες Ἄρη,
τρόπον αἰγυπιῶν,
οἵτ' ἐκπατίοις ἄλγεσι παίδων   50
ὕπατοι λεχέων στροφοδινοῦνται
πτερύγων ἐρετμοῖσιν ἐρεσσόμενοι,
δεμνιοτήρη
πόνον ὀρταλίχων ὀλέσαντες·
ὕπατος δ' ἀΐων ἤ τις Ἀπόλλων,   55
ἢ Πάν, ἢ Ζεύς, οἰωνόθροον
γόον ὀξυβόαν τῶνδε μετοίκων
ὑστερόποινον
πέμπει παραβᾶσιν Ἐρινύν.
Οὕτω δ' Ἀτρέως παῖδας ὁ κρείσσων   60
ἐπ' Ἀλεξάνδρῳ πέμπει ξένιος
Ζεύς, πολυάνορος ἀμφὶ γυναικὸς
πολλὰ παλαίσματα καὶ γυιοβαρῆ
γόνατος κονίαισιν ἐρειδομένου
διακναιομένης τ' ἐν προτελείοις   65
κάμακος θήσων Δαναοῖσιν,
Τρωσί θ' ὁμοίως. Ἔστι δ' ὅπῃ νῦν
ἔστι· τελεῖται δ' ἐς τὸ πεπρωμένον.
Οὔθ' ὑποκλαίων οὔθ' ὑπολείβων

45. χιλιοναύταν libri. -ην Dind., probante Engero.
47. ἀρωγάτην M. sec. Dind. -ήν Eng. v. 73 cit.
57. Omnino abjiciendum comma. τ. μ. pendet ab Ε.: sic τέκνων Ἐρινύς, Eur. Med. 1389.
64. ἐριδομένου M. ἐρειπομένου Fl.

holding from Zeus twin-throned twin-sceptred

honour, a firm-paced pair of Atreidae,

45   launched from this land an army of Argives

borne in a thousand barks,

an avenging legion of heroes:

sending forth from the soul loud clamour of war,

like two vultures

50   which in distracting grief for their offspring

to the utmost height over their nests float in curves,

rowing themselves with their oars of pinions,

having lost the brood-care

which before at the nest had detained them:

55   and in the highest some *dweller*, Apollo,

or Pan, or Zeus, hearing the shrill-voiced

wail of the mourning birds sends the departed

fledgelings' Erinnys

with a late levied doom 'gainst the sinners.

60   So doth the master Zeus, patron of host and guest,

'gainst Alexander send the Atreidae,

and for the lady of many a lover

will impose on Achaeans and Trojans alike

many encounters fatiguing the sinews

65   where the knee *of the hero* is pressed in the dust

and the spear-shaft snapt in the foremost

orgies *of battle*. And now things are —

as they are; but will end in the issue decreed.

Not by burnt nor drink offering after *the sin*

δ ad π supra scripto; ut vulg. Bess.

66. κάμακος — ὁμοίως; hæc in mo-
nom. et paroem. digessit Eng.

67. ὅπη vulg. ὅπη Herm.

69. οὐδ᾽ ὕποκ, Herm., quod necessarium sit; sed licet per me poetis
asyndeto uti. ὑποκλαίων libri, ὑποκαίων
Casaubon, (-όων Dind.)

οὔτε δακρύων ἀπύρων ἱερῶν   70
ὀργὰς ἀτενεῖς παραθέλξει.
Ἡμεῖς δ' ἀτίται σαρκὶ παλαιᾷ
τῆς τότ' ἀρωγῆς ὑπολειφθέντες
μίμνομεν, ἰσχὺν
ἰσόπαιδα νέμοντες ἐπὶ σκήπτροις.   75
ὅ τε γὰρ νεαρὸς μυελὸς στέρνων
ἐντὸς ἀνάσσων
ἰσόπρεσβυς, Ἄρης δ' οὐκ ἔνι χώρᾳ.
τί θ' ὑπεργήρως, φυλλάδος ἤδη
καταακαρφομένης; τρίποδας μὲν ὁδοὺς   80
στείχει, παιδὸς δ' οὐδὲν ἀρείων
ὄναρ ἡμερόφαντον ἀλαίνει.
Σὺ δέ, Τυνδάρεω
θύγατερ, βασίλεια Κλυταιμνήστρα,
τί χρέος; τί νέον; τί δ' ἐπαισθομένη   85
τίνος ἀγγελίας
πευθοῖ περίπεμπτα θυοσκνεῖς;
πάντων δὲ θεῶν τῶν ἀστυνόμων,
ὑπάτων, χθονίων,
τῶν τε θυραίων τῶν τ' ἀγοραίων   90
βωμοὶ δώροισι φλέγονται·
ἄλλη δ' ἄλλοθεν οὐρανομήκης
λαμπὰς ἀνίσχει
φαρμασσομένη χρίματος ἁγνοῦ

---

70. ἀπύρων ἱερῶν. Vide Comment.
72. ἀτίται M. ἀτίται Fl., et sic recte recentt., 'vacantes militiæ munere'.
76. ὅτε libri. ὅ τε Auratus.
77. ἀνάσσων libri. corr. Herm., recentt.

78. χωρᾶι M. χώρᾳ vulg. 'in puerorum pectore non est deus indiges'. Sic γυνή, οὐκ ἔνεστ' Ἄρης Æsch. Supp. 749.
79. τίθιπεργήρως M. corr. Martin.; præclara eademque diu desiderata emendatio.

70 nor by tears will he charm the intensified wrath
 which he roused by contempt of religion.

But we (for our old flesh exempt from the war)
 left behind by the vengeful-armada that day
 stay at home, and apply
75 to our staves a strength equal to childhood's.
 For the young vital juice throbbing up in the breast
 of a child is as weak
 as old age, nor does Ares inhabit the spot:
 and what of the man past old age, when the leaves
80 are now fading away? on his three-footed walks
 he goes, and no more fit for war than a child,
 like a dream in the daylight, he wanders.

But thou, Tyndareus' child,
 Clytemnestra queen-*regent*, what is the cause?
85 what the news? what intelligence hast thou received?
 on what tidings' report
 dost thou serve out and kindle the incense?

for of all the town-governing gods, the most high,
 those of the underworld,
90 gods of the doorway, and gods of the market,
 the altars with gifts are illumined:

and on every side darting its rays to the sky
 rises a flambeau
 drenched with the virgin nard's guileless and *undefiled*

---

82. ἡμερόφατον M. corr. in cet.
87. πειθοῖ vulgo, πυθοῖ Fl. πευθοῖ
Scaliger, probantibus Herm., Dind.
cet. θυοσκινεῖς libri, nisi quod M.
sec. Dind. θυοσκνεῖς a pr. m.; id ab
Ahrente commendatum recepit Eng.

90. τῶν τ' οὐρανίων libri. Huuc
versum ejecit Porsonus, Engerus
emeudatum restituit.
91. Sic F. δώροις cet.
94. χρίσματος Fl., vulg. χρίματος
M. Herm., recentt.

μαλακαῖς ἀδόλοισι παρηγορίαις,   95
πελάνῳ μυχόθεν βασιλείῳ.
   Τούτων λέξαις ὅ τι καὶ δυνατὸν
   καὶ θέμις αἰνεῖν,
   παίων τε γενοῦ τῆςδε μερίμνης,
   ἢ νῦν τότε μὲν κακόφρων τελέθει,   100
   τότε δ᾽ ἐκ θυσιῶν ἀγανὰ φαίνουσ᾽
   ἐλπὶς ἀμύνει φροντίδ᾽ ἄπληστον
   τὴν θυμοβόρον φρενὶ λύπην.

στρ. Κύριός εἰμι θροεῖν ὅδιον κράτος αἴσιον ἀνδρῶν
   ἐκτελέων· ἔτι γὰρ θεόθεν καταπνείει   105
   πειθὼ μολπᾶν
   ἀλκᾷ σύμφυτος αἰών·
   ὅπως Ἀχαιῶν δίθρονον κράτος, Ἑλλάδος ἥβας
   ξύμφρονα ταγάν,   110
   πέμπει σὺν δορὶ καὶ χερὶ πράκτορι θούριος ὄρνις
   Τευκρίδ᾽ ἐπ᾽ αἶαν·
   οἰωνῶν βασιλῆς βασιλεῦσι νεῶν, ὁ κε-
     λαινός, ὅ τ᾽ ἐξόπιν ἀργᾶς,   115
   Φανέντες ἴκταρ μελάθρων χερὸς ἐκ δορυπάλτου
   παμπρέπτοις ἐν ἕδραισιν   .
   βοσκόμενοι λαγίναν ἐρικύμαδα φέρμα τε γένναν

---

96. πελάνῳ vulgo, sed M. sec.
Franzii apographon -ῳ, quod Eng.
recepit. Ego πάντοθεν πληθύνομαι scri-
bere πελάνῳ.
97. λέξας· vulgo. corr. Hartung.
98. εἰπεῖν Fl.
102. Sic. Fl. ἄπλειστον M.
103. τὴν θυμοφθόρον λύπης φρένα
M. τὴν θυμοβόρον λύπης φρένα Fl.
Schol. M. legit θυμοβόρον. Sermo

ex Hesiodeo illo sumptus περύλαξο δὲ
θυμῷ ἄλγεα θυμοβορεῖν Op. 795. Verris-
simam Pauwii corr. recepi Porsono
probatam. Junge: ἀμύνει φρενί. φρὴν
ap. Æsch. diaphragma est, s. fons co-
gitationis; minime vero ipsa cogitatio.
105. ἐκτελέων libri, quo nihil melius si modo recordaris Hes. Op. 464
et 472.
107. μολπᾶν M. a p. m.

95   soft *and essentially odorous* blandishments,

with the treasure-room's *rich* royal unguent.

Tell me of these things whatever to utter is

lawful and possible,

and be healer for me of this *inward* concern,

100   which now at one moment sadly forebodes,

and then again hope, from the frankincense-fires

kindly beaming, repels the insatiate care,

this heart-gnawing grief, from my bosom.

I have full powers to tell of the strong men's omen of conquest

105 seen on the march; (for my being still one with its birthmate

vigour of harmony

breathes forth god-given eloquence;)

how martial bird sends with the spear and the sentence-exacting

110 arm to the Teucrian

land the Achaeans' twin-throned royalty, Hellas's soldiers

one-hearted chiefdom:

kings of birds to the kings of the galleys appearing, the

115   dark one, and he with tail argent,

before the halls, fast by the hand that poises the spear-shaft,

on conspicuous perches,   [burden

feasting themselves on the full-wombed child of the hare and her

---

109. ἦβαν libri. corr. ex Ar. Ran. 1284 opt. codd..

110. τὰν γᾶν M. corr. in Fl.

111. ξὺν Fl. καὶ libris omissum ex. Ar. Ran. 1289 revocatum est.

114. βασιλεύς libri. βασιλεῖς Karsten, -ῆς ego, ut βραβῆς v. 230, βασιλῆς Soph. Ai. 189.

115. ἀργίας libri. ἀργᾶς Blomf., ἀργᾷς Dind., recentt.

116. δορυπάλτου libri, Enger. δοριπάλτου cum T. V. vulgo.

117. παμπρέποις ἐν ἕδραισιν M. παμπρέποισιν ἕδραις Fl. παμπρέποις ἐν ἕδραισι Boss.

119. ἐρικύματα φέρματι M. ἐρικύμονα φέρβοντο Fl. ἐρικυμάδα ex Hesychii glossa receperunt Karst., Dind., Eng. φέρμα τε Ahr., quem sequor, voce βλαβέντα ductus.

2

βλαβέντα λοισθίων δρόμων.　　　　120
Αἴλινον, αἴλινον εἰπέ, τὸ δ᾽ εὖ νικάτω.

ἀντ.　Κεδνὸς δὲ στρατόμαντις ἰδὼν δύο λήμασιν ἴσους
Ἀτρεΐδας μαχίμους ἐδάη λαγοδαίτας
πομπᾶς ἀρχούς·
οὕτω δ᾽ εἶπε τεράζων·　　　　125
χρόνῳ μὲν ἀγρεῖ Πριάμου πόλιν ἅδε κέλευθος,
πάντα δὲ πύργων
κτήνη πρόσθε τὰ δημιοπληθέα Μοῖρα λαπάξει
πρὸς τὸ βίαιον.　　　　130
Οἶον μή τις ἄγα θεόθεν κνεφάσῃ προτυ-
πὲν στόμιον μέγα Τροίας
στρατωθέν· ὅσσον γὰρ ἐπίφθονος Ἄρτεμις ἀγνὰ　　135
πτανοῖσιν κυσὶ πατρὸς
αὐτότοκον πρὸ λόχου μογερὰν πτάκα θυομένοισι,
στυγεῖ δὲ δεῖπνον αἰετῶν·
αἴλινον, αἴλινον εἰπέ, τὸ δ᾽ εὖ νικάτω·

ἐπῳδ.　τόσσον περ εὔφρων ἀ καλὰ　　　　140
δρόσοισι λέπτοις μαλερῶν λεόντων,
πάντων τ᾽ ἀγρονόμων Φιλομάστοις
θηρῶν ὀβρικάλοισι, τερπνὰ
τούτων αἰτεῖ ξύμβολα κρᾶναι.

122. Probabile mihi videtur voc. δὲ, hoc genus versus pronunciando, ἰδὲ factam esse. λήμασι δίσσους libri; recte Dind. λήμασιν ἴσους.
123. Ἀτρεΐδας vulgo. Ἀτρεΐδας Monk.
124. πομποὺς τ᾽ ἀρχάς M., acc. illo corr., ἀρχούς Fl. πομπᾶς ἀρχούς Karst.,

Weil., Dind. Vera lectio incerta.
129. προσθετὰ M. πρόσθετὰ Bess. πρόσθε τὰ vulgo. Mutare nolim. δημιοπληθῆ libri, δημιοπληθέα O. Muller, Eng.; nec desunt aliæ epicæ formæ in hoc carmine. Μοῖρ᾽ ἀλαπάξει vulgo. Ut editur, F., recentt.
131. ἄτα libri, ἄγα Herm.

120 from further running all debarred.

    Speak the refrain of the dirge, but may good prove victo r

    And the shrewd army-diviner, observing the two gallant Atreids

    matched in mood, was apprised of the cavalcade-leading

    hare-tribe butchers;

125 and thus spake he divining:

    "in time this route bindeth its quarry the city of Priam;

    then all its towers'

    substance hitherto stored by the people fate shall in violent

130   · fashion demolish:

    granted only no grudge from the deities tarnish the

      bit for Troy forged and in grandeur

135 embattled; since undefiled Artemis hating as much these

    feathered hounds of her father,

    butchering, litter and all, the poor trembler before her deliv'ry,

    (for she abhors the eagles' food) —

    speak the refrain of the dirge, but may good prove victor: ---

140 as she, the beauteous one, delights

    in tiny cubs dropped by the fierce-souled lions;

    and all ravening animals' pap-fond

    younglings, prays *her sire* to accomplish

    mystic omens pleasing these *fav'rites.*

---

134. οἴκῳ libri, vulgo. ὅσσον ego; quo recepto, τόσσον περ v. 140 tolerari potest.

140. εὔρρων καλὰ M. ἁ καλὰ Fl., vulgo.

141. δρόσοισιν ἀέλπτοις M. δρόσοισιν ἀέπτοις Fl., Boss. δρόσοισι λεπτοῖς Wellauer. ʌ pro ʌ posita est, ʌ

supra scripta, et schol. M. confictum. μαλερῶν ὄντων M. λεόντων Stanleius, ex E. M. sub v. ἔραχι. Dind. inseruit τε m. c. Ahr. mavult λεόντων.

143. ὀβρικάλοισι M., sed ου in οι mutato. τερπνά cum glossa ᾽Αρτεμις in F.; sed cum ξύμβολα jungi debet.

144. κράναι M. κρᾶναι Fl.

2 *

Δεξιὰ μέν, κατάμομφα δὲ φάσματα Φανῶν.   145
Ἰήϊον δὲ καλέω Παιᾶνα,
μή τινας ἀντιπνόους Δαναοῖς χρονί-
    ας ἐχενῇδας τεύξῃ ἀπλοίας,   150
σπευδομένα θυσίαν ἑτέραν, ἄνομόν τιν', ἄδαιτον,
νεικέων τέκτονα σύμφυτον, οὐ δεισήνορα, μίμνει
    γὰρ Φοβερὰ παλίνορτος
οἰκονόμος δολία μνάμων μῆνις τεκνόποινος.   155
Τοιάδε Κάλχας ξὺν μεγάλοις ἀγαθοῖς ἀπέκλαγξεν
μόρσιμ' ἀπ' ὀρνίθων ὁδίων οἴκοις βασιλείοις·
    τοῖς δ' ὁμόφωνον
αἴλινον, αἴλινον εἰπέ, τὸ δ' εὖ νικάτω.

στρ.ά. Ζεύς, ὅστις ποτ' ἐστίν, εἰ τόδ' αὐ-   160
        τῷ φίλον κεκλημένῳ,
    τοῦτό νιν προςεννέπω·
    οὐκ ἔχω προςεικάσαι
        πάντ' ἐπισταθμώμενος,
    πλὴν Διός, εἰ τὸ μάταν ἀπὸ Φροντίδος ἄχθος   165
    χρὴ βαλεῖν ἐτητύμως.

ἀντ.ά. ‾ Οὐδ' ὅστις πάροιθεν ἦν μέγας,
        παμμάχῳ θράσει βρύων,
    οὐδὲ λέξεται πρὶν ὤν·   170
    ὃς δ' ἔπειτ' ἔφυ τρια-
        κτῆρος οἴχεται τυχών·
    Ζῆνα δέ τις προφρόνως ἐπινίκια κλάζων
    τεύξεται φρενῶν τὸ πᾶν·   175

---

145. φάσματα στρουθῶν M. τῶν
στρουθῶν Fl. φάσματα φανῶν Heimsoeth. quam certissimam emend. Engerus non recepit.

149. ἐχενῇδας libri. corr. Blomf.
150. ἀπλοίας M. τεύξῃ ἀπλοίας

145 Good is the vision of eagles, but chequered with evil.
But I invoke the deliv'rer Pacan
lest she should work for the Greeks any foul-blowing,
150   lingering, ship-staying, adverse-weather,
craving a different victim, unlawful, not yielding a banquet,
cognate framer of bickerings, no poor craven, for housewife-
rancour is waiting to-break-out-
155 afterwards, dire, ever-mindful, treach'rous, offspring-avenging."
Such were the fates which, mixed with large benisons, learnt from the omens
seen at the starting, Calchas rehearsed to imperial households:
whereto in concert
speak the refrain of the dirge, but may good prove victor.

160 Zeus (if, whosoeer he is, he be
titled thus acceptably
by this name I speak of him:
I've no power to strike a balance,
when I bring each plea to scale,
165 whether *or not* I should truly reject from my thought as
idle burden all but Zeus:

not he, who in former times was great,
with all-bearding boldness full,
170 ev'n as 'one who was' will be
named; and he who next arose
met his conqu'ror and is gone)
Zeus is he whom if man heartily greet with ovations
175 he will reach the sum of wit:

Eng., m. c.; fortasse recte. ἀπλοίας   165. εἰ τόδε libri. corr. Pauw.
T. Vict.   170. οὐδὲν λέξαι libri οὐδὲ λέξεται
  157. ἀπέκλαιεν M.   Ahr. a recentt. receptum.

22 ΑΓΑΜΕΜΝΩΝ.

στρ.β'. τὸν φρονεῖν βροτοὺς ὁδώ-
σαντα, τὸν πάθει μάθος
θέντα κυρίως ἔχειν.
Στάζει δ' ἔν θ' ὕπνῳ πρὸ καρδίας
μνησιπήμων πόνος, καὶ παρ' ἄ- 180
κοντας ἦλθε σωφρονεῖν·
δαιμόνων δέ που χάρις βιαίως
σέλμα σεμνὸν ἡμένων.

ἀντ.β'. Καὶ τόθ' ἡγεμὼν ὁ πρέσβυς νεῶν Ἀχαιικῶν 185
μάντιν οὐδένα ψέγων,
ἐμπαίοις τύχαισι συμπνέων,
εὖτ' ἀπλοίᾳ κεναγγεῖ βαρύ-
νοντ' Ἀχαιικὸς λεώς,
Χαλκίδος πέρχν ἔχων παλιρρό- 190
χθοις ἐν Αὐλίδος τόποις,

στρ.γ'. πνοαὶ δ' ἀπὸ Στρυμόνος μολοῦσαι
κακόσχολοι, νήστιδες, δύσορμοι,
βροτῶν ἄλαι, νεῶν τε καὶ πεισμάτων ἀφειδεῖς, 195
παλιμμήκη χρόνον τιθεῖσαι
τρίβῳ κατέξαινον ἄνθος Ἀργείων·
ἐπεὶ δὲ καὶ πικροῦ
χείματος ἄλλο μῆχαρ
βριθύτερον πρόμοισιν 200
μάντις ἔκλαγξεν, προφέρων
Ἄρτεμιν, ὥστε χθόνα βά-

177. τῷ libri. τὸν Schutz. recentt.   quam ap. Thucydidem.
179. τε est 'etiam' ut nonnun-   190. παλιρρόθοις libri; dedi Ahren-

him who guides in wisdom's way
    mortals, who makes absolute
teaching *which is got* with pain.
    There drop ev'n in sleep by conscience seen·
180 qualms that rouse thought of pain, so to men
    wisdom comes against their will;
such, I trow, the daemons' grace, superbly
    seated on majestic thrones.

    Thereupon the elder-born
185   captain of Achaean ships,
blaming now no seer, but with
chances veering as they caught his sails;
when the Greek fighting-men lay depressed
    by the store-exhausting gales
190 off the Chalcid land on Aulis' shores of
    flowing and receding tides:

and Strymon-blasts coming with disastrous
repose and dearth, making unsafe moorings,
195 men's path-perplexers, heeding not cost of ships and tackle,
a twice-told length of time expended
in waste, and tore all to shreds the Argives' flow'r:
and when the seer one plan
yet to the leaders chanted
200 ev'n than the bitter storm-wind
harder to bear, urging in plea
    Artemis, such plan that the two

tis em.; alii alia.   cum Pors. recentt.

  195. ναῶν καὶ libri. νεῶν τε καὶ   201. ἔκλαγξε libri. corr. Pors.

κτροις ἐπικρούσαντας Ἀτρεί-
δας δάκρυ μὴ κατασχεῖν·

ἀντ.γ'. ἄναξ δ' ὁ πρέσβυς τότ' εἶπε Φωνῶν·   205
βαρεῖα μὲν κὴρ τὸ μὴ πιθέσθαι·
βαρεῖα δ', εἰ τέκνον δαΐξω, δόμων ἄγαλμα,
μιαίνων παρθενοσφάγοισιν
ῥείθροις πατρῴους χέρας πέλας βωμοῦ.   210
Τί τῶνδ' ἄνευ κακῶν;
Πῶς λιπόναυς γένωμαι,
ξυμμαχίας ἁμαρτών;
παυσανέμου γὰρ θυσίας
    παρθενίου θ' αἵματος ὀρ-   215
    γᾷ περιοργῶς ἐπιθυ-
    μεῖν θέμις· εὖ γὰρ εἴη.

στρ.δ'. Ἐπεὶ δ' ἀνάγκας ἔδυ λέπαδνον,
Φρενὸς πνέων δυσσεβῆ τροπαίαν
ἄναγνον, ἀνίερον, τόθεν   220
τὸ παντότολμον Φρονεῖν μετέγνω.
Βροτοὺς θρασύνει γὰρ αἰσχρόμητις
τάλαινα παρακοπὰ πρωτοπήμων.
Ἔτλα δ' οὖν θυτὴρ γενέ-   225
    σθαι θυγατρὸς γυναικοποί-
    νων πολέμων ἀρωγὰν
καὶ προτέλεια ναῶν.

205. τόδ' libri. τότ' Stanl., ab
Herm. aliisque merito receptum.
210. ῥείθροις et βωμοῦ πέλας libri.
hoc Blomf., illud Pors. corr.: sed
spondæum illic sedere nefas; itaque
Eng. πόροις, aut simile quid susp.
212. τί πῶς; M. Fl. τε et τί γένωμαι M. Fl. Ut vulg. F.

kings with their staves smiting the ground
did not refrain from weeping:

205 the elder lord thus replied, exclaiming:
"a grievous doom — that of non-compliance —
and grievous if I slay my child, beauty of the palace,
and stain with streams of maiden-murder —
210 her father's hands — nigh the altar. Which of these
is free from wrong? *But* how
be by the ships deserted,
losing the leaguers' aid? *No!*
for that we crave with a desire
215　　passing desire off'ring of maid's
wind-lulling blood, this is god's-will;
Yes! for I hope fair issue."

And when he donned destiny's *broad* collar
and breathed a mood impious, unholy,
220 impure, his former love's reverse,
he then resolved any deed to venture.
It makes men bold, shameful-deeds-contriving
unblest fanaticism, grief's fore-runner.
225 Thus he had the heart to turn
woman-child-slayer, aid in wars
woman-avenging, *dared* this
voyage-inauguration.

---

215. περιόργως libri. acc. corr.
Blomf.
217. γὰρ εὖ εἴη Fl. Non opus
erit mutato, si versionem recte in-
telligas.
222. βροτοῖς libri. βροτοὺς Schulz.
Herm. autem primus ante βρ. interpunxit.

ἀντ.δ'. Λιτὰς δὲ καὶ κληδόνας πατρῴους
παρ' οὐδὲν αἰῶ τε παρθένειον   230
ἔθεντο φιλόμαχοι βραβῆς·
Φράσεν δ' ἀόζοις πατὴρ μετ' εὐχὰν
δίκαν χιμαίρας ὕπερθε βωμοῦ
πέπλοισι περιπετῆ παντὶ θυμῷ
προνωπῆ λαβεῖν ἀέρ-   235
        δην στόματός τε καλλιπρώ-
        ρου φυλακὰν κατασχεῖν
Φθόγγον ἀραῖον οἴκοις

στρ.ε'. βίᾳ χαλινῶν τ' ἀναύδῳ μένει.
Κρόκου βαφὰς δ' ἐς πέδον χέουσα
ἔβαλλ' ἕκαστον θυτή-   240
        ρων ἀπ' ὄμματος βέλει φιλοίκτῳ·
πρέπουσά θ', ὡς ἐν γραφαῖς, προςεννέπειν
θέλουσ', ἐπεὶ πολλάκις
πατρὸς κατ' ἀνδρῶνας εὐτραπέζους
ἔμελψεν, ἁγνᾷ δ' ἀταύρωτος αὐδᾷ πατρὸς
Φίλου τριτόσπονδον εὔποτμον παι-   245
        ᾶνα φίλως ἐτίμα.

ἀντ.ε'. Τὰ δ' ἔνθεν οὔτ' εἶδον οὔτ' ἐννέπω·
τέχναι δὲ Κάλχαντος οὐκ ἄκραντοι.
Δίκα δὲ τοῖς μὲν παθοῦ-
        σιν μαθεῖν ἐπιρρέπει τὸ μέλλον·   250
τὸ προκλύειν, πρὶν γένοιτο, χαιρέτω·

230. αἰῶνα παρθένιον M. αἰῶ τε
O. Muller. παρθένειον Fl. ultima syll.
est anceps.

236. φυλακᾷ Blomf., fortasse recte.
238. τ' in δ' mutavit Tricl., δ'
in prox. v. omisso. Quippe impe-

The chieftains *then* lusting for the battle
230 set down as naught prayers and *wild* appeals to
her father, and her virgin life.
The father bade, after prayer, the priestly
esquires to lift high upon the altar,
like mountain-goat, the maid *who* with outspread
235 attire, sense and all, *had sunk*
prone; and to keep a guard on *those*
lips of her lovely face 'gainst
family-cursing accents

by force and *rude* might of speech-bridling bands.
And shedding her crocus-tinctured *tunic*
240 to earth, she smote each of her
slayers with a pity-kissing eye-dart;
and made a show, as in painted forms, as fain
to speak; for she many a time
within her sire's rich-spread hero-guest-halls
had sung, and with voice *all* pure, free from mate, trilled with love
245 her loving sire's hymn of praise for happy
fortune, at third-bowl-mixing.

I neither saw what ensued nor relate;
but Calchas' schemes failed not of completion.
The law-of-right turns the scale
250 then to know the future when you 've felt it:
farewell to news ere the thing has been, I say,

ritum offendit sermonis continuatio.   245. αἰῶνα M. παιῶνα Hartung;
  244. ἀγνὰ libri. ἀγνᾷ Schutz. Mox   formam tragicam Eng.
αὐδὰ M.   249. παθοῦσι libri.

ἴσον δὲ τῷ προστένειν·
τορὸν γὰρ ἥξει σύνορθρον αὐγαῖς.
Πέλοιτο δ' οὖν τἀπὶ τούτοισιν εὔπραξις, ὡς   255
θέλει τόδ' ἄγχιστον Ἀπίας γαί-
ας μονόφρουρον ἕρκος.

Ἥκω σεβίζων σόν, Κλυταιμνήστρα, κράτος·
δίκη γάρ ἐστι φωτὸς ἀρχηγοῦ τίειν
γυναῖκ', ἐρημωθέντος ἄρσενος θρόνου.   260
Σὺ δ' εἴ τι κεδνὸν εἴτε μὴ πεπυσμένη
εὐαγγέλοισιν ἐλπίσιν θυηπολεῖς
κλύοιμ' ἂν εὔφρων· οὐδὲ σιγώσῃ φθόνος.

ΚΛΥΤΑΙΜΝΗΣΤΡΑ.

Εὐάγγελος μέν, ὥσπερ ἡ παροιμία,
ἕως γένοιτο μητρὸς εὐφρόνης πάρα.   265
Πεύσει δὲ χάρμα μεῖζον ἐλπίδος κλύειν·
Πριάμου γὰρ ᾑρήκασιν Ἀργεῖοι πόλιν.

ΧΟΡΟΣ.

Πῶς φῇς; πέφευγε τοὖπος ἐξ ἀπιστίας.

ΚΛΥΤΑΙΜΝΗΣΤΡΑ.

Τροίαν Ἀχαιῶν οὖσαν· ἢ τορῶς λέγω;

ΧΟΡΟΣ.

Χαρά μ' ὑφέρπει δάκρυον ἐκκαλουμένη.   270

---

252. τὸ δὲ προκλύειν ἐπιγένοιτ' ἂν κλύοις προχαιρέτω M. idem Fl. nisi quod ἐπεὶ γένοιτ'. τὸ δὲ προκλύειν omisit F. ἂν κλύοις corrupte legitur ἀπηλύοις in A., ἂν ἡ λύσις in T. V. Fuerunt qui glossam adeo corrup-

tam in textum receperint. Scilicet x et η literae similes sunt. Rectissime, mea sententia, Heimsoeth., quae dedi. τὸ μέλλον δ' ἐπεὶ γένοιτ' ἂν κλύοις προχαιρέτω (s. πρὸ χαιρέτω) Bamberg., Schn., Dind., Weil., Ahr.,

as equalling grief before:
all bright 't will come dawning with the morn-beams.
255 At least in all after this may there be fortune-fair
as wishes you puissant sole-protecting
tow'r of the land of Apis.

With homage, Clytemnestra, to your rule
I come: 'tis right a royal chieftain's dame
260 to honour, when the male's state-seat is void.
Whether you 're burning incense having heard
good, or, if not, in hope of cheering news,
I'd gladly hear, nor, if you 're mute, bear grudge.

CLYTEMNESTRA.

May there be born from mother of good cheer,
265 as says the proverb, morning of good news.
You 'll hear a joy passing your hope to hear:
the Argive men have taken Priam's town.

CHORUS.

How say you? through mistrust the word escaped.

CLYTEMNESTRA.

That Troy is the Achaeans': do I speak plain?

CHORUS.

270 Joy steals upon me, calling forth a tear.

Eng. An credam igitur Æsch. dixisse
ἐπεὶ γένοιτ' ἄν? At πρὶν γένοιτο recte
sequitur vocem χαιρέτω, quæ valet
χαίρειν λέγοιμ' ἄν.
254. συνορθὸν αὐταῖς M. σύναρθρον
αὐταῖς Fl. F. σύνορθρον Wellauer.,

αὐγαῖς Herm.
255. εὔπραξις libri. quam vocem
quum Lobeck. Græcitati abjudicet,
εὖ πρᾶξις scribunt Eng., Karst.
261. εἴτε libri. in M. ultima ε e
correctione. εἰ τι Aur., recentt.

ΚΛΤΤΑΙΜΝΗΣΤΡΑ.

Εὖ γὰρ φρονοῦντος ὄμμα σοῦ κατηγορεῖ.

ΧΟΡΟΣ.

Τί γάρ; Τὸ πιστὸν ἔστι τῶνδέ σοι τέκμαρ;

ΚΛΤΤΑΙΜΝΗΣΤΡΑ.

Ἔστιν· τί δ' οὐχί; μὴ δολώσαντος θεοῦ.

ΧΟΡΟΣ.

Πότερα δ' ὀνείρων φάσματ' εὐπειθῆ σέβεις;

ΚΛΤΤΑΙΜΝΗΣΤΡΑ.

Οὐ δόξαν ἂν λάβοιμι βριζούσης φρενός.   275

ΧΟΡΟΣ.

Ἀλλ' ἦ σ' ἐπίανέν τις ἄπτερος φάτις;

ΚΛΤΤΑΙΜΝΗΣΤΡΑ.

Παιδὸς νέας ὧς κάρτ' ἐμωμήσω φρένας.

ΧΟΡΟΣ.

Ποίου χρόνου δὲ καὶ πεπόρθηται πόλις;

ΚΛΤΤΑΙΜΝΗΣΤΡΑ.

Τῆς νῦν τεκούσης φῶς τόδ' εὐφρόνης λέγω.

ΧΟΡΟΣ.

Καὶ τίς τόδ' ἐξίκοιτ' ἂν ἀγγέλων τάχος;   280

---

272. τί γὰρ τὸ libri. τί γάρ;   280. Sic libri; sed in M. sec.
Schutz: alia dici poterant, hoc apte.   Franzii apographon post λ litera

CLYTEMNESTRA.

The look of one well pleased accuses you.

CHORUS.

Of course: but have you the sure proof of it?

CLYTEMNESTRA.

I have: how not? unless a god played false.

CHORUS.

Do you esteem dream phantoms credible?

CLYTEMNESTRA.

275 I would not take belief from slumbering sense.

CHORUS.

Has some unfledged report inflated you?

CLYTEMNESTRA.

You greatly blame my wit as some young girl's.

CHORUS.

Since what time has the city been destroyed?

CLYTEMNESTRA.

This night, I tell you, mother of yon dawn.

CHORUS.

280 And pray what herald could attain this speed?

erasa est; quapropter ἀγγέλλων Karst. est valde probabilis correctio.
corr.; Dind., Ahr. recoperunt. Sane

ΚΛΥΤΑΙΜΝΗΣΤΡΑ.

Ἥφαιστο:, Ἴδης λαμπρὸν ἐκπέμπων σέλας·
Φρυκτὸς δὲ Φρυκτὸν δεῦρ' ἀπ' ἀγγάρου πυρὸς
ἔπεμπεν· Ἴδη μὲν πρὸς Ἑρμαῖον λέπας
Λήμνου, προςαιθρίζουσα πόμπιμον Φλόγα
πεύκης· μέγαν δὲ πανὸν ἐκ νήσου τρίτον
Ἀθῷον αἶπος Ζηνὸς ἐξεδέξατο·   285
ὑπερτελής τε πόντον ὥστε νωτίσαι
ἰσχὺς πορευτοῦ λαμπάδος πρὸς ἡδονὴν
ἧξεν, τὸ χρυσοφεγγὲς ὥς τις ἥλιος
σέλας παραγγείλασα Μακίστου σκοπάς·
ὁ δ' οὔτι μέλλων οὐδ' ἀφρασμόνως ὕπνῳ   290
νικώμενος παρῆκεν ἀγγέλου μέρος·
ἑκὰς δὲ Φρυκτοῦ Φῶς ἐπ' Εὐρίπου ῥοὰς
Μεσσαπίου φύλαξι σημαίνει μολόν·
οἱ δ' ἀντέλαμψαν καὶ παρήγγειλαν πρόσω
γραίας ἐρείκης θωμὸν ἅψαντες πυρί.   295
Σθένουσα λαμπὰς δ' οὐδέπω μαυρουμένη,
ὑπερθοροῦσα πεδίον Ἀσωποῦ, δίκην
Φαιδρᾶς σελήνης, πρὸς Κιθαιρῶνος λέπας,
ἤγειρεν ἄλλην ἐκδοχὴν πομποῦ πυρός.
Φάος δὲ τηλέπομπον οὐκ ἠναίνετο   300
Φρουρά, πλέον καίουσα τῶν εἰρημένων·
λίμνην δ' ὑπὲρ Γοργῶπιν ἔσκηψεν Φάος,
ὄρος τ' ἐπ' Αἰγίπλαγκτον ἐξικνούμενον

---

282. ἀπαγγέλου M. a pr. m., ἀπ'
ἀ., a. sec. m. Schutz ex E. M.,
cet. restituit ἀπ' ἀγγάρου.
284. Hic Heims. intexuit frag. a
Dind. primo ex Hesych. allatum,
προςαιθρίζουσα πόμπιμον φλόγα: non

tamen ut v. ἔπεμπεν, cum Ahr.,
mutaret, sed v. πεύκη (i. e. πεύκης),
ad v. 288 injuria deturbatam, proximo versui praeficeret. Res tantum
non certa, me judice. Mox φανὸν
libri. πανὸν Pors.

CLYTEMNESTRA.

Hephaestus, who from Ida sent bright flame:
and beacon kept despatching beacon here,
with fire as courier: Ida to Hermes' cliff
in Lemnos, darting high a carrier blaze
of pine wood: thirdly Athos, steep of Zeus,
285 received a mighty flambeau from the isle,
and rising high to clear the sea's *broad* back
the travelled lamplight's strength with transport sprang,
and ushered in the rays of golden sheen
like a sun-*rising* to Makistus' peaks.
290 And he, no loiterer, nor unheedfully
subdued by sleep, sent on his share of news:
and far the fire-sign to Euripus' streams
came, and gave notice to Messapion's guards.
They lit in turn and sent the watchword on,
295 kindling with fire a heap of grizzled heath.
And the stark lamplight, even yet not dimmed,
o'erleaping Asop's plain, in manner of
the radiant moon*beam*, to Cithaeron's rock,
awaked a fresh relay of fire express.
300 The frontier-guard spurned not the light despatched
from far, but lit up more than was imposed:
so the light flashed across Gorgopis' lake
and having reached the mountain Ægiplanct

285. ἄθωον libri. corr. Blomf.
286. ρωτίσαι Musgr.; id quod
quivis alius, praeter Æsch., dixisset.
288. πεύκη τὸ libri. ἧξεν, τὸ ego
in locum absentis renunciavi. cf. Pers.
469 παραγγείλας ἧξε, et Comment.

301. Hic Dind. posuit fragm.
illud, de quo dixi; eum enim offendit frigida locutio πλέον τῶν εἰρημένων. Immo vivida est: vigiles, ne
desint operæ, immoderate abundant.

3

ὤτρυνε θεσμὸν μὴ μεγαίρειν μοι πυρός.

Πέμπουσι δ' ἀνδαίοντες ἀφθόνῳ μένει 305
φλογὸς μέγαν πώγωνα καὶ Σαρωνικοῦ
πορθμοῦ κάτοπτον πρῶν' ὑπερβάλλειν πρόσω
φλέγουσαν· εἶτ' ἔσκηψεν ἔς τ' ἀφίκετο
Ἀραχναῖον αἶπος, ἀστυγείτονας σκοπάς·
κἄπειτ' Ἀτρειδῶν ἐς τόδε σκήπτει στέγος 310
φάος τόδ' οὐκ ἄπαππον Ἰδαίου πυρός. .
Τοιοίδε τοί μοι λαμπαδηφόρων νόμοι·
νικᾷ δ' ὁ πρῶτος καὶ τελευταῖος δραμών,
ἄλλος παρ' ἄλλου διαδοχαῖς πληρούμενοι.
Τέκμαρ τοιοῦτο σύμβολόν τε σοὶ λέγω, 315
ἀνδρὸς παραγγείλαντος ἐκ Τροίας ἐμοί.

ΧΟΡΟΣ.

Θεοῖς μὲν αὖθις, ὦ γύναι, προςεύξομαι·
λόγους δ' ἀκοῦσαι τούςδε κἀποθαυμάσαι
διηνεκῶς θέλοιμ' ἂν ὡς λέγοις πάλιν.

ΚΛΥΤΑΙΜΝΗΣΤΡΑ.

Τροίαν Ἀχαιοὶ τῇδ' ἔχουσ' ἐν ἡμέρᾳ. 320
Οἶμαι βοὴν ἄμικτον ἐν πόλει πρέπειν.
Ὄξος τ' ἄλειφά τ' ἐγχέας ταὐτῷ κύτει
διχοστατοῦντ' ἄν, οὐ φίλω, προςεννέποις.
Καὶ τῶν ἁλόντων καὶ κρατησάντων δίχα

304. μὴ χαρίζεσθαι πυρός libri. Sed χαρίζεσθαι est glossa ad μὴ μεγαίρειν adscripta, et postea in libros recepta non sine μὴ. Habes ἀφθονήτῳ prox. v. Est autem signum in Megaride, quod argumentum melius erit non contemnere. Vide infra v.

347 et 478. μὴ miserum, toties consortis viduum; quotiescumque, nisi me fallit, corrigunt πῆ.
307. κάτοπτρον libri. κάτοπτον Canter.
308. εἶτ' ἀφίκετο libri. ἔς τ' Stanl. ἔςτ' alii. vera l. incerta.

roused up the edict not to stint me fire:

305 they made a blaze, and sent with zeal ungrudged

a mighty beard of flame even to o'ershoot

the headland that looks down on Saron's frith

illuming it: then flashed *until* it reached

the Arachnaean steep, heights near the town.

310 Then to the Atreids' roof, there, shot the flame

not without far descent from Ida's fire.

Such my lamp-bearing racers' rules o' the course:

each wins, the first-stage-runner and the last,

all run the full course by relief of each.

315 Such proof I give you and concerted sign,

my lord transmitting it from Troy to me.

CHORUS.

Anon, o lady, I'll address the gods;

for I would have you speak these words throughout

again, that I may listen and admire.

CLYTEMNESTRA.

320 The Greeks hold Troy this day; and in the town

I fancy cries incongruous are rife.

If you poured oil and verjuice in one jar

you 'd style them as dissentients, and not friends:

the captives' and the conquerors' cries one may

310. ἐστὸγε M.

312. τοιοίδ' ἕτοιμοι Bess., F. τοιοίδ' ἕτυμοι Fl., Vict. Schutz. corr.

313, 314 inverso ordine leguntur in libris. Olim reposui, ut syntaxis recte incederet.

315. τοιοῦτον FL F.

319. Vulg. dubitanter recepi, nam Both. οὓς pro ὡς commendat. Verti cum Heims.

322. ἐχχίας libri. corr. Canter.

323. οὐ φίλως libri. φίλω Stanl. Sunt qui illud interpretari possint.

3 *

φθογγὰς ἀκούειν ἔστι συμφορᾶς διπλῆς.   325

Οἱ μὲν γὰρ ἀμφὶ σώμασιν πεπτωκότες

ἀνδρῶν κασιγνήτων τε, καὶ φυταλμίων

παῖδες γερόντων, οὐκέτ᾽ ἐξ ἐλευθέρου

δέρης ἀποιμώζουσι φιλτάτων μόρον.

Τοὺς δ᾽ αὖτε νυκτίπλαγκτος ἐκ μάχης πόνος   330

νήστεις πρὸς ἀρίστοισιν ὧν ἔχει πόλις

τάσσει, πρὸς οὐδὲν ἐν μέρει τεκμήριον,

ἀλλ᾽ ὡς ἕκαστος ἔσπασεν τύχης πάλου.

Ἐν αἰχμαλώτοις Τρωϊκοῖς οἰκήμασιν

ναίουσιν ἤδη, τῶν ὑπαιθρίων πάγων   335

δρόσων τ᾽ ἀπαλλαγέντες· ὡς δ᾽ εὐδαίμονες

ἀφύλακτον εὐδήσουσι πᾶσαν εὐφρόνην.

Εἰ δ᾽ εὐσεβοῦσι τοὺς πολισσούχους θεοὺς

τοὺς τῆς ἁλούσης γῆς θεῶν θ᾽ ἱδρύματα

οὔ τὰν ἑλόντες αὖθις ἀνθαλοῖεν ἄν.   340

Ἔρως δὲ μή τις πρότερον ἐμπίπτῃ στρατῷ

πορθεῖν ἃ μὴ χρή, κέρδεσιν νικωμένους·

δεῖ γὰρ πρὸς οἴκους νοστίμου σωτηρίας

κάμψαι διαύλου θάτερον κῶλον πάλιν.

Θεοῖς δ᾽ ἀναμπλάκητος εἰ μόλοι στρατὸς   345

ἐγρηγορὸς τὸ πῆμα τῶν ὀλωλότων

γένοιτ᾽ ἄν, εἰ πρόσπαια μὴ ἁμάρτοι κακά.

327, 328. Sic libri. φυτάλμιοι παί- δων γέροντες Weil., ab Enger. receptum. Sed et senes interfici oportet, ut nemo nisi pueri mulieresque supersint; nec nisi vulg. retento Priami cadaver spectare possum.

331. νῆστις Fl. νήστεις F., recentt. νῆστις Ahr.

333. Enger. primus post πάλον interpunxit. Idem ἐν δ᾽ prox. v.; sed nescio an Æschyli proprium sit omittere v. δέ.

336. ὡς δυσδαίμονες libri. ὡς δ᾽ εὐδ. Stanl. Verti cum Martino. cf. v. 1236.

340. οὐκ ἄν γ᾽ Fl. οὐκ ἀνελόντες Bess. οὔ τὰν Herm. οὐκ ἂν tuetur Abr. ἂν enim ex ἢ ἂν ortum esse, ut ἄρα ex ἢ ἄρα. Utinam consentire possem. Deinde αὖ θάνοιεν Fl. ἂν θάνοιεν Bess. ἀνθάλοιεν Aurat. accentum corr. Blomf.

341. ἐμπίπτοι F. sic Dind., alii;

325 hear, *each* distinct, rising from different lots:

those, sunk *with arms* around a husband's corse

or brother's, children *clasping the dead forms*

of aged sires, no longer through free throats,

as heretofore, bemoan the loved one's fate:

330 but these night-wandering turmoil after fight

sets hungry down at meals of what the place

holds, with no ticket to admit in turn

but as each drew the billet of his luck.

In captive Trojan homesteads they dwell now,

335 from hoarfrosts underneath the clear cold sky

and dews released; and how luxuriously

they 'll sleep the night out with no watch to keep!

And if they reverence city-guarding gods,

those of the captured land, and gods' abodes,

340 the captors will not in their turn be caught.

But let no lust meanwhile befal the host

to long for things unfit, o'ercome by gain:

there's need of home-arriving safe-return,

and to bend back the bistade's other limb.

345 Ev'n if the host come sinless towards the gods

the lost ones' woe will be awake to see

if unexpected ills can hit the mark.

---

sed monito opus est, non voto.

342. πορθεῖν libri, excepto quod Vict., et Fl. sec. Herm. ποθεῖν.

345. ἀν ἀμπλάκητος Fl. θεοῖσι δ' ἀμπλάκητος cum Stanl., Herm. alii. Sed nexus est; 'Esto: deorum numina non læscrunt; homicidii tamen (Iphigeniæ et Trojanorum) pœna daude est'. Nam salutem in neutram partem augurari vult Clyt. Prætendit quidem τὸ δ' εὖ κρατοίη; ad quæ

Chorus, ut illa, parum ex animo, respondet εὐφρόνως λέγεις 'bene ominaris'. Addo quod ἀμπλάκητος (s. potius -τός) est vox nihili, ut videtur.

346. ἐγρήγορον libri. corr. Pors., tuetur Ahr.

347. μὴ τύχοι libri. πῃ τεύχοι Ahr., Eug. Weil. Sed, ut ego vidi, μὴ satis frugi est; at v. τύχοι nequam, quae vocis ἀμάρτοι sedem præoccupaverit, contempta voce μή.

Τοιαῦτά τοι γυναικὸς ἐξ ἐμοῦ κλύεις·
τὸ δ' εὖ κρατοίη, μὴ διχορρόπως ἰδεῖν,
πολλῶν γὰρ ἐσθλῶν τὴν ὄνησιν εἱλόμην.   350

ΧΟΡΟΣ.

Γύναι, κατ' ἄνδρα σώφρον' εὐφρόνως λέγεις·
ἐγὼ δ' ἀκούσας πιστά σου τεκμήρια
θεοὺς προςειπεῖν εὖ παρασκευάζομαι,
χάρις γὰρ οὐκ ἄτιμος εἴργασται πόνων.

'Ω Ζεῦ βασιλεῦ, καὶ νὺξ Φιλία   355
    μεγάλων κόσμων κτεάτειρα,
ἥτ' ἐπὶ Τροίας πύργοις ἔβαλες
    στεγανὸν δίκτυον ὡς μήτε μέγαν
    μήτ' οὖν νεαρῶν τιν' ὑπερτελέσαι
    μέγα δουλείας   360
    γάγγαμον ἄτης παναλώτου.
Δία τοι ξένιον μέγαν αἰδοῦμαι
    τὸν τάδε πράξαντ', ἐπ' Ἀλεξάνδρῳ
    τείνοντα πάλαι τόξον ὅπως ἂν
    μήτε πρὸ καιροῦ μήθ' ὑπὲρ ἄσσον   365
    βέλος ἠλίθιον σκήψειεν.

στρ.ά.   Διὸς πλαγὰν ἔχουσιν, εἰπεῖν
          πάρεστιν, τοῦτο δ' ἐξιχνεῦσαι.

---

348. κλύοις FL κλύεις Bess., nec   360. Versus suspectus Schutzio,
aliter infra v. 1431 ἀκούεις.   Eng. cet., sed sensus integer: 'ser-
   350. πολλῶν ἰσθλῶν et sexcenta alia   vitutis rete jaculum, exitii instru-
in hac fabula Hesiodo derivata sunt.   mentum'. Sic infra v. 771 θράσος
   353. εὖ cum παρ. vel caesura duce   ἄτας 'temeritas exitii effectrix'.
conjungo.   363. Interpunctionem post Ἀλ.

Such woman's words you hear from me; but may

good win, in no mere equipoise with ill,

350 for I prefer the bliss of plenteous joys.

CHORUS.

Lady, like man of judgement, cheerfully

you speak; and I, hearing your trusty proofs,

duly prepare me to address the gods,

for grace is wrought well worth the task of praise.

355 O Zeus, *prime* king, and thou Night the beloved

  of glories majestic possessor!

who also didst fling on the bulwarks of Troy

  a fast-holding net, so that no full-grown,

  no, nor a young one rose *and emerged* from

360   slavery's drop-net

  immense, of all-trapping perdition!

I venerate Zeus, great lord of the board,

  who accomplished these deeds; who has long had his bow

  levelled at Paris in order to launch no

365   fatuous arrow whizzing onward before

  opportunity's hint, nor behind it.

'A stroke from Zeus' we *now* can warrant

'they have', and trace this story's progress.

Herm. pr. delevit.

365. ὑπὲρ ἄστρων libri, quod defendi nequit. ὑπερᾷσσον Weil. Scripsi divisim. Jam optimum sensum habes, sicut verti; ἄστρων autem correctio erat.

367. Sic libri. ego commata apposui ut sit: 'hoc habent; Jovis ictum': vox ab arena tralata.

368. πάρεστι libri. corr. Karst., Heims. τοῦτ' ἰξ. Fl. τοῦτο δ' Eng.

Ἔπραξαν ὡς ἔκριναν. Οὐκ ἔφα τις
θεοὺς βροτῶν ἀξιοῦσθαι μέλειν   370
ὅσοις ἀθίκτων χάρις
πατοῖθ'· ὁ δ' οὐκ εὐσεβής.
Πέφανται δ' ἐγγενὴς
ἀτολμήτων Ἄρης   375
πνεόντων μεῖζον ἢ δικαίως,
φλεόντων δωμάτων ὑπέρφευ,
ὑπὲρ τὸ βέλτιστον· ἔστω δ' ἀπή-
μαντον, ὥςτ' ἀπαρκεῖν
εὖ πραπίδων λαχόντι·   380
οὐ γὰρ ἔστιν ἔπαλξις
πλούτου πρὸς κόρον ἀνδρὶ
λακτίσαντι μέγαν Δίκας
βωμὸν εἰς ἀφάνειαν.

ἀντ.ἀ.   Βιᾶται δ' ἁ τάλαινα πειθώ, ·   385
πρόβουλος παῖς ἄφερτος ἄτας·
ἄκος δὲ πᾶν μάταιςν· οὐκ ἐκρύφθη,
πρέπει δέ, φῶς αἰνολαμπές, σίνος.
Κακοῦ δὲ χαλκοῦ τρόπον   390
τρίβῳ τὲ καὶ προσβολαῖς
μελαμπαγὴς πέλει
δικαιωθείς· ἐπεὶ
διώκει παῖς ποτανὸν ὄρνιν,

369. ὡς ἔπραξεν ὡς ἔκρανεν libri. Prius ὡς delevit Herm. ἔπραξαν Franz., Herm. alii: necessario; nam hic generaliter loqui oportet, non de Paride. Ego ἔκριναν, ut κρίνω δ' ἄφθονον ὄλβον v. 471. Neque enim ἔκρανεν de Jove dici potest, neque ἔκραναν intransitive de Trojanis; ceterum de Paride non loquitur poeta, sed ad v. 400. Tentare possis ἐχρῆν νιν. licenter.

373. Locus misere vexatus. Legendum ἐγγενὴς et Ἄρης ut ego et Karst. vidimus (ἐγγόνους et ἀρη libri). Sic omnia prospere eveniunt. Et ἔκγονος optime conveniret, sed veri

They fared as they made choice. One said 'the gods, they
370 deign not to heed men by whom homage due
to things debarred *mortal* touch
is spurned': but he prayed not well.
A strife for things denied
375 to lust is proved innate
in men unduly breathing pride,
in houses overwell o'erflowing,
beyond what 's best: let *the good* painless be,
such as to suffice him
380 who has his share of wisdom;
for there rises no refuge
when, through fulness of wealth, man
kicks at Justice's altar high,
kicks it, to his exstinction.

385 But sad Temptation drags him onward,
foreplotting, fatal child of ruin:
and cure is all-abortive; 'tis not hidden,
the bane, but shines clear, a dire-gleaming light:
390 like metal base, which by wear
and testing stone's touch assayed
displays black streaks; for he 's
a child in chase of bird
swift-winged, who brings a fatal taint on

similius est postremam partem vocis
ἐγγόνους corruptam esse. Ἄρης ἀτολμήτων dictum est ut ἔρις ἀγαθῶν.
'ferocitas (quæ propria est Τρώων
ὑπερριάλων, μάχης ἀκορήτων, Cic. Div.
2. 39. 82) rerum inconcessarum cap-
tatrix'. Sententia e Menelai oratione
est sumpta, Hom. Il. τι. 13. 620 sq.

379. ὥστε κἀπαρκεῖν F. Triclinii
infausta correctio.
380. λαχόντα libri. corr. Ahr.
383. μεγάλα libri. corr. Canter.
386. προβουλόπαις libri. πρόβουλος
παῖς Karst. Res manifesta.
391. προβολαῖς libri. corr. Stanl.

πόλει πρόςτριμμ' ἄφερτον ἐνθείς· 395
λιτᾶν δ' ἀκούει μὲν οὔτις θεῶν·
   τὸν δ' ἐπίστροφον δὴ
φῶτ' ἄδικον καθαιρεῖ.
Οἷος καὶ Πάρις, ἐλθὼν
ἐς δόμον τὸν Ἀτρειδᾶν 400
ᾔσχυνε ξενίαν τράπε-
ζαν κλοπαῖσι γυναικός.

στρ.β'. Λιποῦσα δ' ἀστοῖσιν ἀσπίστορας
κλόνους τε καὶ λογχίμους, ναυβάτας θ' ὁπλισμούς, 405
ἄγουσά τ' ἀντίφερνον Ἰλίῳ φθοράν,
βέβακεν ῥίμφα διὰ πυλᾶν,
ἄτλητα τλᾶσα. Πολλὰ δ' ἔστενον
τόδ' ἐννέποντες δόμων προφῆται·
ἰώ, ἰὼ δῶμα, δῶμα καὶ πρόμοι· 410
ἰὼ λέχος καὶ στίβοι φιλάνορες.
Πάρεστι σιγᾶς, ἀτίμως, ἀλοιδόρως,
ἄδιστ' ἀδημονῶν ἰδεῖν·
πόθῳ δ' ὑπερποντίας
φάσμα δόξει δόμων ἀνάσσειν. 415
Εὐμόρφων δὲ κολοσσῶν
ἔχθεται χάρις ἀνδρί,

395. πτανὸν libri. corr. Schutz.
395. θείς Fl. corr. Triclin.
397. τῶνδε libri. δὴ ego, ejecto
τῶν. 'cultorem scilicet'. τῶν est scrip-
toris librarii peccatum.
400. τῶν Fl. Vict. τὸν F.
405. τε καὶ, post ἀσπίστορας in
libris lectum, in ordinem coegit
Ahr., θ' post ναυβάτας addito.
407. βέβακε Fl. corr. in F. Vict.
408. πολὺ δ' ἀνέστενον Fl. Quod

Pauw. conjecerat, πολλὰ δ' ἔστενον,
id F. præbet, omnes receperunt.
409. τόδ' Fl Vict. τάδ' Aur.
410. ἰὼ δῶμα, utrumque semel,
Fl. (Eugeri typographus omisit alterum δῶμα.)
412. πάρεστι σιγᾶς ἄτιμος ἀλοίδορος
ἄδιστος ἀρεμένων ἰδεῖν libri. Vides
σιγᾶς perisp. esse. Sit σιγᾶς; ut ἀργᾶς;
supra: magnum posco; sit tamen.
ἀτίμως est οὐκ ἐπιτιμῶν. Deinde Schol.

395 his state, *then seeks for expiation*:

    for *now* no god hears his prayers, none; but each

        sweeps away the guilty

    man who, forsooth, turns towards him.

    Such was Paris; to Atreus'

400 sons' abode having come, he

    outrage foul to the friendly board

        did by theft of the host's wife.

    And leaving her country-men battle shocks

405 with shields and spears, ships to mount, fleets to build and furnish,

    and bearing for a dowry ruin to Ilion

    she lightly goes the gates between;

    ill-daring darer. Much they mourned —

    the palace-seers — mourned with exclamation:

410 "Alas, sad home! *sad* the home and *sad* the chiefs!

    sad bed! and form where she fondled her *true* lord!

    he stands by mute, breathing not vengeance nor reproach,

    aghast at sights most sweet *before;*

    and missing her *now*-beyond-

415 seas a ghost seems to rule the palace.

    Now the charms of her statues

    fair is loathed by the husband,

F., qui ἥδιστη interpretatur, legit ἄδιστα. Jam velim adeas Med. cod. apographon quod Dindorfius, vir optimus, nobis in manus dedit. Non-ne quævis litera ρ eadem est quæ δ, recta lineola per mediam postea demissa? Hinc ego ἀδημονῶν 'obstupe-factus'. Putes et δαιμονῶν, formam tragicam, sed vox notior mansisset, illa injuriæ obnoxia erat. ἄδιςτ' cum ἰδεῖν conjungo. Et lectus jugalis quidem, et Helenæ corporis vestigia ἄδιστα fuerant ἰδεῖν. Aliorum conjecturae ap. Engeri ed. prostant.

416. κολοσσοί, ut aperte enarrem quare vir. doct. conjecturas spreverim, sunt Helenæ statuæ ligneæ, e quibus una in locto Menelai sub noctem posita est; quemadmodum Admetus conjugi pollicitus est Eur. Alc. 348 sq. ψυχρὸν παραγκάλισμα.

ὀμμάτων δ᾿ ἐν ἀχηνίαις
ἔρρει πᾶσ᾿ Ἀφροδίτα.

ἀντ.β΄. Ὀνειρόφαντοι δὲ πενθήμονες   420
πάρεισι δόξαι φέρουσαι χάριν ματαίαν·
μάταν γάρ, εὖτ ἂν ἐσθλά τις δοκῶν ὁρᾷ,
παραλλάξασα διὰ χερῶν
βέβακεν ὄψις οὐ μεθύστερον   425
πτεροῖς ὀπαδοῦσ᾿ ὕπνου κελεύθοις.
Τὰ μὲν κατ᾿ οἴκους ἐφεστίους ἄχη
τάδ᾿ ἐστὶ καὶ τῶνδ᾿ ὑπερβατώτερα.
Τὸ πᾶν δ᾿ ἀφ᾿ Ἕλλανος αἴας συνορμένοις
πένθεια τλησικάρδιος   430
δόμῳ ᾿ν ἑκάστῳ πρέπει.
Πολλὰ γοῦν θιγγάνει πρὸς ἧπαρ·
οὓς μὲν γάρ τις ἔπεμψεν
εἶδεν· ἀντὶ δὲ φώτων
τεύχη καὶ σποδὸς εἰς ἑκά-   435
στου δόμους ἀφικνεῖται.

στρ.γ΄. Ὁ χρυσαμοιβὸς δ᾿ Ἄρης σωμάτων,
ὁ καὶ ταλαντοῦχος ἐν μάχῃ δορός,
πυρωθὲν ἐξ Ἰλίου   440
φίλοισι πέμπει βαρὺ
ψῆγμα δυσδάκρυτον ἀν-

---

418. ἀχηνίαις hic, me judice, a
voce κέχηνα derivatur.
419. Ἀφροδίτη Fl.
422. δοκῶν ὁρᾶν libri. ὁρᾷ Prienius.
426. ὀπαδοῖς libri. ὀπαδοῦσ᾿ Dobræus.

427. ἐφ᾿ ἑστίας libri. corr. Voss.
428. Sic libri, vulg. Hahn. non
probat mihi τὰ δ᾿ et interpunct. suam
post ἄχη.
429. Ἑλλάδος libri. Ἕλλανος Franz.
431. τλησικάρδιος unice verum est;

and for lack of the love-lit eyes
rapture perishes wholly.

420 And, seen in dreams, fancies fair *dashed* with fond
regret are there, bringing joys empty of fruition:
for hope-deluding, when in thought one sees delight,
the dream-sprite gliding from the embrace
425 is gone, and afterwards returns on wings
no more, the *next* slumber's paths attending.
The griefs at home, home with *consecrated* hearth,
are these, and more, these surpassing; but the full
amount — for those who from Greece sailed in company
430 death-wail from hearts inured to grief
in each one's home rises clear.
Much in truth, pierces to the marrow:
whom each sent, he remembers
but, in place of the *stalwart*
435 heroes, urns and the burnt-remains
back return to each homestead.

For Mars who discounts the slain warrior's corpse,
and holds the scales also in the fight with spears,
440 to friends from Troy sends the dust
with fire refined, weighty dust,
˙cause of weeping, when he freights

---

vox enim usitata inter Pythagoreos,
τέτλαθι δὴ κραδίη.
  431. δόμων libri. At hic Halmio
manus do; præcepit enim δόμῳ 'ν.
ἑκάστου libri. ἑκάστῳ Eng.

433. Pors. inseruit τις.
436. εἰξαριχνεῖται Fl. corr. Pors.
439. ὁ addidit Weilius.
441. Inviolata v. βαρύ.

τήνορος σποδοῦ γεμί-
ζων λέβητας εὐθέτους.

Στένουσι δ' εὖ λέγοντες ἄν-   445
    δρα τὸν μὲν ὡς μάχης ἴδρις·
τὸν δ' ἐν φοναῖς καλῶς πεσόντ'
    ἀλλοτρίας διαὶ γυναι-
    κός· τάδε σῖγά τις βαΰ-
ζει· φθονερὸν δ' ὑπ' ἄλγος ἕρ-   450
πει προδίκοις 'Ατρείδαις.

Οἱ δ' αὐτοῦ περὶ τεῖχος
θήκας 'Ιλιάδος γᾶς
εὔκαλοι κατέχουσιν ἐχ-
θρὰ δ' ἔχοντας ἔκρυψεν.   455

ἀντ.γ'. Βαρεῖα δ' ἀστῶν φάτις ξὺν κότῳ,
τὸ δημοκράντου δ' ἀρᾶς τίνει χρέος.
Μένει δ' ἀκοῦσαί τί μου
μέριμνα νυκτηρεφές·   460
τῶν πολυκτόνων γὰρ οὐκ
    ἄσκοποι θεοί· κελαι-
    ναὶ δ' 'Ερινύες χρόνῳ
τυχηρὸν ὄντ' ἄνευ δίκας
    παλιντυχεῖ τριβᾷ βίου   465
τιθεῖσ' ἀμαυρόν· ἐν δ' ἀΐστοις τελέθοντος οὔτις ἀλ-
κά· τὸ δ' ὑπερκόπως κλύειν

444. εὐθέτου libri. corr. Auratus.
448. διὰ libri. διαὶ Herm., 'et ita
legitur in Crameri Anecd. I. p. 119
13 Oxon.' Eng.
454. εὔμορροι Fl. V. εὐμόρρως F.

Vulgatum servari non posse in
Comment. ostendi. Glossema est
εὔμορροι, cujus in locum restitui
veram lect. εὔκαλοι, quod Dorice
scriptum pro εὔκηλοι corrector a voce

lightly wielded urns with burnt-
ashes representing men.
445 This man they mourn and, lauding, say
how skilled he was in fight; and this
as nobly fall'n in bloody fray
(*all* for another's wife;) but one
silently murmurs this; and woe
450   mixed with dislike assails the king-
principals in the quarrel.
Others round the redoubts, there,
resting peacefully, tenant
tombs of Ilian earth, and with
455   hate it covered its winners.

The townsmen's talk joined with spite carries weight,
and claims the debt sanctioned by a people's curse.
My care abides *yet* to hear
460 a something now screened by night:
for of these great homicides
not unwatchful are the gods;
and in time the Furies dark
by fate-reversing blotting-out
465   of mortal life his light eclipse
who prospers not with right; and for
him who exists among th' unseen
help there is none; and praise beyond

καλός derivari opinatus est. Vide
Comment.
458. τὸ ipse addidi, post κότῳ
omissum. δημοκράτου libri. corr. Pors.

462. ἀπόσκοποι Fl.
465. παλιντυχῆ Fl. corr. Scaliger.
468. ὑπερχότως libri. corr. Gro-
tius.

εὖ βαρύ· βάλλεται γὰρ ὄ-
γκοις Διόθεν κεραυνός.   470
Κρίνω δ' ἄφθονον ὄλβον·
μήτ' εἴην πτολιπόρθης,
μήτ' οὖν αὐτὸς ἀλοὺς ὑπ' ἄλλων βίον κατίδοιμι.

δ.ά ἐπῳδ. Πυρὸς δ' ὑπ' εὐαγγέλου   475
πόλιν διήκει θοὰ
βάξις· εἰ δ' ἐτήτυμος,
τίς οἶδεν, ἤ τι θεῖόν ἐστι μὴ οὐ σαφές;
δ.β'. τίς ὧδε παιδνὸς ἢ φρενῶν κεκομμένος
φλογὸς παραγγέλμασιν   480
νέοις πυρωθέντα καρδίαν, ἔπειτ'
ἀλλαγᾷ λόγου καμεῖν;
δ.γ'. Γυναικὸς αἰχμᾷ πρέπει
πρὸ τοῦ φανέντος χάριν ξυναινέσαι.
δ δ'. Πιθανὸς ἄγαν ὁ θῆλυς ὅρος ἐπινέμεται   485
ταχύπορος· ἀλλὰ ταχύμορον
γυναικογήρυτον ὄλλυται κλέος.

Τάχ' εἰσόμεσθα λαμπάδων φαεσφόρων
φρυκτωριῶν τε καὶ πυρὸς παραλλαγὰς   490
εἴτ' οὖν ἀληθεῖς, εἴτ' ὀνειράτων δίκην

---

469. ὄσσοις libri. ὄγκοις Hartung.
Hoc meum feci; dignissimum enim
est quod in amissæ vocis locum acci-
piatur. Et quidni verum sit, quum
plurale in mathematicis libellis adhuc
exstet, et Æsch. Pythagoreus fuerit?
474. κατέδοιμι libri. corr. Valck.
ὑπ' ἄλλων sicut ὑπ' ὀρφανιστῶν Soph.

Ai. 512.
477. ἐτητύμως libri. corr. Aur.
478. ἤ, τοι θεῖόν ἐστιν μὴ ψῦθος
Fl. ἤ τοι F. V. ἤ τι Diud. Ridiculum est ut vertunt; Paleius enim
'quis novit utrum verum sit, au verum?' sic utique debebat 'not-a-
deception'. Hermannus, (qui εἴ τι

meed is a load; at thing of size
470   thunder from Zeus is vollied.

I choose wealth without-envy:

no town-captor would I be,

no, nor, captive myself, behold

    my life subject to others.

475 But *see*, a swift rumour roused

by fire the glad messenger

through the city speeds, but if

'tis true, who knows? or some mysterious work divine.

Who is so childish or in sense so dull of edge

480 as from the pass-words of flame

to catch at heart fever-heat and afterwards

    languish on the story's change?

It seems to suit woman's mood

t' assent to what pleases ere the thing appears:

485 too fond, the female field of faith is trespassed on

and soon o'errun, but, soon defunct,

a rumour dies when by woman heralded.

We shall soon know of these relays of fire,

490 of cresset signals and light-wafting lamps,

if, as she says, they 're true, or like *some* dreams

correxit,) etiam festivius: 'verumne sit, quis novit?' nisi deorum men- dacium est; continuo enim colligi posset verum esse'. Abr. apponit πη, toujours πη. Quid multa? ψύθος est glossa ad οὐ σαφὲς adscripta. Quæ dedi verto 'an divinum aliquid sit, ut ne sit recte intellectum'.

480. πρὸ τοῦ, (vide Comment.), est πρὸ τινός. Verto: 'mulieris est, antequam gratia evidenter accepta est, acceptam referre'.

485. γυναικοκήρυκτον Vict.

489. Hos versus libri Clytemne- stræ tribuunt, Scaliger Choro: res non incerta.

τερπνὸν τόδ' ἐλθὸν φῶς ἐφήλωσεν φρένας·

Κῆρυκ' ἀπ' ἀκτῆς τόνδ' ὁρῶ κατάσκιον
κλάδοις ἐλαίας· μαρτυρεῖ δέ μοι κάτις
πηλοῦ ξύνουρος διψία κόνις τάδε·   495
ὡς οὔτ' ἄναυδος οὔτε σοι δαίων φλόγα
ὕλης ὀρείας σημανεῖ καπνῷ πυρός,
ἀλλ' ἢ τὸ χαίρειν μᾶλλον ἐκβάξει λέγων·
τὸν ἀντίον δὲ τοῖςδ' ἀποστέργω λόγον·
εὖ γὰρ πρὸς εὖ φανεῖσι προσθήκη πέλοι.   500
Ὅςτις τάδ' ἄλλως τῇδ' ἐπεύχεται πόλει
αὐτὸς φρενῶν καρποῖτο τὴν ἁμαρτίαν.

ΚΗΡΥΞ.

Ἰὼ πατρῷον οὖδας Ἀργείας χθονός,
δεκάτου σε φέγγει τῷδ' ἀφικόμην ἔτους,
πολλῶν ῥαγεισῶν ἐλπίδων μιᾶς τυχών.   505
Οὐ γάρ ποτ' ηὔχουν τῇδ' ἐν Ἀργείᾳ χθονὶ
θανὼν μεθέξειν φιλτάτου τάφου μέρος.
Νῦν χαῖρε μὲν χθών, χαῖρε δ' ἡλίου φάος,
ὕπατός τε χώρας Ζεύς, ὁ Πύθιός τ' ἄναξ
τόξοις ἰάπτων μηκέτ' εἰς ἡμᾶς βέλη·   510
ἅλις παρὰ Σκάμανδρον ἦσθ' ἀνάρσιος·
νῦν δ' αὖτε σωτὴρ ἴσθι καὶ παιώνιος,
ἄναξ Ἄπολλον. Τούς τ' ἀγωνίους θεοὺς
πάντας προςαυδῶ, τόν τ' ἐμὸν τιμάορον
Ἑρμῆν, φίλον κήρυκα, κηρύκων σέβας,   515
ἥρως τε τοὺς πέμψαντας, εὐμενεῖς πάλιν
στρατὸν δέχεσθαι τὸν λελειμμένον δορός.

---

492. ἐφήλωσε libri. corr. Pors.   terpunxit post πυρός; nam vulgo
496. ὣς Fl.   plene interpungebatur.
497. Dind. primus commate in-   504. δεκάτου libri. δεκάτῳ Wund.

that pleasing light which came befooled the mind.

Yonder I see a herald *bound* from shore

brow-screened with olive-sprays; and thirsty dust

495 mud's sister and next neighbour bears me out:

since not as mute nor lighting you a flame

of mountain wood he 'll teach by smoke of fire;

but speaking will proclaim superior joy

or — but I disallow that tale's reverse.

500 Fair may the adjunct be to fair displays.

Who for our state prays thus in other sense,

may he, alone, reap fruit from his thought's sin.

HERALD.

Hail to thee, Argive land's paternal soil!

thus have I reached thee in this tenth year's light,

505 and after many hopes were wrecked, gained one.

I never fancied in this Argive earth

to die and get my grave-land share most sweet.

Now hail! my land, and hail! sunlight, to thee;

to Zeus the land's Most High, and Pytho's king,

510 who with his bow aims shafts at us no more:

unkind enough thou cam'st, Apollo king,

to the Scamander; now our Saviour be

and Leech again. The gods of combat all

I next invoke, and my own patron-god

515 Hermes, dear herald, herald's reverence,

and the conducting heroes, with good will

to take again the spear-surviving host.

---

511. ἦλθ' supra scripto ες Fl.
ἦλθες F. V. ἦσθ' Bl. ἦσθ' Herm. 'at
veniendi notio non apta' Eng. Immo

Graeci aptam esse existimabant, quod
e Soph. Ai. 702 intelligi potest.
512. παγώνος Fl. corr. Dobraeus.

4 *

ΑΓΑΜΕΜΝΩΝ.

Ἰὼ μέλαθρα βασιλέων, φίλαι στέγαι,
σεμνοί τε θᾶκοι, δαίμονές τ' ἀντήλιοι,
εἴ που πάλαι φαιδροῖσι τοισίδ' ὄμματι 520
δέξασθε κόσμῳ βασιλέα πολλῷ χρόνῳ·
ἥκει γὰρ ὑμῖν φῶς ἐν εὐφρόνῃ φέρων
καὶ τοῖσδ' ἅπασι κοινὸν Ἀγαμέμνων ἄναξ.
Ἀλλ' εὖ νιν ἀσπάσασθε, καὶ γὰρ οὖν πρέπει,
Τροίαν κατασκάψαντα τοῦ δικηφόρου 525
Διὸς μακέλλῃ, τῇ κατείργασται πέδον,
καὶ σπέρμα πάσης ἐξαπόλλυται χθονός.
Τοιόνδε Τροίᾳ περιβαλὼν ζευκτήριον
ἄναξ Ἀτρείδης πρέσβυς εὐδαίμων ἀνὴρ 530
ἥκει, τίεσθαι δ' ἀξιώτατος βροτῶν
τῶν νῦν· Πάρις γὰρ οὔτε συντελὴς πόλις
ἐξεύχεται τὸ δρᾶμα τοῦ πάθους πλέον·
ὀφλὼν γὰρ ἁρπαγῆς τε καὶ κλοπῆς δίκην
τοῦ ῥυσίου θ' ἥμαρτε καὶ πανώλεθρον 535
αὐτόχθονον πατρῷον ἔθρισεν δόμον·
διπλᾶ δ' ἔτισαν Πριαμίδαι θἀμάρτια.

ΧΟΡΟΣ.

Κῆρυξ Ἀχαιῶν χαῖρε τῶν ἀπὸ στρατοῦ.

ΚΗΡΤΞ.

Χαίρω τε, τεθνάναι τ' οὐκέτ' ἀντερῶ θεοῖς.

ΧΟΡΟΣ.

Ἔρως πατρῴας τῆςδε γῆς σ' ἐγύμνασεν; 540

520. ἤπου libri. εἴ που Aur., recentt. inde a Stanl. Deinde ἰδόντες Aur.; sed praeco τοισίδ' injecit ominis evitandi causa.
527. Huc vulgo obtrusus βωμοὶ δ' ἄιστοι καὶ θεῶν ἰδρύματα ex Pers. 811. Immane peccatum; quod Salzmannus primus notavit. Scilicet poeta sacrilegii reum Agamemnonem sedulo non facit.

Hail! mansions of our kings, beloved roofs,
and awful thrones, and gods who face the sun;
520 if ever erst ye did, with bright eyes, these,
receive in state the king after long time:
king Agamemnon comes with light in night
for you and all in common who stand here.
Yea, greet him kindly, for indeed 'tis fit,
525 who hath dug up the Troad with the spade
. of right-restoring Zeus; with it the soil
is tilled, and all the land's seed quite cleared out.
Having cast such a yoke-band over Troy
530 the elder king Atreides, hero blest,
is come, of living men most worthy fame.
Not Paris, nor the country co-assessed
boasts that the act outdid the suffering *dealt:*
cast in the suit for rape and theft he both
535 has lost the goods he seized and with the land
mowed down in ruin full his father's house;
and Priam's folk paid double mulct-for-sin.

CHORUS.

Rejoice, thou herald of the embattled Greeks.

HERALD.

I do; I'll say no more to heaven 'gainst death.

CHORUS.

540 Love of this fatherland kept you sore tried?

534. ὅρλων libri. corr. Bl.   F. et Palcio 'facinoris pretium'.
536. ἐθρίσεν a sec. m. in Fl. su-   539. χαίρω· τεθνᾶναι δ' libri (ἔτ' in
pra scriptum.   Fl. omissum) χαίρω τε Herm. olim,
537. θἀμάρτια. Verto cum Sch.   quod Heims. recepit, δ' in τ' mutato.

ΚΗΡΥΞ.

῞Ωςτ᾽ ἐνδακρύειν γ᾽ ὄμμασιν χαρᾶς ὕπο.

ΧΟΡΟΣ.

Τερπνῆς ἄρ᾽ ἦστε τῆςδ᾽ ἐπήβολοι νόσου.

ΚΗΡΥΞ.

Πῶς δή; διδαχθεὶς τοῦδε δεσπόσω λόγου.

ΧΟΡΟΣ.

Τῶν ἀντερώντων ἱμέρῳ πεπληγμένοι.

ΚΗΡΥΞ.

Ποθεῖν πcθοῦντα τήνδε γῆν στρατὸν λέγεις;   545

ΧΩΡΟΣ.

῾Ως πόλλ᾽ ἀμχυρᾶς ἐκ Φρενός μ᾽ ἀναστένειν.

ΚΗΡΥΞ.

Πόθεν τὸ δύσφρον τοῦτ᾽ ἐπῆν στένος λεῷ;

ΧΟΡΟΣ.

Πάλαι τὸ σιγᾶν Φάρμακον βλάβης ἔχω.

ΚΗΡΥΞ.

Καὶ πῶς; ἀπόντων κοιράνων ἔτρεις τινάς;

541. ἐκδακρύειν T.   whitt.
542. ἴστε Fl. ἦτε F. ἦστε Ahr.   546. μ᾽ Scaliger addidit.
543. Interpunxit Schutz.   547. στύγος στρατῷ libri. Nebu-
544. πεπληγμένος libri. corr. Tyr-   lones ambo. στένος ego, vocibus ἀνασ-

HERALD.

So that tears start within my eyes for joy.

CHORUS.

Then you were smit with that delightful pain.

HERALD.

How so? when taught I 'll own to that remark.

CHORUS.

Pierced with desire for those who loved again.

HERALD.

545 You say this land pined for its pining host.

CHORUS.

So that I often sighed from gloomy thought.

HERALD.

Whence this sad sigh that weighed upon the state?

CHORUS.

I 've long held silence mischief's remedy.

HERALD.

Why? feared you any, with the masters gone?

τένειν et ἐπῆν ductus; λεῷ Heims.
549. τυράννων Fl. V. κοιράνων F. Hæc suspicor correctoris esse purpureos pannos. Malim δεσποτῶν,

quinetiam verum esse puto; et βλάβη supra erat 'malum'. Cf. proverbium 'absente domino strepunt servuli'.

ΧΟΡΟΣ.

Ὡς νῦν, τὸ σὸν δή, καὶ θανεῖν πολλὴ χάρις.　　550

ΚΗΡΥΞ.

Εὖ γὰρ πέπρακται. Ταῦτα δ᾽ ἐν πολλῷ χρόνῳ
τὰ μέν τις ἂν λέξειεν εὐπετῶς ἔχειν
τὰ δ᾽ αὖτε κἀπίμομφα. Τίς δὲ πλὴν θεῶν
ἅπαντ᾽ ἀπήμων τὸν δι᾽ αἰῶνος χρόνον;
μόχθους γὰρ εἰ λέγοιμι καὶ δυσαυλίας,　　555
σπαρνὰς παρήξεις καὶ κακοστρώτους — τί δ᾽ οὐ
στένοντες, οὐ λαχόντες ἤδεος μέρος;
τὰ δ᾽ αὖτε χέρσῳ, καὶ προσῆν πλέον στύγος·
εὐναὶ γὰρ ἦσαν δαΐων πρὸς τείχεσιν·
ἐξ οὐρανοῦ δὲ κἀπὸ γῆς λειμωνίας　　560
βόλοι κατεψέκαζον, ἔμπεδον σίνος
ἐσθημάτων τιθέντες ἐν θηρῶν τριχί.
Χειμῶνα δ᾽ εἰ λέγοι τις οἰωνοκτόνον
οἷον παρεῖχ᾽ ἄφερτον Ἰδαία χιών,
ἢ θάλπος εὖτε πόντος ἐν μεσημβριναῖς　　565
κοίταις ἀκύμων νηνέμοις εὗδοι πεσών —
τί ταῦτα πενθεῖν δεῖ; παροίχεται πόνος·
παροίχεται δὲ τοῖσι μὲν τεθνηκόσιν

---

550. ὧν νῦν libri. corr. Scaliger.
556. κακοστρώτους Fl. V. corr. in F.
557. οὐ λαχόντες ἤματος libri, corrupte. At quid, malum, ἤδεος? Dicam: editores certatim castigant insontem λάχοντες quum, me judice, noxam admiserit v. ἤματος. Expecto ἡδονῶν μέρος, ut πραπίδων μέρος v. 380.; sed tum, unde ἤματος? Cedo ἤδεος, jamque apparet ἤματος supra scriptum esse, ut simile ψιλώσεως exemplum, quemadmodum laudatur in E. M. s. v. ἤδος. Velim mihi reddas unde unde extricatum v. ἤδμα vel simile quid; nam Hesychius nondum ad me devertit.
559. δηίων libri. corr. Dind.
560. γὰρ libri. δὲ Pearson.; quod ni recipias, hæreo. λειμωνίαι Fl. V. corr. Schutz.

CHORUS.

550 So that death now were, as you say, quite sweet.

HERALD.

True: for we 've tasted good. Thus in long time
one might declare that some things fall out well,
and some again not faultless: save the gods
who through his lifetime is quite free from pain?
555 If I should tell of toils and sorry berths,
the close and ill-spread deckways — but at what
did we not sigh? getting no share of joy.
Then things on land were horrors greater yet:
for close by hostile walls our beds were laid,
560 and pelting drops from heaven and meadowy earth
besprinkled us, and to the wild-beast's fur
of our apparel searching damage caused.
And should one tell of the bird-killing cold
past-bearing which Idaean snows brought on,
565 or melting heat whene'er the waveless deep
in breezeless rest at noontide dropped asleep —
but why deplore it? now the pain is past;
aye, for the dead so past that they no more

---

560. ὀρόσοι libri. βόλοι ego. Vox
desideratur quæ ἀπὸ κοινοῦ sit, et
pluviam, rorem, grandinem, prui-
nam, nives significet, qualis est βέλη
Soph. Ant. 358. Suidas βόλος· ἡ
ὀρόσος. Glossæ igitur ὀρόσοι quæ
diu se male habuit, tandem vale
dictum est.

561. κατεψάκαζον mavult Dind.

562. ἔνθηρον τρίχα libri. ἀνθηρὸν

Stanl.; hanc vocem si quis noverit
vertet 'crispatam et nitido colore
florentem'. Vix id voluit præco. Ego
nihil melius quam ἐν θηρῶν τριχί reperire potui. ἐν θεῶν κρίσει infra v.
1289. Cave suspiceris vocem τιθέντες:
valde eam amat Æsch. Locus ex
Hesiodo sumptus ut ostendam in
Comment.

τὸ μήποτ' αὖθις μηδ' ἀναστῆναι μέλειν.
Τί τοὺς ἀναλωθέντας ἐν ψήφῳ λέγω;   570
τὸν ζῶντα δ' ἀλγεῖν χρή· τύχης παλιγκότου
καὶ πολλὰ χαίρειν συμφορὰς καταξιῶ.
Ἡμῖν δὲ τοῖς λοιποῖσιν Ἀργείων στρατοῦ
νικᾷ τὸ κέρδος, πῆμα δ' οὐκ ἀντιρρέπει·
ὡς κομπάσαι τῷδ' εἰκὸς ἡλίου φάει   575
ὑπὲρ θαλάσσης καὶ χθονὸς ποτωμένοις·
Τροίαν ἑλόντες δήποτ' Ἀργείων στόλος
θεοῖς λάφυρα ταῦτα τοῖς καθ' Ἑλλάδα
δόμοις ἐπασσάλευσαν ἀρχαῖον γάνος.
Τοιαῦτα χρὴ κλύοντας εὐλογεῖν πόλιν   580
καὶ τοὺς στρατηγούς· καὶ χάρις τιμήσεται
Διὸς τάδ' ἐκπράξασα. Πάντ' ἔχεις λόγον.

ΧΟΡΟΣ.

Νικώμενος λόγοισιν οὐκ ἀναίνομαι·
ἀεὶ γὰρ ἡβᾷ τοῖς γέρουσιν εὖ μαθεῖν.
Δόμοις δὲ ταῦτα καὶ Κλυταιμνήστρᾳ λέγειν   585
εἰκὸς μάλιστα, σὺν δὲ πλουτίζειν ἐμοί.

ΚΛΥΤΑΙΜΝΗΣΤΡΑ.

Ἀνωλόλυξα μὲν πάλαι χαρᾶς ὕπο,
ὅτ' ἦλθ' ὁ πρῶτος νύχιος ἄγγελος πυρὸς
φράζων ἅλωσιν Ἰλίου τ' ἀνάστασιν·
καί τίς μ' ἐνίπτων εἶπε, Φρυκτωρῶν δία   590

---

570. λέγειν libri. λέγω, cum sign.
interrog., ego. v. μέλειν, ut solet,
injuriam intulit. Subinde colon ad
χρή posui, interpunct. post καταξιῶ
delevi. Manet asyndeton ut supra
v. 567.

572. συμφοραῖς libri. συμφορὰς Bl.
utpote qui probe sciret verbum λέγειν
cum dat., v. καταξιοῦν cum acc. con-
strui. Et hic et saepius Herm. sibi
persuasit, et multis aliis, nil intra
oleam esse duri.

retain a wish ever to rise again:
570 and why count up the lost ones in my list?
the living ought to grieve: nay, to the turns
of wayward fate I wish a long goodbye:
since for us remnants of the Argive host
the good prevails and pain does not outweigh:
575 so that we fairly crow to yon sunbeam,
we fliers over sea and land: "Of yore
a host of Argives having taken Troy
through Hellas to the gods within their fanes
nailed up these spoils, a trophy of the past."
580 Hearing these things 'tis fit ye laud the state
and its host-leaders; honoured too shall be
Jove's grace which wrought the deed. Thou hast the whole tale.

CHORUS.

Won by your words I cavil not: one thing
is always young with old men, learning well.
585 But 'tis most fit you tell it to the house
and to the queen, and with me enrich them.

CLYTEMNESTRA.

I shouted praise for joy a while ago
when came the first night messenger of fire
reporting Ilion's sack and overthrow:
590 and one said chiding me: "by signal-men

577. τροίην Fl. corr. in F.
585. μέλειν libri. Frigide, immo absurde dictum; cujus vice λέγειν reposui, nam μέλειν est glossema ad α-λέγειν adscriptum. Deinde ἐμοί ego, (libri. ἐμέ); nec dubium est quin Chorum illud dicere oportet.
587. ἀναλολύξαμεν libri. corr. Steph.
590. ἐνίππων Fl. φρυκτώρων διὰ libri. corr. Schutz et Dind.

πεισθεῖσα Τροίαν νῦν πεπορθῆσθαι δοκεῖς;
ἢ κάρτα πρὸς γυναικὸς αἴρεσθαι κέαρ.
Λόγοις τοιούτοις πλαγκτὸς οὖσ' ἐφαινόμην·
ὅμως δ' ἔθυον, καὶ γυναικείῳ νόμῳ
ὀλολυγμὸν ἄλλος ἄλλοθεν κατὰ πτόλιν   - 595
ἔλασκον εὐφημοῦντες ἐν θεῶν ἕδραις
θυηφάγον κοιμῶντες εὐώδη φλόγα.
Καὶ νῦν τὰ μάσσω μὲν τί δεῖ σ' ἐμοὶ λέγειν;
ἄνακτος αὐτοῦ πάντα πεύσομαι λόγον·
ὅπως δ' ἄριστα τὸν ἐμὸν αἰδοῖον πόσιν   600
σπεύσω πάλιν μολόντα δέξασθαι· τί γὰρ
γυναικὶ τούτου φέγγος ἥδιον δρακεῖν,
ἀπὸ στρατείας ἄνδρα σώσαντος θεοῦ
πύλας ἀνοῖξαι; ταῦτ' ἀπάγγειλον πόσει·
ἥκειν ὅπως τάχιστ' ἐράσμιον πόλει·   605
γυναῖκα πιστὴν δ' ἐν δόμοις εὕροι μολὼν
οἵανπερ οὖν ἔλειπε, δωμάτων κύνα
ἐσθλὴν ἐκείνῳ, πολεμίαν τοῖς δύσφροσιν,
καὶ τἄλλ' ὁμοίαν πάντα, σημαντήριον
οὐδὲν διαφθείρασαν ἐν μήκει χρόνου.   610
Οὐδ' οἶδα τέρψιν οὐδ' ἐπίψογον φάτιν
ἄλλου παρ' ἀνδρὸς μᾶλλον ἢ χαλκοῦ βαφάς.

ΚΗΡΥΞ.

Τοιόσδ' ὁ κόμπος τῆς ἀληθείας γέμων
οὐκ αἰσχρὸς ὡς γυναικὶ γενναίᾳ λακεῖν.

<hr />

597. κοιμῶντες libri. Hoc nemo explicavit. Conjecerunt καίοντες Casaub., κοιῶντες Herm., κινοῦντες Ahr. Dedi καινοῦντες 'inaugurantes'.

612. Sic libri. Neque erit cur haereas si modo memoria retineas quae scholl. dixerunt ad Hes. Op. 161, et Plut. de Pyth. or. p. 102 Tauchn. Proverbium est antiquae cupri στομώσει alludens, quae multis

cheated, dost think that Troy is now destroyed?

this heart-excitement is full womanish".

By such remarks I was shown up as crazed:

but still they offered; and in woman's key

595 on each side some one through the city raised

the cry of joy, and with fair words renewed

on the gods' altars spice-fed fragrant flame.

As for the larger news — why tell it me?

I 'll hear the whole tale from the king himself.

600 Now will I haste to greet as best I can

my honoured lord on his return; for what

light's sweeter for a wife to see than this,

to ope the gates when god has brought back safe

her husband from the war. Bear him back word

605 to come at his best speed, the city's love;

and let him find at home, having come, his wife

true, such as her he left, a house-dog staunch

to him, at war with those who wish him ill;

and in all else the same; her, who in length

610 of time has tampered with no signet stamp.

Of cheer or word of shame from other man

I know no more than of bronze-tempering.

HERALD.

That sort of boast freighted with truth is not

unseemly for a true wife to proclaim.

---

ante sæculis usu interciderat. Tem-
perantiam dico, neutiquam vero tinc-
turam, ut Paleius perperam. Rectius Kingsleii Argonautæ sibi induunt
'swords of tempered bronze'.

613, 14. in libris præconi tri-
buuntur. Mirere si quis innovare
velit; fuerunt tamen, Hermanno ipso, quem e longinquo veneror, præ-
ludente.

ΧΟΡΟΣ.

Αὕτη μὲν οὕτως εἶπε μανθάνοντί σοι   615
τοροῖσιν ἑρμηνεῦσιν εὐπρεπῶς λόγον.
Σὺ δ' εἰπέ, κῆρυξ, Μενέλεων δὲ πεύθομαι,
εἰ νόστιμός τε καὶ σεσωσμένος πάλιν
ἥξει σὺν ὑμῖν, τῆςδε γῆς φίλον κράτος.

ΚΗΡΥΞ.

Οὐκ ἔσθ' ὅπως λέξαιμι τὰ ψευδῆ καλὰ   620
ἐς τὸν πολὺν φίλοισι καρποῦσθαι χρόνον.

ΧΟΡΟΣ.

Πῶς δῆτ' ἂν εἰπὼν κεδνὰ τἀληθῆ τύχοις·
σχισθέντα δ' οὐκ εὔκρυπτα γίγνεται τάδε.

ΚΗΡΥΞ.

Ἀνὴρ ἄφαντος ἐξ Ἀχαιικοῦ στρατοῦ,
αὐτός τε καὶ τὸ πλοῖον· οὐ ψευδῆ λέγω.   625

ΧΟΡΟΣ.

Πότερον ἀναχθεὶς ἐμφανῶς ἐξ Ἰλίου,
ἢ χεῖμα, κοινὸν ἄχθος, ἥρπασε στρατοῦ;

ΚΗΡΥΞ.

Ἔκυρσας ὥστε τοξότης ἄκρος σκοποῦ,
μακρὸν δὲ πῆμα συντόμως ἐφημίσω.

---

615. 'Sic tibi tironi verba dedit periti judicis sententia pulchre'.
619. γε libri. τε Herm.

622. τύχης Fl. τύχης V. τυχ, ς supra scripto F. τύχοις corr. Pors.

CHORUS.

615 For you, a novice, she thus framed her tale
to shrewd exponents with propriety.
But, herald, say — I ask of Menelaûs —
if he is to return and safe again
will come with you, this land's beloved chief.

HERALD.

620 I could not so report fair tidings false
as that my friends would long reap *pleasant* fruit.

CHORUS.

Would you might chance to tell us true good news;
but, sundered, these two things are hard to hide.

HERALD.

That man is missing from the Achaean fleet,
625 he and his ship. I speak things not untrue. -

CHORUS.

Left he Troy openly alone, or did
some common storm-grief tear him from the host?

HERALD.

Like first-rate archer you have hit the mark,
and curtly stated a long tale of woe.

---

624. ἀνήρ libri. corr. Herm.   sc de Homerica narratione declinare.
626. Hoc versu ostendit poeta   628. τοξότας Fl.

ΧΟΡΟΣ.

Πότερα γὰρ αὐτοῦ ζῶντος ἢ τεθνηκότος   630
Φάτις πρὸς ἄλλων ναυτίλων ἐκλῄζετο;

ΚΗΡΥΞ.

Οὐκ οἶδεν οὐδείς, ὥςτ' ἀπαγγεῖλαι τορῶς,
πλὴν τοῦ τρέφοντος Ἡλίου χθονὸς φύσιν.

ΧΟΡΟΣ.

Πῶς γὰρ λέγεις χειμῶνα ναυτικῷ στρατῷ
ἐλθεῖν τελευτῆσαί τε δαιμόνων κότῳ;   635

ΚΗΡΥΞ.

Εὔφημον ἦμαρ οὐ πρέπει κακαγγέλῳ
γλώσσῃ μιαίνειν· χωρὶς ἡ τιμὴ θεῶν.
Ὅταν δ' ἀπευκτὰ πήματ' ἄγγελος πόλει
στυγνῷ προσώπῳ πτωσίμου στρατοῦ φέρῃ,
πόλει μὲν ἕλκος ἕν τὸ δήμιον τυχεῖν,   640
πολλοὺς δὲ πολλῶν ἐξαγισθέντας δόμων
ἄνδρας διπλῇ μάστιγι, τὴν Ἄρης φιλεῖ,
δίλογχον ἄτην, φοινίαν ξυνωρίδα,
τοιῶνδε μέντοι πημάτων σεσαγμένον
πρέπει λέγειν παιᾶνα τόνδ' Ἐρινύων.   645
Σωτηρίων δὲ πραγμάτων εὐάγγελον
ἥκοντα πρὸς χαίρουσαν εὐεστοῖ πόλιν
πῶς κεδνὰ τοῖς κακοῖσι συμμίξω λέγων
χειμῶν' Ἀχαιοῖς οὐκ ἀμήνιτον θεῶν;
Ξυνώμοσαν γάρ, ὄντες ἔχθιστοι τὸ πρίν,   650

---

644. σεσαγμένον libri. corr. Pors. τόνδ', v. 645, est τόνδ' ἄγγελον.

CHORUS.

630 Wait: was there no report of him alive
or dead by other sailors talked about?

HERALD.

No one knows aught, so as to clearly tell,
save the earth's offspring nurser Helios.

CHORUS.

What account give you how the storm came on
635 the fleet and ended through the daemons' spite?

HERALD.

Day of fair words with ill-news-telling tongue
to soil beseems not: to each god apart
is homage paid; and when a messenger
with dismal face brings word of woes accursed
640 of a lost host, — that one, a public wound,
befals the state — of many men, from homes
many, lashed gravewards by the double whip
that Ares loves, his two-barbed death, his team
of two blood-reds, — saddled with such distress
645 one should repeat the Furies' hymn of joy.
But I, returning to a state in weal
rejoicing, with good news of things which leave
life safe, how can I mix kind words with cross
and tell of tempests not-uncaused-by-wrath
650 of gods to Greeks: for two conspired, before

649. Ἀχαιῶν et θεοῖς libri. Correxerunt Dobræus, Herm., Bl., plerique.

πῦρ καὶ θάλασσα, καὶ τὰ πίστ' ἐδειξάτην
Φθείροντε τὸν δύστηνον Ἀργείων στρατόν.
Ἐν νυκτὶ δυσκύμαντα δ' ὠρώρει κακά·
ναῦς γὰρ πρὸς ἀλλήλαισι Θρήκιαι πνοαὶ
ἤρεικον· αἱ δὲ κεροτυπούμεναι βίᾳ   655
χειμῶνι τυφῶ σὺν ζάλῃ τ' ὀμβροκτύπῳ
ᾤχοντ' ἄφαντοι, ποιμένος κακοῦ στρόβῳ.
Ἐπεὶ δ' ἀνῆλθε λαμπρὸν ἡλίου φάος
ὁρῶμεν ἀνθοῦν πέλαγος Αἰγαῖον νεκροῖς
ἀνδρῶν Ἀχαιῶν ναυτικοῖς τ' ἐρειπίοις.   660
Ἡμᾶς γε μὲν δὴ ναῦν τ' ἀκήρατον σκάφος
ἤτοι τις ἐξέκλεψεν ἢ 'ξῃτήσατο
θεός τις, οὐκ ἄνθρωπος, οἴακος θιγών·
Τύχη δὲ σωτὴρ ναῦν θέλουσ' ἐφέζετο,
ὡς μήτ' ἐν ὅρμῳ κύματος ζάλην ἔχειν   665
μήτ' ἐξοκεῖλαι πρὸς κραταίλεων χθόνα.
Ἔπειτα δ' ᾅδην πόντιον πεφευγότες,
λευκὸν κατ' ἦμαρ, οὐ πεποιθότες τύχῃ,
ἐβουκολοῦμεν φροντίσιν νέον πάθος
στρατοῦ καμόντος καὶ κακῶς σποδουμένου.   670
Καὶ νῦν ἐκείνων εἴ τις ἐστὶν ἐμπνέων
λέγουσιν ἡμᾶς ὡς ὀλωλότας· τί μή;
ἡμεῖς τ' ἐκείνους ταῦτ' ἔχειν δοξάζομεν.
Γένοιτο δ' ὡς ἄριστα. Μενέλεων γὰρ οὖν
πρῶτόν τε καὶ μάλιστα προσδόκα μολεῖν·   675
εἰ δ' οὖν τις ἀκτὶς ἡλίου νιν ἱστορεῖ

---

654. ἀλλήλῃσι Fl. V. corr. in F.
655. κερωτυπούμεναι libri. corr.
Wassius.
660. ναυτικῶν τ' ἐρπτίων Fl. F.
ἐρειπίων V. Aurati correctionem re-

ceperunt recentt. Etenim scriba vocis
νεκροῖς oblitus erat.
662. Sic emendatus ab Æschylo
profectus est.
664. ναυστολοῦσ' Casaubon, quem

most hostile, fire and sea, and proved their troth

by havoc of the woebegone Greek fleet.

Wild-billowy troubles in the night arose,

for Thracian squalls dashed foul our vessels one

655 against another, and they, rudely gored

by typhoon's tempest with its rain-lashed surge,

as in a crush caused by an awkward swain

passed out of view. And when the sun's bright light

came up we saw the Ægæan main in bud

660 with Grecian corpses and the wrecks of ships.

Us, and our ship, at least, unharmed in hull,

some being stole away or begged us off —

a god, it was no man, — and held our helm,

and Luck, prompt Saviour, took a seat on board.

655 So at our moorings we had no wave-swell,

and struck against no shore of stubborn rock.

Then, having 'scaped the death-god of the sea,

in the white dawn, mistrusting our own fate,

in thought we watched a flock of recent woes

670 of our disabled and hard-battered fleet.

And now, if any one of them yet breathes,

they speak of us as lost; of course: and we

conjecture that they 've got as much. But may

the best betide: first and most fondly look

675 for Menelaus to return; and if

some sunbeam, as I said, knows him to be

nonnulli secuti sunt; temere, me judice.

670. κατεσποδημένου Meineke, quod non multum abest quin mihi persuadeat; nam hiems mane desierat.

σποδεῖν est ἀμαθύνειν, sed non sine lusu vocem πόδας adhibente.

674. δ᾽ ἄρ᾽ οὖν Aur. fortasse recte. οὖν autem revocat v. 617, ut proximum οὖν (v. 676) v. 633.

χλωρόν τε καὶ βλέποντα μηχαναῖς Διὸς
οὔπω θέλοντος ἐξαναλῶσαι γένος
ἐλπίς τις αὐτὸν πρὸς δόμους ἥξειν πάλιν.
Τοσαῦτ᾽ ἀκούσας ἴσθι τἀληθῆ κλύων.   680

ΧΟΡΟΣ.

στρ.ά. Τίς ποτ᾽ ὠνόμαζεν ὧδ᾽
              ἐς τὸ πᾶν ἐτητύμως —
       μή τις ὄντιν᾽ οὐχ ὁρῶ-
       μεν προνοίαισι τοῦ πεπρωμένου
       γλῶσσαν ἐν τύχᾳ νέμων; —   685
       τὰν δορίγαμβρον ἀμφινει-
              κῆ θ᾽ Ἑλέναν; ἐπεὶ πρεπόν-
       τως ἑλενᾶς, ἕλανδρος, ἑλέπτολις ἐκ
       τῶν ἁβροπήνων προκαλυμμάτων ἔπλευ-   690
       σε ζεφύρου γίγαντος αὔ-
       ρᾳ· πολύανδροί τε φεράσπιδες κυνα-
       γοὶ κατ᾽ ἴχνος πλατᾶν ἄφαντον   695
       κελσάντων Σιμόεντος ἀκ-
              τὰς ἐπ᾽ ἀεξιφύλλους,
       δι᾽ ἔριν αἱματόεσσαν.

ἀντ.ά. Ἰλίῳ δὲ κῆδος ὀρ-   700
              θώνυμον τελεσσίφρων
       μῆνις ἤλασεν, τραπέ-

677. καὶ ζῶντα καὶ libri. Toupius
correxit ex Hesychio; recentt.
680. κλύων Fl. ειν ab eadem manu
supra scripto.
681. Herm. dubitat an ὠνόμαξεν
dixerit poeta, ut σφετεριξάμενοι Supp.
38, et fortasse σεβίξω infra v. 785.

Et est sane cur hœreas in v. ὠνόμαζεν.
689. ἐλένας libri. ἐλέναυς Elmsl.,
ut λιπόναυς. Schneid. olim ἐλενᾶς, ut
ἐχενῆς. Vera lectio incerta.
690. ἁβροτίμων libri. corr. Salmasius, recentt.
695. πλάταν libri, πλατᾶν Heath.

both hale and living, by device of Zeus

not willing yet to extirpate his race,

there is some hope that he 'll come back again.

630 Hearing so much, know that you hear the truth.

CHORUS.

Who, I wonder, named her thus

    altogether truthfully,

(was it one whom we behold

    not by sight, who with prescience of the doom

685 deftly modulates the tongue?)

named the spear-wedded, gage of strife,

    Helena? since conformably,

    knell-like to navies cities and men, from between

690   daintily-worked curtains she *came and* sailed away,

    borne by the earth-born Zephyr's breeze:

    so, with a band numberless, huntsmen bearing shields

635   *sailed* on their oar-blades' vanished footprint —

(*theirs*, who now had attained the *fair*

    Simoïs' verdure-swelling

banks) for bloody contention.

700 And the wrath of Gods, to Troy,

    bent on full reprisals, sped

marring-marriage, not misnamed,

ab hac voce pendet κελσάντων. Impedita structura, sensus haud obscurus, ut verti.

698. ἐπ' ἀξιφύλλους Fl. V. εἰς ἀεξιφύλλους F. Nihil verius Pauwii correctione, quam dedi; Paleius ta-

men ἀκριτοφύλλους, montis epitheton, corrupto antistr. v. motus.

701. τελεσίφρων Fl. V. corr. in F.

702. ἔλασε et ἀτίμως ἱν' Fl. V. ἤλασε et ἀτίμως absque ἱν' F. illud Pors. hoc Canter. corr.

ζας ἀτίμωσιν ὑστέρῳ χρόνῳ
καὶ ξυνεστίου Διὸς
πρασσομένα τὸ νυμφότι-   705
μον μέλος ἐκφάτως τίον-
τάς γ᾽ ὑμέναιον, ὃς τότ᾽ ἐπέρρεπε γαμ-
βροῖσιν ἀείδειν. Μεταμανθάνουσα δ᾽ ὕμνον Πριάμου πόλις γεραι-   710
ὰ πολύθρηνον μέγα που στένει κικλή-
σκουσα Πάριν τὸν αἰνόλεκτρον·
λαμπρῶς θην πολύθρηνον αἰῶνα διαὶ πολιτᾶν   _   715
μέλεον αἷμ᾽ ἀνατλᾶσα.

στρ.β΄. Ἔθρεψεν δὲ λέοντος ἶ-
νιν δόμοις ἀγάλακτον
οὕτως ἀνὴρ φιλόμαστον,
ἐν βιότου προτελείοις   720
ἄμερον εὐφιλόπαιδα
καὶ γεραροῖς ἐπίχαρτον.
Πολέα δ᾽ ἔσχ᾽ ἐν ἀγκάλαις
νεοτρόφου τέκνου δίκαν,
φαιδρωπὸς ποτὶ χεῖρα σαί-   725
νων τε γαστρὸς ἀνάγκαις.

707. γ᾽ inserui, metro flagitante; simul et meliorem sensum præbui: 'etsi facinus ipsi non patraverunt tamen a Paride factum ad se receperunt'. ἐπερρεῖπ Fl. ἐπέρρεπεν Vict. ἐπέπρεπεν F. ἐπέρρεπεν Herm., recentt., metro pessumdato. Weil. dedit ἐπέρρεπε, nescio an primus. 714. παμπρόσθη libri. Impavidus innovavi. Et λαμπρῶς et θην ap. Æsch. inveniuntur. Illud autem φανερῶς non ἐνδόξως significare omnibus notum est; et sic Suid. s. v. Quod ad θην attinet, suspicor eam ex iis vocibus esse quas poeta Athenas Syracusis adscivit. Sæpius occurrit ap. Hom., et Theocr.; ap. Hes., non item. Mox πολύθρηνον est me-

for despite done to board and hearth-god Zeus
levying in the time to come
705 payment from those who, voice and soul,
    joined in the madrigal which then
    lauding the bride had fall'n to the dole of her new
    kinsmen to sing. *Then:* but the venerable *queen-*
710   city of Priam learning now
    different notes full of laments, groans much, and styles
    Paris, I trow, 'the sadly-bedded':
for quite clearly she passed a life
715   full of laments for woful
poured-out blood of her people.

So man nurses a lion's cub
    weaned from milk, in his household,
enamoured yet of the mother's
720 pap, in the dawn of existence
gentle, beloved by the children,
and a delight to the aged:
then in the arms it oft reclines
as babes take their first repasts;
725 fawning comes to the hand with eyes
    bright in serfdom of hunger.

---

dulla hujus sententiae.

715. αἰών ἀμφὶ πολίταν libri. πολιτᾶν Aur. αἰῶνα διαὶ Emper. His
receptis, omnia ex mea sententia
procedunt. Vides literas μρι con-
fusas esse et ρ pro δ' scriptam, ut
supra v. 413.

717. λέοντα σίνιν libri. λέοντος ἶνιν
est egregia Coningtoni emendatio,

omnibus probata.

723. ἔσχ' suspectum est. verti
cum Herm., aliis.

724. νεότροφον Fl.

725. Verti cum Boissonad. σαίνων
τε φ. π. χ. Weil. mavult φαιδρωπῶς
et σαίνοντα. Ingeniosissimo ille quidem, sed fortasse paulo violentius.

ἀντ.β΄. Χρονισθεὶς δ' ἀπέδειξεν ἦ-
    θος τρόπους τε τοκήων·
    χάριν τροφᾶς γὰρ ἀμείβων
    μηλοφόνοισι σὺν ἄταις   730
    δαῖτ' ἀκέλευστος ἔτευξεν·
    αἵματι δ' οἶκος ἐφύρθη,
    ἄμαχον ἄλγος οἰκέταις
    μέγα σίνος πολυκτόνον·
    ἐκ θεοῦ δ' ἱερεύς τις ἄ-   735
    τας δόμοις προςεθρέφθη.

στρ.γ΄. Πάραυτα δ' ἐλθεῖν ἐς Ἰλίου πόλιν λέγοιμ'
    ἂν φρόνημα μεν νηνέμου γαλά-   740
    νας ἀκασκαῖόν τ' ἄγαλμα πλούτου,
    μαλθακὸν ὀμμάτων βέλος,
    δηξίθυμον ἔρωτος ἄν-
    θος. Παρακλίνασ' ἐπέκρα-   744
    νεν δὲ γάμου πικρὰς τελευ- .
    τάς, δύσεδρος καὶ δυσόμι-
    λος συμένα Πριαμίδαισιν
    πομπᾷ Διὸς ξενίου
    νυμφόκλαυτος Ἐρινύς.

ἀντ.γ΄. Παλαίφατος δ' ἐν βροτοῖς γέρων λόγος τέτυκ-   750
    ται, μέγαν τελεσθέντα φωτὸς ὄλ-
    βον τεκνοῦσθαι, μηδ' ἄπαιδα θνήσκειν·

728. ἔθος τὸ πρὸς τοκήων Fl. V.
τοκέων F. ἦθος Conington., τρόπους
τε Enger.; uterque felicissime.
729. χάριν γὰρ τροφᾶς Fl. V. τρο-
φεύσιν F. Corr. Pearson.

730. μηλορόνοισιν ἄταις Fl. ἄταισιν
F. V. μηλορόνοισι σὺν ἄταις Fix et
Ahr., ab Eng. receptum. Quotus
quisque est qui vocis ἄτη vim recte
intelligat? ap. Æsch. dico. Hic autem

But he, waiting a while, displays
    bent and mood of his parents;
and, paying fee for his food with
730 havoc of sheep which he slaughters,
makes him a feast uninvited;
home is defiled with the bloodshed;
he the inmates' doughty grief,
killing many, wasting much,
735 by some god was *begot and* reared
    priest of death to the household.

And, I would say, thus to Ilion's state a temper came
740   tuned to breezeless calm; wealth's soft eyes'-delight;
    melting arrow-glances; love's exotic
stinging the soul *to sweet desire.*
But she altered and bitter ends
745   wrought for the match, proving a sad
    sharer of seats and intercourse;
    who on a *fell* mission from Zeus,
    god of the board, sped unto Priam's
folk, like a Fury espoused
bringing tears by her marriage.

750 An ancient saw long pronouced among mankind hath been
    framed, that man's success great and fully grown
    gets an heir, and does not perish childless:

---

rectissime de ovium cæde usurpatur,
ut ap. Soph. Ai. 307.
  733. ἄμαχον δ' Fl. corr. in F.
  736. προςετράφη libri. corr. Heath.
  741. δ' inseruit Pors., τ' Herm.

743. δηξίθυμον integrum est, me
judice.
  747. πριαμίδαισι Fl. V.
  749. Sic Fl. ἐρινύς F. V.

ἐκ δ' ἀγαθᾶς τύχας γένει 755
βλαστάνειν ἀκόρεστον οἰ-
ζύν. Δίχα δ' ἄλλων μονόφρων
εἰμί· τὸ δυσσεβὲς γὰρ ἔρ-
γον μετὰ μὲν πλείονα τίκ-
τει, σφετέρᾳ δ' εἰκότα γέννᾳ. 760
Οἴκων γὰρ εὐθυδίκων
καλλίπαις πότμος ἀεί.

στρ δ'. Φιλεῖ δὲ τίκτειν ὕβρις μὲν παλαι-
ὰ νεάζουσαν ἐν κακοῖς βροτῶν 765
ὕβριν, τότ' ἢ τόθ' ὅταν τὸ κύριον μόλῃ
φάος τόκου·
δαίμονα τίταν, ἄμαχον, ἀπόλεμον,
ἀνίερον θράσος μελαι- 770
νας μελάθροισιν ἄτας
εἰδομέναν τοκεῦσιν.

ἀντ. δ'. Δίκα δὲ λάμπει μὲν ἐν δυσκάπνοις
δώμασιν, τὸν δ' ἐναίσιμον τίει· 775
τὰ χρυσόπαστα δ' ἔδεθλα σὺν πίνῳ χερῶν
παλιντρόποις
ὄμμασι λιποῦσ' ὅσια προςέβαλε·

---

756. ἀιζύν libri. corr. Pauw.
758. τὸ γὰρ libri. corr. Pors.
759. μετὰ libri. μέτα Herm. Nec libet credere, et licet in variis opinionibus.
761. Particula γὰρ quam Aur. mutabat huic loco unice convenit: 'scelus, inquam, exitii parens est; nam justorum hominum sors non nisi felicitatis genetrix est'.
766. Sic libri, et omnia integra:

v. ex anacr., basi, dact., troch. dim. cat. est conflctus. Non vidit hoc Herm., non Eng.; hic tamen proximorum verborum mendas νεαρὰ φάους· κότον acutissime perspectas habuit. νεαρὰ enim primo fuisse νεαρὰν, glossema ad νεάζουσαν adscriptum; deinde cetera, literis in ordinem suum restitutis, prodire φάος τόκου. Hucusque igitur locum olim impeditissimum prorsus emendatum habemus. Quod

755 for to a race from fortune fair

springs a grief that is never full.

I from the rest thinking apart

say that the sin, *and not success*,

afterwards breeds more, to their kind

760 likened; for homes practising-even-

right have a fortune for aye

blest with beautiful offspring.

But Pride grown old loves to breed Pride that spends

765 wanton youth rioting in mortals' ills,

(betimes or later, whene'er th' appointed birth-day comes)

a vengeful fiend

not to be contended with or warred against;

770 in unhallowed recklessness,

families' black perdition,

taking its parents' likeness.

But Justice shines *brightly* on smoke-defiled

775 homes, and pays homage to the upright man:

with eyes averted she, leaving halls picked out with gold

and filthy deeds,

sheds her rays *only* upon holy spots;

reliqua luce clariora sunt gratia re-
ferenda est Heimsoëthio.
768. τε τὰν libri. τίταν Heims.
Jam nunc interprete vix opus est:
'Lasciviam, quoad impiam temeri-
tatem domibus exitiosam, parentium
instar'. Ὕβρις est pater, mater, fi-
lia; sed non intelligunt haec in Æschylea dictione ὀψιμαθεῖς.
775. δώμασι Fl. corr. in F. post
τίει libri ingerunt βίον. ejecit Ahr.

776. ἐσθλὰ libri. ἔσεθλα Auratus,
qua una correctione optime de pos-
teris meriturus erat.
779. προςέβα τοῦ libri. προςέβαλε
olim Herm., quo nihil verius; nam
Δίκη adumbratur ut quae Homerici
Ἡελίου instar sit, qui προςβάλλει
ἀρούρας. τοῦ autem est pars post-
erior v. πλούτου. Ceterum et hic et
alibi pro virili parte versus rectius
distinxi.

δύναμιν οὐ σέβουσα πλού-   780
    του παράσημον αἴνῳ ·
πᾶν δ᾽ ἐπὶ τέρμα νωμᾷ.

Ἄγε δή, βασιλεῦ, Τροίας πτολίπορθ᾽,
    Ἀτρέως γένεθλον,
πῶς σε προςείπω, πῶς σε σεβίζω,   785
μήθ᾽ ὑπεράρας μήθ᾽ ὑποκάμψας
    καιρὸν χάριτος;
πολλοὶ δὲ βροτῶν τὸ δοκεῖν εἶναι
    προτίουσι, δίκην παραβάντες.

Τῷ δυσπραγοῦντί τ᾽ ἐπιστενάχειν   790
    πᾶς τις ἕτοιμος, δῆγμα δὲ λύπης
    οὐδὲν ἐφ᾽ ἧπαρ προςικνεῖται ·
καὶ ξὺν χαίρουσιν ὁμοιοπρεπεῖς
    ἀγέλαστα πρόσωπα βιῶνται.

Ὅςτις δ᾽ ἀγαθὸς προβατογνώμων   795
    οὐκ ἔστι λαθεῖν ὄμματα φωτὸς
    τὰ δοκοῦντ᾽ εὔφρονος ἐκ διανοίας
    ὑδαρεῖ σαίνει φιλότητι.

Σὺ δέ μοι τότε μὲν στέλλων στρατιὰν
    Ἑλένης ἕνεκ᾽, οὐ γάρ σ᾽ ἐπικεύσω,   800
κάρτ᾽ ἀπομούσως ἦσθα γεγραμμένος,
    οὐδ᾽ εὖ πραπίδων οἴακα νέμων
    ἄρος ἀκούσιον

783. πολίπορθ᾽ libri. corr. BL

785. σεβίξω Fl. hanc formam Herm. adamavit non tamen amplexatus est. σεβίζω F. V. Hoc systema in sex vv. redigunt, ut responsionem efficiant, quæ effici non potest nisi lacunis illatis ubi sensus integer est.

790. δ᾽ libri. corr. Herm.

791. δεῖγμα Fl. V. δῆγμα F. et Stobæus.

793, 794. καὶ ξυγχαίρουσιν — βιαζόμενοι libri. Recepi Weilii conjecturam, Pers. p. 120. χαίρουσιν est participium.

797. τὰ est relativum.

798. σαίνειν libri. Casauboni conj.

780 courting not the pow'r of wealth
  falsely impressed with honour
  guides to its goal each action.

  Come now my king, Troy's city-destroyer,
   offspring of Atreus,
785 how shall I greet thee and do thee obeisance,
   so as to neither run wide nor turn short of
   honour's due measure?
   many of mortal men practise by preference
   the appearing to be, and transgress truth:
790 and to bemoan in response to the hapless
   each one is ready; but from their sorrow
   no sting finds its way to the bosom:
  and along with the joyful taking the same mien
   they constrain features which laugh without gladness.
795 But whoever is skilful in noting his sheep,
   the face of a man cannot be hid from him
   which seeming to do so from feelings of joy
   but smiles with a watery affection.
  Then when you led forth the army for Helen's
800 sake, for I will not keep it concealed from you,
   to my eye you were very ungracefully drawn;
   not as skilfully wielding the tiller of thought,
   when you brought 'gainst their will

σαίνει necessaria est.

800. Musgr. inseruit σ'. Sed fortasse οὐδ' ἐπικεύσω vera lectio est, nam poeta ob oculos habuisse videtur Il. 5. 816 τῷ τοι προφρονέως ἐρέω ἔπος οὐδ' ἐπικεύσω. Cf. infra v. 805.

803. θράσος ἑκούσιον libri. ἀκούσιον Canter. ἄρος Heims. 'ὄφελος καὶ βλάβος ἀκούσιον'. Hesych. Vox est Æschylea huic loco optime conveniens. Cf. Il. 1. 410 ἐπαύρωνται βασιλῆος, et Hes. Op. 258, unde hæc sumpta sunt.

ἀνδράσι θνήσκουσι κομίζων.

Νῦν δ' οὐκ ἀπ' ἄκρας φρενὸς οὐδ' ἀφίλως 805
εὔφρων νόος εὖ τελέσασιν.

Γνώσει δὲ χρόνῳ διαπευθόμενος
τόν τε δικαίως κλὶ τὸν ἀκαίρως
πόλιν οἰκουροῦντα πολιτῶν.

ΑΓΑΜΕΜΝΩΝ.

Πρῶτον μὲν Ἄργος καὶ θεοὺς ἐγχωρίους 810
δίκη προςειπεῖν, τοὺς ἐμοὶ μεταιτίους
νόστου, δικαίων θ' ὧν ἐπραξάμην πόλιν
Πριάμου· δίκας γὰρ οὐκ ἀπὸ γλώσσης θεοὶ
κλύοντες ἀνδροθνῆτας Ἰλίου φθορᾶς
ἐς αἱματηρὸν τεῦχος οὐ διχορρόπως 815
ψήφους ἔθεντο· τῷ δ' ἐναντίῳ κύτει
ἐλπὶς προςῄει χέρσος οὐ πληρουμένῳ.
Καπνῷ δ' ἁλοῦσα νῦν ἔτ' εὔσημος πόλις·
ἄτης θύελλαι ζῶσι· συνθνήσκουσα δὲ
σποδὸς προπέμπει πίονας πλούτου πνοάς. 820
Τούτων θεοῖσι χρὴ πολύμνηστον χάριν
τίνειν· ἐπείπερ κὰλλαγὰς ὑπερκόπους
ἐπραξάμεσθα. καὶ γυναικὸς οὕνεκα
πόλιν διημάθυνεν Ἀργεῖον δάκος,
ἵππου νεοσσός, ἀσπιδηφόρος λεώς, 825

806. πόνος libri. πνόος Weil. νόος
Heims.
813. Cf. Supp. 934.
814. φθορὰς libri. corr. Dobræus.
Cetera sana sunt.
817. χειρὸς libri. χέρσος ego. Nem-
pe χέρσος primo fuit, non ita pridem
χέρρος, jamdiu χειρός. Ecce egregium
Æschyleæ ubertatis exemplum: κύτος

est γαστήρ (ἄκυτος· ἡ μὴ κύουσα E.
M. s. v.), προςῄει dicitur ut προςιέναι
γυναικί, χέρσος nimirum est 'sterilis'.
denique πληρουμένῳ refert phrasin
πληροῦν γυναῖκα. Imago: dii de Trojæ
aut salute aut exitio suffragia ferunt:
adstant duæ urnæ, altera salutaris,
altera letalis: hanc, inquit, cruore
virorumque necis implent, sed illam

on the dying the fruit of your actions.

805 Now with no surface-thought nor unlovingly
    my mind is rejoiced that you end well:
    and in time by a thorough inquiry you 'll know
    him who uprightly and him who unfittingly
    of the people keeps house in the city.

AGAMEMNON.

810 First Argos and the country's gods 'tis fit
    that I address, parties along with me
    in my return and the redress I've won
    from Priam's state. For gods who hear not suits
    by word of mouth dropped no mere make-weight votes
815 in bloody ballot-box for Ilion's sack,
    votes dooming men to death: dry, barren Hope
    came to the opposite vase which was not filled.
    The town still certifies its fall by smoke:
    only death's storm-wrack lives; the embers too
820 dying gasp out rich breath from wealth *devoured*.
    For this we must repay the gods a meed
    of long remembrance; since we claimed and took
    monstrous reprisals, and for a woman's sake
    the Argive beast, a horse's colt in form
825 of a shield-bearing host, has razed a town

ne uuum quidem vitæ germen gravidem reddit. At sic maris vice fungitur Spes. Ita: id voluit poeta. Ceterum confer, si tanti est, plura in Comment.

819. Sic libri. κακῇ θύουσιν ἀέλλη Hes. Th. 874. Hic hujus fabulæ correctores admoncro libet, pluris esse Hesiodi, Theoguidis, Solonis si quæ extent ter pure legisse, quam cetera omnia.

822. καὶ πάγας ὑπερκότους libri. Illud Ahr., hoc Heath., emend. Quum vero certum mihi videretur καὶ πάγας corrupta esse, non opus erat Paleii, Hermanni cet. ἐρρα-ξάμεσθα falsi arguere. Junge: καὶ ὑπ.

825. ἀσπιδηστρόφος Fl. V. ἀσπιδοστρόφος F. Corr. Bl.

πήδημ᾽ ὀρούσας ἀμφὶ Πλειάδων δύσιν·
ὑπερθορὼν δὲ πύργον ὠμηστὴς λέων
ἄδην ἔλειξεν αἵματος τυραννικοῦ.
Θεοῖς μὲν ἐξέτεινα φροίμιον τόδε·
τὰ δ᾽ ἐς τὸ σὸν φρόνημα, μέμνημαι κλύων   830
καὶ φημὶ ταῦτα καὶ συνήγορόν μ᾽ ἔχεις.
Παύροις γὰρ ἀνδρῶν ἐστι συγγενὲς τόδε
φίλον τὸν εὐτυχοῦντ᾽ ἄνευ φθόνου σέβειν·
δύσφρων γὰρ ἰὸς καρδίαν προσήμενος
ἄχθος διπλοΐζει τῷ πεπαμένῳ νόσον,   835
τοῖς τ᾽ αὐτὸς αὑτοῦ πήμασιν βαρύνεται
καὶ τὸν θυραῖον ὄλβον εἰσορῶν στένει.
Εἰδὼς λέγοιμ᾽ ἄν· εὖ γὰρ ἐξεπίσταμαι
ὁμιλίας κάτοπτρον, εἴδωλον σκιᾶς,
δοκοῦντας εἶναι κάρτα πρευμενεῖς ἐμοί.   840
Μόνος δ᾽ Ὀδυσσεύς, ὅσπερ οὐχ ἑκὼν ἔπλει,
ζευχθεὶς ἕτοιμος ἦν ἐμοὶ σειραφόρος·
εἴτ᾽ οὖν θανόντος εἴτε καὶ ζῶντος πέρι
λέγω. Τὰ δ᾽ ἄλλα, πρὸς πόλιν τε καὶ θεούς,
κοινοὺς ἀγῶνας θέντες ἐν πανηγύρει   845
βουλευσόμεσθα· καὶ τὸ μὲν καλῶς ἔχον
ὅπως χρονίζον εὖ μενεῖ βουλευτέον.
Ὅτῳ δὲ καὶ δεῖ φαρμάκων παιωνίων,
ἤτοι κέαντες ἢ τεμόντες εὐφρόνως
πειρασόμεσθα πῆμ᾽ ἀποστρέψαι νόσου.   850
Νῦν δ᾽ ἐς μέλαθρα καὶ δόμους ἐφεστίους
ἐλθὼν θεοῖσι πρῶτα δεξιώσομαι

826. ὀρούσας Fl. Temeritatis est, me judice, hujusmodi versus corrigere.
827. ὑπερθορῶν Fl. F. ὑπερθορών V.

831. ταῦτα libri. corr. Aur.
833. φθόνων Fl. corr. in F. V. ψόγου Stobæus.

taking its spring just as the Pleiads set.

And, having cleared the wall, like lion fed

on raw flesh, lapped to surfeit royal blood.

I have stretched out this prelude to the gods:

830 as for your sentiments; I heard and bear

in mind, and say the same; in me you have

a fellow-pleader. 'Tis innate in few

to court a prosperous friend without dislike.

Ill-natured venom seated at the heart

835 doubles the load for him who has got the sore,

for he is both oppressed by his own woes,

and sighs at sight of wealth outside his door.

I'll speak from knowledge: well I wot that those

who seemed to be quite complaisant to me

840 were only friendship's mirror, a shade's ghost.

But one, Ulysses, who was loth to sail,

when harnessed was a trace-horse prompt at call.

Thus, whether of a living man or dead,

I speak. As for the rest touching the state

845 and gods we'll summon public courts in full

assembly and consult; and must contrive

that what is sound may last and well abide.

And if a man needs healing remedies

by cautery or by cutting kindlily

850 we'll strive to avert the pain of his disease.

Now having reached my halls and chambers round

my hearth, I will first clasp the gods' right hands

835. πεπαμμένῳ libri. corr. Pors.　　850. πήματος τρέψαι νόσον. Dedi
836. αὑτοῦ et πήμασι Fl.　　praeclaram Porsoni em. omnibus,
842. σειρχαφόρος V.　　praeter Herm., probatam.

οἷπερ πρόσω πέμψαντες ἤγαγον πάλιν·
νίκη δ' ἐπείπερ ἔσπετ' ἐμπέδως μένοι.

ΚΛΤΤΑΙΜΝΗΣΤΡΑ.

Ἄνδρες πολῖται, πρέσβος Ἀργείων τόδε,   855
οὐκ αἰσχυνοῦμαι τοὺς φιλάνορας τρόπους
λέξαι πρὸς ὑμᾶς· ἐν χρόνῳ δ' ἀποφθίνει
τὸ τάρβος ἀνθρώποισιν. Οὐκ ἄλλων πάρα
μαθοῦσ', ἐμαυτῆς δύσφορον λέξω βίον
τοσόνδ' ὅσονπερ οὗτος ἦν ὑπ' Ἰλίῳ.   860
Τὸ μὲν γυναῖκα πρῶτον ἄρσενος δίχα
ἧσθαι δόμοις ἔρημον ἔκπαγλον κακόν,
πολλὰς κλύουσαν κληδόνας παλιγκότους·
καὶ τὸν μὲν ἥκειν, τὸν δ' ἐπεισφέρειν κακοῦ
κάκιον ἄλλο, πῆμα λάσκοντας δόμοις.   865
Καὶ τραυμάτων μὲν εἰ τόσων ἐτύγχανεν
ἀνὴρ ὅδ', ὡς πρὸς οἶκον ὠχετεύετο
φάτις, τέτρηται δικτύου πλέω λέγειν.
Εἰ δ' ἦν τεθνηκώς, ὡς ἐπλήθυον λόγοι,
τρισώματός τἂν Γηρυὼν ὁ δεύτερος   870
πολλὴν ἄνωθεν, τὴν κάτω γὰρ οὐ λέγω,
χθονὸς τρίμοιρον χλαῖναν ἐξηύχει λαβών,
ἅπαξ ἑκάστῳ κατθανὼν μορφώματι.
Τοιῶνδ' ἕκατι κληδόνων παλιγκότων
πολλὰς ἄνωθεν ἀρτάνας ἐμῆς δέρης   875
ἔλυσαν ἄλλοι πρὸς βίαν λελημμένης.
Ἐκ τῶνδέ τοι παῖς ἐνθάδ' οὐ παραστατεῖ,

---

863. ἡδονὰς libri. Auratus ille
correxit.
864, 865. Satis placent, ut verti,
    commate post ἄλλο posito.
    867. ἀνὴρ libri. Corr. Herm. ὠχε-
τεύετο libri. Corr. Heath.

who sent me forth and brought me back, and since
victory went with me may she fast abide.

CLYTEMNESTRA.

855 Men citizens, the Argives' senate here,
I'll not be shamed from telling you the traits
of my love for my lord: in time *that* fear
withers for mortals. Not by others taught,
shall I describe my own untoward life
860 so much as passed when he was *camped* at Troy.
First, for a wife abandoned by the male
to sit forlorn at home is frightful woe,
and hear word-omens many unassuaged;
croakers of home-distress — one just come in,
865 when, lo, a second loads bad news with worse.
And if this man received as many wounds
as rumour's watercourse led streaming home;
he 's punctured, so to speak, more than a net:
and had he died as swoln tidings ran
870 truly this second Geryon with three forms
would boast of getting thrice his share of thick
upper mould-blanket — of the under one
I speak not — if he died in each shape once.
Because of these word-omens unassuaged
875 others, when I was caught, unloosed perforce
above me many a neck-encircling noose.
And hence the boy is not here standing by,

868. φάσις Fl. τέτρωται libri.
τέτρηται Ahr.
869. ἐπλήθυνον libri. Formam At-
ticam Pors.
870. τ' ἄν libri. Corr. Wellauer.
871. Facete loquitur insidiatrix.

6*

ἐμῶν τε καὶ σῶν κύριος πιστωμάτων,
ὡς χρῆν, Ὀρέστης· μηδὲ θαυμάσῃς τόδε·
τρέφει γὰρ αὐτὸν εὐμενὴς δορύξενος   880
Στρόφιος ὁ Φωκεύς, ἀμφίλεκτα πήματα
ἐμοὶ προφωνῶν, τόν θ' ὑπ' Ἰλίῳ σέθεν
κίνδυνον, εἴ τε δημόθρους ἀναρχία
βουλὴν καταρρίψειεν· ὥστε σύγγονον
βροτοῖσι τὸν πεσόντα λακτίσαι πλέον.   885
Τοιάδε μέντοι σκῆψις οὐ δόλον φέρει.
Ἔμοιγε μὲν δὴ κλαυμάτων ἐπίσσυτοι
πηγαὶ κατεσβήκασιν, οὐδ' ἔνι σταγών·
ἐν ὀψικοίτοις δ' ὄμμασιν βλάβας ἔχω,
τὰς ἀμφὶ σοὶ κλαίουσα λαμπτηρουχίας   890
ἀτημελήτους αἰέν. Ἐν δ' ὀνείρασιν
λεπταῖς ὑπαὶ κώνωπος ἐξηγειρόμην
ῥιπαῖσι θωΰσσοντος, ἀμφὶ σοὶ πάθη
ὁρῶσα πλείω τοῦ ξυνεύδοντος χρόνου.
Νῦν ταῦτα πάντα τλᾶσ', ἀπενθήτῳ φρενί —   895
τερπνὸν δὲ τἀναγκαῖον ἐκφυγεῖν ἅπαν —   902
λέγοιμ' ἂν ἄνδρα τόνδε τῶν σταθμῶν κύνα,
σωτῆρα ναὸς πρότονον, ὑψηλῆς στέγης
στῦλον ποδήρη, μονογενὲς τέκνον πατρί,
γαῖαν φανεῖσαν ναυτίλοις παρ' ἐλπίδα,
κάλλιστον ἦμαρ εἰσιδεῖν ἐκ χείματος,   900
ὁδοιπόρῳ διψῶντι πηγαῖον ῥέος.
Τοιοῖςδέ τοί νιν ἀξιῶ προςφθέγμασιν·

878. πιστευμάτων libri. Corr.
Herm. coll. Eum. 214.
   888. κατεσβήκασιν, θ supra τ et
τ supra β adscriptis Fl., ut sit κα-
θεοστήκασιν.

889. κλάβας Fl.
   896. Hic versus vulgo post v. 901
legitur: transposuit Eng.
   897. Sunt quos articulus offendat.
τόνδ' ἐγὼ Weil.

who holds the pledge of my good faith and yours,
Orestes, as he ought; be not surprised;
880   our kind ally is entertaining him,
the Phocian Strophius, who forewarned me of
sorrow's dilemma, your own risk at Troy,
and — should the people's clamorous rioting
fling down the senate; since it is innate
885   in man to spurn the fallen all the more.
A plea of this kind surely bears no guile.
And now for me the gushing founts of tears
are quenched; there is not *even* one trickling drop:
I've weakness in my late-reposing eyes,
890   for your sake weeping the fire-signal-stacks
ever, *it seemed*, neglected: then, in dreams
while in my fear for you I saw more woes
than my sleep-fellow time *could bring*, I waked
at the light wing-strokes of the buzzing gnat.
895   Now having borne all this, with mind ungrieved —
902   for sweet is flight from all that comes perforce —
I'd call this man a watch-dog of the folds;
a stay, the vessel's saviour; a high roof's
firm-footed prop; to a father, his one child;
the land descried by sailors past all hope;
900   after a storm a day most fair to see;
a fountain's stream to thirsty traveller.
Such are the titles which I deem his due:

---

898. στόλον Fl. στύλον F. V. Acc.
corr. Dind.

899. καὶ γῆν libri. Sed quum certum sit hæc ab Homerico illo sumpta
esse γαῖαν ἄελπτα δῶκεν ἰδέσθαι, nam

et δῶμ' ἄελπτον v. 911, dubitari non
potest quid sit scribendum.

902. τοιοῖςδε τοίνυν libri. Corr.
Schutz.

Φθόνος δ' ἀπέστω· πολλὰ γὰρ τὰ πρὶν κακὰ
ἠνειχόμεσθα. Νῦν δέ μοι, φίλον κάρα,   905
ἔκβαιν' ἀπήνης τῆςδε μὴ χαμαὶ τιθεὶς
τὸν σὸν πόδ', ὦναξ, Ἰλίου πορθήτορα.
Δμωαί, τί μέλλεθ', αἷς ἐπέσταλται τέλος
πέδον κελεύθου στρωννύναι πετάσμασιν;
εὐθὺς γενέσθω πορφυρόστρωτος πόρος   910
ἐς δῶμ' ἄελπτον ὡς ἂν ἡγῆται δίκη.
Τὰ δ' ἄλλα φροντὶς οὐχ ὕπνῳ νικωμένη
θήσει δικαίως σὺν θεοῖς εἱμαρμένα.

ΑΓΑΜΕΜΝΩΝ.

Λήδας γένεθλον, δωμάτων ἐμῶν φύλαξ,
ἀπουσίᾳ μὲν εἶπας εἰκότως ἐμῇ,   915
μακρὰν γὰρ ἐξέτεινας· ἀλλ' ἐναισίμως
αἰνεῖν, παρ' ἄλλων χρὴ τόδ' ἔρχεσθαι γέρας.
Καὶ τἄλλα μὴ γυναικὸς ἐν τρόποις ἐμὲ
ἅβρυνε, μηδὲ βαρβάρου φωτὸς δίκην
χαμαιπετὲς βόημα προσχάνῃς ἐμοί,   920
μηδ' εἵμασι στρώσας' ἐπίφθονον πόρον
τίθει· θεούς τοι τοῖςδε τιμαλφεῖν χρεών·
ἐν ποικίλοις δὲ θνητὸν ὄντα κάλλεσιν
βαίνειν ἐμοὶ μὲν οὐδαμῶς ἄνευ φόβου.
Λέγω κατ' ἄνδρα, μὴ θεόν, σέβειν ἐμέ.   925
Χωρὶς ποδοψήστρων τε καὶ τῶν ποικίλων
κληδὼν ἀϋτεῖ· καὶ τὸ μὴ κακῶς φρονεῖν
θεοῦ μέγιστον δῶρον· ὀλβίσαι δὲ χρὴ
βίον τελευτήσαντ' ἐν εὐεστοῖ φίλῃ.

let envy keep aloof, for many were
905 the ills we bore before. Now, my beloved,
step from this car, and set not on the ground
thy foot, my king, that ravager of Troy.
Why wait ye, maids, for whom the task is set
to spread his pathway's ground with draperies?
910 let the way instantly be purple-spread,
that his desert may lead him to a home
unhoped for. By god's help my care, sleep-proof,
shall justly settle, as ordained, the rest.

AGAMEMNON.

Leda's descendant, guardian of my halls,
915 you 've made such speech as suits my absence well;
you stretched it to great length: but fittingly
to praise — that prize from others must proceed.
And, for the rest, treat me not softly like
a woman, nor as suits a Phrygian chief
920 mouth out to me a lowly-bent address:
nor make my path by spreading it with cloth
a mark for envy; we must court the gods
with these; and, sooth, that I a mortal man
should tread on broidered beauties is no way
925 devoid of fear. I bid you worship me
as man, not god. Without these carpetings
and figured-cloths fame talks. God's largest gift
is, not to cherish pride. We must count blest
him who has closed his life in sweet welfare.

---

908. τέλος Fl. V. τάδε F.   βόημα F. βόαμα V. vulgo. Illud
920. βόαμα Fl., η supra scripto.   tuentur Rost. et Enger.

Εἶπον τάδ' ὡς πράσσοιμ' ἂν εὐθαρσὴς ἐγώ. 930

ΚΛΥΤΑΙΜΝΗΣΤΡΑ.

Καὶ μὴν τόδ' εἰπὲ μὴ παρὰ γνώμην ἐμήν.

ΑΓΑΜΕΜΝΩΝ.

Γνώμην μὲν ἴσθι μὴ διαφθεροῦντ' ἐμέ.

ΚΛΥΤΑΙΜΝΗΣΤΡΑ.

Ηὔξω θεοῖς δείσας ἂν ὧδ' ἔρδειν τάδε.

ΑΓΑΜΕΜΝΩΝ.

Εἴπερ τις, εἰδώς γ' εὖ τόδ' ἐξεῖπον τέλος.

ΚΛΥΤΑΙΜΝΗΣΤΡΑ.

Τί δ' ἂν δοκεῖ σοι Πρίαμος, εἰ τάδ' ἤνυσεν; 935

ΑΓΑΜΕΜΝΩΝ.

Ἐν ποικίλοις ἂν κάρτα μοι βῆναι δοκεῖ.

ΚΛΥΤΑΙΜΝΗΣΤΡΑ.

Μή νυν τὸν ἀνθρώπειον αἰδεσθῇς ψόγον.

ΑΓΑΜΕΜΝΩΝ.

Φήμη γε μέντοι δημόθρους μέγα σθένει.

ΚΛΥΤΑΙΜΝΗΣΤΡΑ.

Ὁ δ' ἀφθόνητος οὐκ ἐπίζηλος πέλει.

---

930. εἰ πάντα δ' ὡς πράσσοιμ' ἂν, libri. πράσσοιμεν Dind., ἂν εἴην, si diis placet, subaudito. Rem perspexit

Weilius: 'hæc dixi sic ut equidem agendo fidenter periclitarer'.

933. Rectissime interpretatus est

930 Thus have I said and thus should boldly act.

CLYTEMNESTRA.

Pray do not speak so as to thwart my will.

AGAMEMNON.

My will be sure that I shall not corrupt.

'CLYTEMNESTRA.

In fear you might have vowed the gods this act.

AGAMEMNON.

None more; I spoke to that end well advised.

CLYTEMNESTRA.

935 What think you Priam, this achieved, had done?

AGAMEMNON.

Walked on the damask certainly, I think.

CLYTEMNESTRA.

Be not abashed then at mere human blame.

AGAMEMNON.

Yet much the commons' murmuring talk prevails.

CLYTEMNESTRA.

At least the unenvied man is not admired.

Bl., εἰ ἔδεισας, ηὔξω ἄν.   937. αἰδεσθείς; Fl. αἰδεσθῆς; F. αἰδε-
   935. δοκῇ libri. Corr. Stanl.   σθῆς Aur.
   936. δοκῇ Fl. V. Corr. in F.

ΑΓΑΜΕΜΝΩΝ.

Οὖτοι γυναικὸς ἔστιν ἱμείρειν μάχης.　　　940

ΚΛΥΤΑΙΜΝΗΣΤΡΑ.

Τοῖς δ' ὀλβίοις γε καὶ τὸ νικᾶσθαι πρέπει.

ΑΓΑΜΕΜΝΩΝ.

Ἦ καὶ σὺ νίκην τήνδε δήριος τίεις;

ΚΛΥΤΑΙΜΝΗΣΤΡΑ.

Πιθοῦ· κράτος μέντοι πάρες γ' ἑκὼν ἐμοί.

ΑΓΑΜΕΜΝΩΝ.

Ἀλλ' εἰ δοκεῖ σοι ταῦθ', ὑπαί τις ἀρβύλας
λύοι τάχος, πρόδουλον ἔμβασιν ποδός.　　　945
Καὶ τοῖςδε μ' ἐμβαίνονθ' ἁλουργέσιν θεῶν
μή τις πρόσωθεν ὄμματος βάλοι φθόνος.
Πολλὴ γὰρ αἰδὼς δωματοφθορεῖν ποσὶν
φθείροντα πλοῦτον ἀργυρωνήτους θ' ὑφάς.
Τούτων μὲν οὕτω. Τὴν ξένην δὲ πρευμενῶς　　950
τήνδ' ἐςκόμιζε· τὸν κρατοῦντα μαλθακῶς
θεὸς πρόσωθεν εὐμενῶς προςδέρκεται·
ἑκὼν γὰρ οὐδεὶς δουλίῳ χρῆται ζυγῷ.
Αὕτη δὲ πολλῶν χρημάτων ἐξαίρετον
ἄνθος, στρατοῦ δώρημ', ἐμοὶ ξυνέσπετο.　　955
Ἐπεὶ δ' ἀκούειν σου κατέστραμμαι τάδε,
εἶμ' ἐς δόμων μέλαθρα πορφύρας πατῶν.

---

942. Sic libri. Verto: 'egone solus, an tu quoque hanc certaminis
victoriam affectas?

946. Sic Fl. σὺν τοῖσδε F. V.
Deinde ἐμβαίνοντ' αλ. Fl. F. corr.
in V.

AGAMEMNON.

940 'Tis not a woman's part to court dispute.

CLYTEMNESTRA.

On fortune's favourites ev'n defeat looks well.

AGAMEMNON.

Do you too prize such victory in a strife?

CLYTEMNESTRA.

Comply: yet freely yield the palm to — me.

AGAMEMNON.

Well, if it please you, some one quickly loose
945 *these* shoes, the foot's mock-lacquey stepping-place.
And may no god's eye's envy, as I tread
these sea-dyed tissues, smite me from afar.
It is great scandal to despoil the house
by spoiling treasure with one's feet, the webs
950 weighed against silver. Thus *I deem* of this.
But greet this maiden-stranger courteously:
the gentle conquerer god regards from far
with favour; for none willingly puts on
the slavish yoke. She followed me, the flower
955 selected from much wealth, an army's gift.
And since I'm bent to obey you in this act,
I'll pace the purple to my palace-halls.

948. σωματοφθορεῖν πόσιν libri. ποσίν Scaliger. δωματοφθορεῖν Schutz., quem Bl., Herm., Eng. secuti sunt.

Sensus est, quem dedi in versione.
950. τοὐμὸν μὲν οὕτω Emper.; Eng.
954. αὐτὴ libri. αὕτη Aur.

ΚΛΤΤΑΙΜΝΗΣΤΡΑ.

Ἔστιν θάλασσα, τίς δέ νιν κατασβέσει;
τρέφουσα πολλῆς πορφύρας ἰσάργυρον
κηκῖδα παγκαίνιστον, εἱμάτων βαφάς.   960
Οἴκῳ δ᾽ ὑπάρχει τῶνδε σὺν θεοῖς, ἄναξ,
πλουτεῖν· πένεσθαι δ᾽ οὐκ ἐπίσταται δόμος.
Πολλῶν πατησμὸν δ᾽ εἱμάτων ἂν ηὐξάμην
δόμοισι προὐνεχθέντος ἐν χρηστηρίοις,
ψυχῆς κόμιστρα τῆσδε μηχανωμένη.   965
Ῥίζης γὰρ οὔσης φυλλὰς ἵκετ᾽ ἐς δόμους,
σκιὰν ὑπερτείνασα Σειρίου κυνός.
Καὶ σοῦ μολόντος δωματῖτιν ἑστίαν,
θάλπος μὲν ἐν χειμῶνι σημαίνεις μολόν·
ὅταν δὲ τεύχῃ Ζεὺς ἀπ᾽ ὄμφακος πικρᾶς   970
οἶνον, τόθ᾽ ἡδὺ ψῦχος ἐν δόμοις πέλει,
ἀνδρὸς τελείου δῶμ᾽ ἐπιστρωφωμένου.
Ζεῦ, Ζεῦ τέλειε, τὰς ἐμὰς εὐχὰς τέλει·
μέλοι δέ τοι σοὶ τῶνπερ ἂν μέλλῃς τελεῖν.

ΧΟΡΟΣ.

στρ.ά.   Τίπτε μοι τόδ᾽ ἐμπέδως   975
δεῖμα προστατήριον
καρδίας τερασκόπου ποτᾶται,

959. εἰς ἄργυρον libri. Corr. Salmasius.
960. οἶκος libri. οἴκῳ, quod BL conjecerat, ego scripsi. Scilicet ὑπάρχει est Atticum illud, quod valet 'contigit' ut Dem. Ph. 1. ὑπάρχει ὑμῖν χρῆσθαι et passim. Deinde vocabula τῶνδε et πένεσθαι satis demonstrant ἔχειν esse glossam ad πλουτεῖν

adscriptam. Eng. conj. γέμων. Possis et βρύειν vel πλήθειν, inepta omnia; nam πλουτεῖν unice respondet voci πένεσθαι.
962. ἔχειν libri. πλουτεῖν ego.
963. δειμάτων libri. Corr. Aur., et Canter.
965. μηχανωμένης libri. Corr. Aur. Huic mendæ causam præbuit v. τῆσδε.

CLYTEMNESTRA.

There is the sea — and who shall dry it up? —
which for much purple cloth breeds juice as dear
960 as silver, ever fresh for use, robe-dyes.
Of this our house, sire, by god's grace, can boast
rich store; the house knows not to lack. I would
have vowed much raiment-trampling, had that been
prescribed the house by oracles, when I
965 was planning means to escort thy life safe home.
For, now the root lives, leaves come to the house,
spreading a screen against dog Sirius;
and by your coming to the family hearth
you notify that warmth has come in frost:
970 and when Zeus makes the wine from unripe grapes,
then is there coolness sweet at home, if in
the house a husband fully blest sojourns.
O Zeus, fulfilment's god, fulfil my prayers,
and see to that which thou wilt now fulfil.

CHORUS.

975 Why does this presentiment
domineering steadily
o'er my portent-scanning spirit hover?

967. ὑπερτίνασα Fl. corr. in F. V.
ὑπερτείνουσα Aur., Dind. sine idonea
causa.
969. μόλων libri. Corr. Voss. et Bl.
970. ζεὺς τ᾽ ἀπ᾽ F. V. ζεὺς τᾶπ᾽
Fl. τ᾽ delevit Aur.
971. τότ᾽ ἤδη libri, ut quod maxime, putidum. τόθ᾽ ἠδὺ Aur. recte,
ut illo fere omnia. 'frigus amabile'.

972. ἐπιστρεφωμένου Fl. ἐπιστρο-
φωμένου F. corr. in V.
974. μέλη, supra scripto οι, δέ
σοι Fl. μέλοι δέ τι σοι V. μέλοι δέ
τοι σοι F. σοὶ Pors.
976. δεῖγμα Fl. V. δεῖμα F. sec.
Bekk.; idem conj. Aur. δεῖγμα esset
'indiculum' idque ridiculum.

μαντιπολεῖ δ' ἀκέλευστος ἄμισθος ἀοιδά;

οὐδ' ἀποπτύσαν δίκαν   980

δυσκρίτων ὀνειράτων

θάρσος εὐπειθὲς ἵ-

ζει φρενὸς φίλον θρόνον;

χρόνος δ' ἐπεὶ προὔμνησ' ἰδὼν ἐν ξυμβόλοις

φάσματ' ἄτας παρή-   985

βησεν, εὖθ' ὑπ' Ἴλιον

ὦρτο νκυβάτας στρατός.

ἀντ. ά.   Πεύθομαι δ' ἀπ' ὀμμάτων

νόστον, αὐτόμαρτυς ὤν.

Τὸν δ' ἄνευ λύρας ὅμως μονῳδεῖ   990

θρῆνον Ἐρινύος αὐτοδίδακτος ἔσωθεν

θυμός, οὐ τὸ πᾶν ἔχων

ἐλπίδος φίλον θράσος.

Σπλάγχνα δ' οὔτοι ματᾴ-   995

ζει πρὸς ἐνδίκοις φρεσίν,

τελεσφόροις δίναις κυκλούμενον κέαρ.

Εὔχομαι δ' ἐξ ἐμᾶς

ἐλπίδος ψύθη πεσεῖν

ἐς τὸ μὴ τελεσφόρον.   1000

στρ. β'.   Μάλα γέ τοι τὸ πολέος γ' ὑγιίας

980. ἀποπτύσας FL V. ἀποπτύσαι F. Corr. Scaliger.

982. εὐπιθὲς libri. Corr. Rossbach et Westphal, m. gr. ἴξει FL ἴξει F. V. Corr. Scaliger.

984. χρόνος δ' ἐπεὶ (ἐπὶ F.) πρυμνησίων ξυνεμβόλοις ψαμμίας ἀκάτα (ἀκάτας F. V.) libri. Hæc miris modis confusa, corrupta, præpostere collocata, tantum non glossis fœdata sunt. Causam præbuit huic ruinæ

perperam scripta prima vox πρυμνησίων, quæ sane satis probabiliter πρυμνησίων correcta est: hinc adeo lintres in arena hærebant, et funibus simul alligatis, vel, remis in numerum adductis, sesquiversus allisus est. Cfr. φάσματα φανῶν supr. v. 145. ἰδὼν est Calchas. Si spondæus in quinta sede offendit, scribe κέαρ κυκλούμενον in v. antist.

990. ὅπως libri. Corr. Stanl. Dein-

why does song play the diviner unbidden, unguerdoned?
980 why, not spurning it like dreams
hard to sift, does confidence
firm in faith not retain
    its own seat within my breast?
and yet the time has passed its prime since he forewarned
985 who in types saw the sprites
    of destruction when to Troy
    sped the ship-ascending host.

From my eyes I learn, my own
witness, of his home-return;
990 yet without the lyre my soul self-lessoned
strikes up within me a solo, a wail of Erinnys;
not retaining its beloved
fullest confidence of hope.

995 Nor for naught starts my breast
    at the midriff's truthful tale, —
my heart, that whirls in rounds which bring an end fulfilled.
But I pray that my fears
    failing promise may in lies
1000 issue, in no end fulfilled.

Truly each stage of health far advanced

de libri ὑμνωὸεῖ, quod ex ὁμνωὸεῖ correctum est, quum μονωὸεῖ debuit. Præterea primo ante se habuit v. ὁμως. Quid si sensus quoque hoc verb. mavult? At si duobus locis corruptis demus syll. ὑμν corripi posse, nihil certi erit usquam.

991. ἐρινὺς libri. Corr. Herm. et Pors.

995. ματάζει libri. Corr. Herm.

998. Sic Fl. nec quisquam cor-rigere voluisset si v. stroph. quem dedi invenisset.

999. ψυὸὴ Fl. F. ψυὸῇ V. Corr. Stephanus.

1001. μάλα γάρ τοι τᾶς πολλᾶς ὑγιείας; Fl. V. μάλα γε (γάρ supra scripto) τοι δὴ cet. F. Hæc Herm. in formulam maxime probabilem redegit, nec multum discrepat, me judice, ab ea quam Æsch. promulgavit.

ἀκόρεστον τέρμα· νόσος γὰρ ἀεὶ γεί-
των ὁμότοιχος ἐρείδει·
καὶ πότμος εὐθυπορῶν   1005
ἀνδρὸς ἔπαισεν πρὸς ἄφαντον ἕρμα.

Καὶ τὸ μὲν πρὸ χρημάτων
κτησίων ὄκνον βαλὼν
σφενδόνας ἀπ' εὐμέτρου   1010
οὐκ ἔδυ πρόπας δόμος
πημονᾶς γέμων ἄγαν,
οὐδ' ἐπόντισε σκάφος.

Πολλά τοι δόσις ἐκ Διὸς ἀμφιλα-   1015
φής τε καὶ ἐξ ἀλόκων ἐπετειᾶν
νῆστιν ὤλεσεν νόσον·

ἀντ.β'.   τὸ δ' ἐπὶ γᾶν πεσὸν ἅπαξ θανάσιμον
προπάροιθ' ἀνδρὸς μέλαν αἷμα, τίς ἂν τοῦτ'
ἀγκαλέσαιτ' ἐπαείδων;   1020
Οὐδὲ τὸν ὀρθοδαῆ
τῶν φθιμένων Ζεὺς ἀνάγειν ἂν εἶρξεν.

Εἰ δὲ μὴ τεταγμένα   1025
Μοῖρα μοῖραν ἐκ θεῶν

1002. Bl. addidit ἀεί, probante
Herm. Ceterorum conj. nequam sunt.
1006. Inserui πρός. Cf. v. antistr.
1008. τὸ μὲν valet τοῦτο μὲν 'hoc
si accidit', cui opponendum erat
τοῦτο δὲ in v. antistr. 'at si illud,
scilicet, homicidium'.
1009. ὄκνος libri. ὄκνον ego. 'do-
mus, inquit, si opes perdendi cunctationem projecit, non tota submer-
gitur'. Junge: ὄκνον πρὸ χρημάτων
(non προβαλὼν τὸ μὲν χρημάτων)
'cunctationem, quæ quasi propugnat
pro salute opum'.

1011. Ap. Hes. est ἅπας βίος,
sensus idem; Op. 687.
1012. πημονὰς Fl. F. corr. in V.
1016. κἀξ Fl corr. in F. V.
1018. πεσόνθ' ἅπαξ libri. Corr.
Pauw. θ' enim ad v. θανάσιμον pertinet: sic Eng., Porsoni corr. spreta.
1019. πρόπαρ Fl. corr. in F. V.
Deinde τίς τ' ἀγκαλέσαιτ' T. omisso
πάλιν quod Fl. V. præbent ante ἀγκ.
Recte: nam glossa erat ad ἀγκ- ad-
cripta. τ' illa superest de pæne
evanido τοῦτ', quod restitui.
1024. ἀνάγειν ζεὺς αὖτ' ἔπαυσεν ἐπ'

is without cloy: sickness, a neighbour who shares one

wall, is for ever assailing.

1005 And a man's state as it sails

fair on its course strikes on an unseen breaker.

Then by casting overboard

fear to lose acquired wealth,

1010 from a wisely-weighted sling,

all the house does not go down

over-freighted with its bane,

nor in deep sea sinks the ship.

1015 Large boon, doubtless, from Zeus in exuberance

and from the furrows which yield in the autumn

kills a famine's *fell* disease:

but if it has first to earth fallen once

giving death place, who can call up any more a

1020　　man's ruddy life-blood by charming?

else would not Zeus have debarred

him who was well skilled to bring back the lost ones.

1025 And if no appointed Doom

barred a god-sent doom from all

<hr>

εὐλαβείᾳ Fl. αὖτ' ἔπαυσ' ἐπ' εὐλαβείᾳ
γε V. αὖτ' ἔπαυσ' ἐπ' ἀβλαβείᾳ γε F.
Jam Canterus hæc magna ex parte
scholio deberi vidit; quem secutus
Herm. scripsit Ζεὺς δὲ τὸν ὀρθοδαῆ
τῶν φθιμένων ἀνάγειν ἔπαυσεν. Sed illa
vocis Ζεὺς transpositio violentior est;
ἔπαυσεν autem est interpretatio; nam
certissimum mihi videtur idem verbum quod v. 1027 usurpatur, et
hic esse restituendum. Itaque scripsi
εἶρξεν cum præeunte ἄν. Jam nihil
aliud opus erat quam ut Ζεὺς ἀνάγειν
scriberem. Verto: 'quippe vetant

Jovis leges; alioqui neque Asclepium
a mortuis arcuisset, ne excitaret'.
1025—1033. Sic libri, σοφώτερον
quam σαφέστερον fateor, sed omnia
prorsus sana; Μοῖρα scripsi (μοῖρα
vulgo) et comma post ἐκτολυπεύσειν
delevi. Vide Comment. Quod autem
ad hoc et cetera Æschyli ænigmata
attinet, non ea sunt quorum sententiam quisquam, etiamsi acerrimo
ingenio præditus in Græcis literis
diu lateque versatus sit, primo im-
petu compertam habere possit.

εἶργε μὴ πλέον φέρειν,
προφθάσασα καρδία
γλῶσσαν ἂν τάδ᾽ ἐξέχει.   1030
Νῦν δ᾽ ὑπὸ σκότῳ βρέμει
θυμαλγής τε καὶ οὐδὲν ἐπελπομέ-
να ποτὲ καίριον ἐκτολυπεύσειν
ζωπυρουμένας φρενός.

ΚΛΤΤΛΙΜΝΗΣΤΡΑ.

Εἴσω κομίζου καὶ σύ· Κασάνδραν λέγω·   1035
ἐπεί σ᾽ ἔθηκε Ζεὺς ἀμηνίτως δόμοις
κοινωνὸν εἶναι χερνίβων, πολλῶν μετὰ
δούλων σταθεῖσαν κτησίου βωμοῦ πέλας.
Ἔκβαιν᾽ ἀπήνης τῆσδε· μηδ᾽ ὑπερφρόνει.
Καὶ παῖδα γάρ τοί φασιν Ἀλκμήνης ποτὲ   1040
πραθέντα τλῆναι δουλίας μάζης θιγεῖν.
Εἰ δ᾽ οὖν ἀνάγκη τῆσδ᾽ ἐπιρρέποι τύχης,
ἀρχαιοπλούτων δεσποτῶν πολλὴ χάρις.
Οἳ δ᾽ οὔποτ᾽ ἐλπίσαντες ἤμησαν καλῶς
ὠμοί τε δούλοις πάντα καὶ παρὰ στάθμην.   1045
Ἔχεις παρ᾽ ἡμῶν οἷάπερ νομίζεται.

ΧΟΡΟΣ.

Σοί τοι λέγουσα παύεται σαφῆ λόγον.

1036. ἀμηνίτως, χερνίβων, κτησίου duplicem sensum habent.
1037. μέτα libri, μετὰ Herm.
421. δουλείας μάζης βίᾳ Fl. καὶ ζυγῶν θίγειν βίᾳ F. V. Quod Bl. scripsit δουλίας μάζης βίον id proxime accessit ad ver. lect. Ex iis δουλίας μάζης 'cibarii panis' omnia ingenui-tatis monimenta præ se fert aptis-simeque dicitur si personas, hanc et illam, consideras. Sed μάζης βίον non potuit dici; nam intelligi potest quid sit λαγὼ βίος sed λαγῴων βίος putidum est. Deinde ζυγῶν θιγεῖν 'jugum attingere' pariter atque illud absurdum est; oportuit esse φέρειν,

mitigation, then my heart,
faster than my tongue could speak,
these *misgivings* would pour out:
1030 now it sighs, in darkness sunk,
spirit-sore, with no hope that it ever will
spin from the flame-enwrapt *distaff of* reason
aught to suit the present need.

CLYTEMNESTRA.

1035 Go you in too, I mean Casandra, since
Zeus not vindictively has made you share
our household's cleansing-rite, with many slaves
placed near the altar of the treasure-god.
Step from this car, and cherish no high thoughts.
1040 They say, you know, that once Alcmena's son
was sold and took the slavish barley dole.
. And if this lot's constraint should turn the scale
great thanks *are due* for lords enriched of old.
Those who, not hoping it, reap largely, pass
1045 the plumb-line and are harsh to slaves all ways;
you get from us just what is usual.

CHORUS.

To you she speaks plain words, and makes a pause;

φορεῖν, καινίζειν, δῦναι. Meæ rationes
hujusmodi sunt: μάζης male sciptum
μάξης, cum interpr. ζυγῶν supra ad-
dita, secuta est vox θιγεῖν; βίᾳ autem
est pars interpretationis ad τλῆναι
pertinentis, quæ nullo modo in
textum recipienda erat.

1044. οἶδ' Fl. οἱ δ' V. Corr. Stanl.
1045. παραστάθμων Fl. παρὰ στάθμην 'ad amussin' Theogn. 543 non
est Attice dictum.
1046. ἕξεις Aur. Sed sensus est:
παρ' ἡμῶν δὲ οἱ δοῦλοι ἔχουσιν ο. ν.
Sic Enger.

7 *

Ἐκτὸς δ᾽ ἂν οὖσα μορσίμων ἀγρευμάτων
πείθοι᾽ ἄν, εἰ πείθοι᾽· ἀπειθοίης δ᾽ ἴσως.

ΚΛΥΤΑΙΜΝΗΣΤΡΑ.

Ἀλλ᾽ εἴπερ ἐστὶ μὴ χελιδόνος δίκην   1050
ἀγνῶτα φωνὴν βάρβαρον κεκτημένη,
ἔσω φρενῶν λέγουσα πείθω νιν λόγῳ.

ΧΟΡΟΣ.

Ἐπεὶ τὰ λῷστα τῶν παρεστώτων λέγει
πείθου, λιποῦσα τόνδ᾽ ἀμαξήρη θρόνον.

ΚΛΥΤΑΙΜΝΗΣΤΡΑ.

Οὔτοι θυραίαν τήνδ᾽ ἐμοὶ σχολὴν πάρα   1055
τρίβειν· τὰ μὲν γὰρ ἑστίας μεσομφάλου
ἕστηκεν ἤδη μῆλα πρὸς σφαγὰς πάρος,
ὡς οὔποτ᾽ ἐλπίσασι τήνδ᾽ ἕξειν χάριν.
Σὺ δ᾽ εἴ τι δράσεις· τῶνδε, μὴ σχολὴν τίθει.
Εἰ δ᾽ ἀξυνήμων οὖσα μὴ δέχει λόγον,   1060
σὺ δ᾽ ἀντὶ φωνῆς φράζε καρβάνῳ χερί.

ΧΟΡΟΣ.

Ἑρμηνέως ἔοικεν ἡ ξένη τοροῦ
δεῖσθαι· τρόπος δὲ θηρὸς ὡς νεαιρέτου.

ΚΛΥΤΑΙΜΝΗΣΤΡΑ.

Ἢ μαίνεταί τε καὶ κακῶν κλύει φρενῶν,

1048. ἐντὸς libri. ἐκτὸς Herm. Et
sane ν et κ literæ simiiles sunt; quod
si non essent tamen hoc reciperem
sententiæ ergo. ἐντὸς δ᾽ ἀλοῦσα conj.

Haupt., Eng., Karst.: 'captiva es, i.
e., non tui juris, itaque utrum mavis
facies'. Quanto rectius: 'si captiva
non esses, tum demum consensus

and, were you free from fatal toils, if you
complied, why, you 'd comply; perhaps not comply.

CLYTEMNESTRA.

1050 Well, if she is not swallow-like possessed
but of some barbarous jargon, then I speak
within her ken, and move her by my words.

CHORUS.

Since she suggests the present turn's best choice
comply, and leave this car-inserted seat.

CLYTEMNESTRA.

1055 I cannot waste this time outside the door:
before the hearth, our house's centre-boss,
now stand the sheep for slaughter; as for those
who never hoped to get this joy: and if
you will do aught of this, make no delay:
1060 but if through ignorance you decline discourse
in lieu of speech make signs with alien hand.

CHORUS.

The stranger seems to need exponents shrewd.
Her ways are like some wild thing's just ensnared.

CLYTEMNESTRA.

Surely she raves and heeds an evil wit,

pro arbitrio foret'.
   1052. πείθω ex iis verbis est quorum praesens tempus fere idem valet
quod perfectum.

1053. ἔπου. τὰ libri. ἐπεὶ τὰ Heims.
1055. σχολὴ libri. Corr. Weiseler.
1057. πυρός libri. Corr. Musgrav.
1064. ἡ Fl. corr. in F. V.

ἥτις λιποῦσα μὲν πόλιν νεαίρετον   1065
ἥκει· χαλινὸν δ' οὐκ ἐπίσταται φέρειν
πρὶν αἱματηρὸν ἐξαφρίζεσθαι μένος.
Οὐ μὴν πλέω ῥίψασ' ἀτιμασθήσομαι.

ΧΟΡΟΣ.

Ἐγὼ δ', ἐποικτείρω γάρ, οὐ θυμώσομαι.
Ἴθ' ὦ τάλαινα, τόνδ' ἐρημώσασ' ὄχον,   1070
εἴκουσ' ἀνάγκῃ τῇδε καίνισον ζυγόν.

ΚΑΣΑΝΔΡΑ.

στρ.ά. Ὀτοτοτοῖ πόποι δᾶ.
Ἀπόλλων, Ἀπόλλων.

ΧΟΡΟΣ.

Τί τοῦτ' ἀνωτότυξας ἀμφὶ Λοξίου;
οὐ γὰρ τοιοῦτος ὥστε θρηνητοῦ τυχεῖν.   1075

ΚΑΣΑΝΔΡΑ.

ἀντ.ά. Ὀτοτοτοῖ πόποι δᾶ.
Ἀπόλλων, Ἀπόλλων.

ΧΟΡΟΣ.

Ἡ δ' αὖτε δυσφημοῦσα τον θεὸν καλεῖ
οὐδὲν προσήκοντ' ἐν γόοις παραστατεῖν.

ΚΑΣΑΝΔΡΑ.

στρ.β'. Ἀπόλλων, Ἀπόλλων   1080

1071. ἑκοῦσ' libri. Corr. Rob.
1072. ὀτοτοτοῖ M. corr. in Fl. qui tamen πομποῖ habet.

1065 who having left her country just ensnared
has come, and knows not how to wear the bit
before she foams away her rage in blood.
I'll vent no further speech and be disdained.

CHORUS.

But, for I pity her, I'll not be wroth.
1070 Come, thou unhappy one, vacate this car,
yield to this fate, and try the new yoke on.

CASANDRA.

Oh woe, woe! alas, earth!
Apollo! Apollo!

CHORUS.

Why shout ye woe for Loxias? he's not
1075 the sort to come into a mourner's hands.

CASANDRA.

Oh woe, woe! alas, earth!
Apollo! Apollo!

CHORUS.

Again with grief she calls upon a god
not bound at wailings to be standing by.

CASANDRA.

1080 Apollo! Destroyer!

1073. ἄπολλον bis M. ἄπολλον bis Fl. et sic infra. Corr. Herm.
1078. ἥδ' M. corr. in cet.

ἀγυιᾶτ᾽, ἀπόλλων ἐμός·
ἀπώλεσας γὰρ οὐ μόλις τὸ δεύτερον.

ΧΟΡΟΣ.

Χρήσειν ἔοικεν ἀμφὶ τῶν αὐτῆς κακῶν.
Μένει τὸ θεῖον δουλίᾳ περ ἐν φρενί.

ΚΑΣΑΝΔΡΑ.

ἀντ.β΄.   Ἀπόλλων, Ἀπόλλων   1085
ἀγυιᾶτ᾽, ἀπόλλων ἐμός·
ἆ ποῖ ποτ᾽ ἤγαγές με; πρὸς ποίαν στέγην;

ΧΟΡΟΣ.

Πρὸς τὴν Ἀτρειδῶν· εἰ σὺ μὴ τόδ᾽ ἐννοεῖς
ἐγὼ λέγω σοι· καὶ τάδ᾽ οὐκ ἐρεῖς ψύθη.

ΚΑΣΑΝΔΡΑ.

στρ.γ΄.   Μισόθεον μὲν οὖν, πολλὰ συνίστορα   1090
αὐτοφόνα τε κακὰ κάρτάνας,
ἀνδροσφαγεῖον καὶ φονορραντήριον.

ΧΟΡΟΣ.

Ἔοικεν εὔρις ἡ ξένη κυνὸς δίκην
εἶναι, ματεύει δ᾽ ὧν ἀνευρήσει φόνον.

1081. ἀγυιᾶτ M. ἀγυιᾶτ᾽ G. F. Fl. (hic sec. Franz. properisp.) ἀγυιᾶτ᾽ Rob. ex Sophiani emend; et sic infra.
1082. οὐ μόλις est 'non parum' Herm.
1083. αὐτῆς codices. αὐτῆς T. Vict.
1084. παρ᾽ ἐν M. παρὸν Fl. παρὸν F. (Herm.) Corr. Schutz.
1086. ἀγυίατ᾽ Fl.; cet. ut v. 1081.

1089. ἆ ἆ praemittit M., om. Fl. ξυνίστορα M. corr. in Fl.
1091. καρτάναι M. Fl. κάρτάνας F. Herm. inseruit τε m. gr. Emperio Kayser., Enger., videtur καρατόμα esse corrigendum, Romano, scilicet, et posteriore more deceptis; nam quis Graecus, praeter Perseum, alteri caput praecidit unquam? quod idem interrogari non potest de sus-

the street-god, my destroying god!

for twice thou hast destroyed me, not almost.

CHORUS.

She seems about to augur her own woes.

God's gift abides though in a bondsman's breast.

CASANDRA.

1085 Apollo! Destroyer!

the street-god, my destroying-god!

Oh whither hast thou led me? to what roof?

CHORUS.

The Atreids': you might know; but if you dont

I tell you; and you 'll say this is not false.

CASANDRA.

1090 No, a god-hating roof, privy to many crimes,

murders of kinsfolk, strangling-cords;

a men's-throat-cutting place, a sink of blood.

CHORUS.

The stranger seems keen-scented like a hound,

and tracks the game she starts by trace of blood.

---

pendio heroinarum. κρεατόμα conj. Weil.

1092. ἀνδρὸς σφάγιον libri, in M. ι in litura. σφάγειον T. σφαγεῖον Pors. ἀνδροσφαγεῖον Dobræ. Deinde πέδον ῥαντήριον libri, sed in M. pr. m. scripserat πέδορ. πεδορραντήριον Dind. at quid hoc significet ab ipso audieris melius. φονορραντήριον Enger. Etenim πέδον est glossa.

1093. εὑρις M. ις in litura. εὑρις Fl. Corr. Pors. Bl. mavult εὑριν.

1094. μαντεύειν M. ματεύει Fl. ματεύειν T. ὧν ἂν εὑρήση M. G. Rob., ἐρευρήσει Fl. F. Vict. ἂν ἀνευρήσει T. Recepi Porsoni em. sed ita ut idem valeat quod ἂν εὑροι. Jampridem Paleius recte vertebat 'quorumcunque cruorem homicidio fusum invenorit, eum investigat'.

ΚΑΣΑΝΔΡΑ.

ἀντ.γ΄. Μαρτυρίοισι γὰρ τοῖςδ᾽ ἐπιπείθομαι · 1095
κλαιόμενα τάδε βρέφη σφαγὰς
ὀπτάς τε σάρκας πρὸς πατρὸς βεβρωμένας.

ΧΟΡΟΣ.

Ἦμεν κλέος σου μαντικὸν πεπυσμένοι,
τούτων προφήτας δ᾽ οὔτινας ματεύομεν.

ΚΑΣΑΝΔΡΑ.

στρ.δ΄. Ἰὼ πόποι, τί ποτε μήδεται; 1100
τί τόδ᾽ ἄχος νέον μέγα
μέγ᾽ ἐν δόμοισι τοῖσδε μήδεται κακὸν
ἄφερτον φίλοισιν, δυσίατον; ἀλ-
κὰ δ᾽ ἑκὰς ἀποστατεῖ.

ΧΟΡΟΣ.

Τούτων ἄϊδρίς εἰμι τῶν μαντευμάτων · 1105
ἐκεῖνα δ᾽ ἔγνων, πᾶσα γὰρ πόλις βοᾷ.

ΚΑΣΑΝΔΡΑ.

ἀντ.δ΄. Ἰὼ τάλαινα, τόδε γὰρ τελεῖς;
τὸν ὁμοδέμνιον πόσιν
λουτροῖσι φαιδρύνασα · πῶς φράσω τέλος;

1095. μαρτυρίοις γὰρ M. μ. μὲν γὰρ Fl. Corr. Pauw. τοῖσδε πεπείθομαι libri. Corr. Abresch.
1096. Sic M. τὰ Fl.
1098. ἦ μὴν a pr. m. M., alia manus, ut videtur, ἦμεν superscripsit. ἦμεν Fl. cet. ἦμεν Rob. ἦ μὴν corr. Pors.
1099. ἦμεν M. Fl. cet. ἦν supra scripto in G., unde ἦ μὴν Ald. Turn. ἦσμεν Pors., Bl., Herm., Dind. Sed neutrum horum hic ferri potest; neque ἦ μὴν ἦσμεν neque πεπυσμένοι ἦσμεν. Weilium solum habeo quem

CASANDRA.

1095 Yes! for I credit these tokens, the crying babes —
these — that wail their own butchery
and roasted flesh of which their father ate.

CHORUS.

True, we had heard of your divining fame,
but these are things for which we seek no seers.

CASANDRA.

1100 O God! what's this? what is she compassing?
what this novel heinous *woe*,
this heinous woe she 's plotting in this house?
an ill past her friends' strength to bear, hard to cure;
help withdraws far away.

CHORUS.

1105 In these revealings I'm unversed, but those
I knew; for all the city talks of them.

CASANDRA.

O hapless one! you will act it out?
having by bathing beautified
your bedmate lord — how shall I tell the end?

sequar, nec meliorem ducem quæro.
Is enim dedit ἦμεν v. 1098 et, pro
prave iterata cadem voce, τούτων,
ut quod solum hic stare potuerit.
Mox μαστεύομεν libri. Corr. Schutz.
  1101. ἄχθος M. ἄχος supra scripto.

Engerus omittit μέγα, et πόσιν in
v. antist.; id quod nondum mihi
veri simile videtur.
  1103. Sic F. φίλοισι cet. ἀλκὰν Fl.
  1106. βοᾷ πόλις Fl.

τάχος γὰρ τόδ' ἔσται· προτείνει δὲ χεὶρ   1110
ἐκ χερὸς ὀρέγματα.

ΧΟΡΟΣ.

Οὔπω ξυνῆκα· νῦν γὰρ ἐξ αἰνιγμάτων
ἐπαργέμοισι θεσφάτοις ἀμηχανῶ.

ΚΑΣΑΝΔΡΑ.

στρ ί.   Ἒ ἔ, παπαῖ παπαῖ, τί τόδε φαίνεται;
ἢ δίκτυόν τί γ' Ἅιδου;   1115
ἀλλ' ἄρκυς ἡ ξύνευνος, ἡ συναιτία
φόνου. Στάσις δ' ἀκόρετος γένει
κατολολυξάτω θύματος λευσίμου.

ΧΟΡΟΣ.

μεσοστρ.ά. Ποίαν Ἐρινὺν τήνδε δώμασιν κέλει
ἐπορθιάζειν; οὔ με φαιδρύνει λόγος.   1120
Ἐπὶ δὲ καρδίαν κροκοβαφὴς δράμε
σταγών, ἅτε καιρίᾳ πτωσίμοις
ξυνανύτει βίου δύντος αὐγαῖς· ταχεῖ-
α δ' ἄτα πέλει.

ΚΑΣΑΝΔΡΑ.

ἀντ.ί.   Ἆ ἆ· ἰδοὺ ἰδού· ἄπεχε τῆς βοὸς   1125
τὸν ταῦρον· ἐν πέπλοισιν
μελαγκέρῳ λαβοῦσα μηχανήματι

1110. χεῖρ' ἐκ χειρὸς ὀρεγομένα M.   1114. ἐέ M.
χεὶρ ἐκ χερὸς ὀρεγμένα Fl. ὀρέγμασι   1115. ἡ M. ἢ Ald.
Schol. Corr. Herm. Cf. Theocr.   1117. ἀκόρεστος libri. Corr. Bothe.
22. 102 ἐτώσια χερσὶ προδεικνύς.   1119. ἐρινῦν M.
1113. Sic M. V. G. ἐπ' ἀ. Fl. F.

1110 for soon that will be. Now she puts forth her hand
      and makes trial-thrusts.

CHORUS.

I don't yet understand: your riddles' end
is that I am posed by cloudy oracles.

CASANDRA.

Oh, oh! good God! good God! what now comes in view
1115 a casting-net of Hades?
      but she the wife, a stake-net, shares the guilt
      of blood. And let a band, ne'er appeased
      by her race, sing for joy while the stoned victim dies!

CHORUS.

What Fury 's this you summon in the house
1120 to raise her cry? your words dont gladden me.
      To my heart has rushed, and left sallow hues,
      the flow which for men struck down mortally
      runs its course along with their life's-sunset-beams;
        then death comes apace.

CASANDRA.

1125 Take care! O take care! the bull, keep 'him from
      the cow! for, having caught him
      in robes, with dark-horned implement she gores

1121. ἴδραμε κροκοβαφὴς libri. ego, monente Engero. δορὶ est glos-
Corr. Enger.   sema.
    1122. καὶ δορία πτώσιμος ξυνανυτεῖ   1127. μελάγκρωι M. ν super ι
M. eadem Fl. nisi quod δωρία. και-   scripta. μελαγκέρων Fl. Sensus: μέλαν
ρία ego; ξυνανυτεῖ Pors., πτωσίμοις   ξίφει ὡςπερεὶ κέρατι.

τύπτει· πίτνει δ' ἐν ἐνύδρῳ κύτει.
Δολοφόνου λέβητος τύχαν σοι λέγω.

ΧΟΡΟΣ.

μεσαντ.ά. Οὐ κομπάσαιμ' ἂν θεσφάτων γνώμων ἄκρος   1130
εἶναι· κακῷ δέ τῳ προςεικάζω τάδε.
Ἀπὸ δὲ θεσφάτων τίς ἀγαθὰ φάτις
βροτοῖς τέλλεται; κακῶν γὰρ διαὶ
πολυεπεῖς τέχναι θεσπιῳδοὶ φόβον
Φέρουσιν μαθεῖν.   1135

ΚΑΣΑΝΔΡΑ.

στρ.ς'. Ἰὼ ἰὼ ταλαίνας κακόποτμοι τύχαι·
τὸ γὰρ ἐμὸν θροῶ πάθος ἐπαγχίσαν.
Ποῖ δή με δεῦρο τὴν τάλαιναν ἤγαγες;
οὐδέν ποτ' εἰ μὴ ξυνθανουμένην· τί γάρ;

ΧΟΡΟΣ.

μεσοςτρ.β'. Φρενομανής τις εἶ θεοφόρητος, ἀμ-   1140
φὶ δ' αὑτᾶς θροεῖς
νόμον ἄνομον, οἷά τις ξουθὰ
ἀκόρετος βοᾶς, φεῦ, ταλαίναις φρεσὶν
Ἴτυν Ἴτυν στένουσ' ἀμφιθαλῆ κακοῖς
ἀηδὼν βίον.   1145

ΚΑΣΑΝΔΡΑ.

ἀντ.ς'. Ἰὼ ἰὼ λιγείας μόρον ἀηδόνος·

1128. ἐν addidit Schutz. τεύχει libri. κύτει Bl., Herm.
1132. τις M.
1133. βροτοῖσι Fl. στέλλεται libri. Corr. Herm., et Emper. διὰ M. δὴ αἱ Fl. Corr. Herm.

1134. πολυετεῖς Fl. θεσπιωιδὸν M. θεσπιωδὸν Fl. θεσπιῳδῶν Casaub. Melius Herm., quod dedi. θεσπιῳδὸν φόβον hic dici non potuit.
1135. φέρουσιν Fl. absque ν cet.

and he within the filled vessel sinks.

I thus tell you the wily pan's fatal hap.

CHORUS.

1130 I would not boast in words inspired to be

nice judge; but this I liken to some harm.

And from words inspired what good tidings spring

to men: for because of men's *present* woes

the seer's god-inspired wordy lore brings a fear

1135   to learn what it means.

CASANDRA.

Alas, alas! the lost one's inauspicious doom!

for I now relate my own following fate.

Oh whither hast thou led me the forlorn?

for nothing but to die with him: what else?

CHORUS.

1140 A mind-maddened one, by god moved art thou,

     and about thyself

chantest tunes tuneless, as some brown

nightingale, alas! mourning with thoughts of grief

Itys, Itys, his story that bloomed with woes

1145   from both parents sprung.

CASANDRA.

Io, io, the portion of shrill nightingale!

1137. ἐπεγχέασα M. ἐπαγχέασα Fl.
Recepi Karsteni em., Heimsoethio
probatam.
1141. αὐτᾶς M. Mox οἶα M.
1143. ἀκόρεστος βοᾶις M. βοᾶς Fl.

ἀκόρετος Ald. ῥεῦ ταλαινᾶς M. ῥιλοίκτοις ταλαί ῥρεσὶν Fl. Glossema
ῥιλοίκτοις ab Herm. receptum est.
1146. ἀηδόνος μόρον libri. Corr.
Herm.

περέβαλον γάρ οἱ πτεροφόρον δέμας
θεοὶ γλυκύν τ' αἰῶνα κλαυμάτων ἄτερ·
ἐμοὶ δὲ μίμνει σχισμὸς ἀμφήκει δορί.

ΧΟΡΟΣ.

μεσαντ.β'. Πόθεν ἐπισσύτους θεοφόρους ἔχεις   1150
   ματαίους δύας,
   τὰ δ' ἐπίφοβα δυσφάτῳ κλαγγᾷ
   μελοτυπεῖς ὁμοῦ τ' ὀρθίοις ἐν νόμοις;
   πόθεν ὅρους ἔχεις θεσπεσίας ὁδοῦ
   κακορρήμονας;   1155

ΚΑΣΑΝΔΡΑ.

στρ.ζ'. Ἰὼ γάμοι γάμοι Πάριδος ὀλέθριοι
   φίλων· ἰὼ Σκαμάνδρου πάτριον ποτόν.
   Τότε μὲν ἀμφὶ σὰς ἀϊόνας τάλαιν'
      ἠνυτόμαν τροφαῖς·
   νῦν δ' ἀμφὶ Κωκυτόν τε κἀχερουσίους   1160
   ὄχθους ἔοικα θεσπιῳδήσειν τάχα.

ΧΟΡΟΣ.

μεσοστρ.γ'. Τί τόδε τορὸν ἄγαν ἔπος ἐφημίσω,
   νεογνὸς ἂν θρόον μάθοι·
   πέπληγμαι δ' ὅπως δάκει φοινίῳ

1147. περεβάλοντο γάρ οἱ M. (Dind. nescit utrum παρ- an περ-) περιβαλόντες γάρ οἱ Fl. Illud -το ex γε pro γάρ quondam scripto ortum est, unde et -τες in Fl. Insolita forma περεβ- confirmatur simili illa Eum. 634 περεσκήνωσεν.

1148. ἀγῶνα libri, sed γρ. αἰῶνα

a librario supra scriptum in M.

1150. τ' ante ἔχεις recte delevit Herm.

1152. ἐπιρόβωι M. ἐπίρόβᾳ Fl. Corr. Aur.

1153. ὁμοῦ τ' jure suspectum est. ἄμουσ' Schoemann. Fortasse νόμοις τ' ὀρθίοις ἐκνόμοις.

for the gods put on her a wing-bearing form,
and let her spend a sweet life free from tears:
for me a gash waits with a two-edged blade.

CHORUS.

1150 *Say* from whence thou hast these fierce god-impelled,
these thine idle griefs;
how thou dost mould to melody
with that ominous scream horrors in high-pitched key,
and find landmarks for this thine inspired path
1155 of ill-omened words.

CASANDRA.

The match! my brother's match! which brought ruin home:
alas, Scamander's stream, drink of my native land!
by thy margin, then, I the ill-fated one
throve on thy nourishings;
1160 but now it seems I soon shall sing my strains
upon Cocytus' banks and Acheron's.

CHORUS.

What this too distinct speech thou hast uttered means,
a child might understand the cry:
and I'm pierced as with deadly sting by thy

1154. ἔχη Fl.
1158. τάλαινα Fl.
1163. ἀνθρώπων libri. ἂν θρόον ego. νεαρὸς ἂν ἀρρενῶν quod Meineke dedit, Enger. recepit, mihi quidem sonat infantem delirum. Iambicus

ordo dochmiis se interposuit, ut saepe.
1164. ὑπὸ δήγματι libri. Corr. Herm. Illud est glossa; nam δάκος σημαίνει καὶ δῆγμα E. M. s. v. Enger. mavult πλήγματι, cujus vocis Æsch., ut mihi videtur, ignarus fuit.

δυσαλγεῖ τύχᾳ μινυρὰ κακὰ θρευμένας,   1165
θαύματ' ἐμοὶ κλύειν.

ΚΑΣΑΝΔΡΑ.

ἀπ.ζ'.   Ἰὼ πόνοι πόνοι πόλεος ὀλομένας
τὸ πᾶν· Ἰὼ πρόπυργοι θυσίαι πατρὸς
πολυκανεῖς βοτῶν ποιονόμων· ἄκος δ'
     οὐδὲν ἐπήρκεσαν,   1170
τὸ μὴ πόλιν μὲν ὥσπερ οὖν ἔχει παθεῖν·
κἀγὼ δὲ θερμόνους τάχ' ἐμπελῶ πέδῳ.

ΧΟΡΟΣ.

μεσαντ.γ'.   Ἑπόμενα προτέροισι τάδ' ἐφημίσω.
Σέ τις κακοφρονῶν τίθη-
     σι δαίμων ὑπερβαρὴς ἐμπίτνων   1175
μελίζειν πάθη γοερὰ θανατηφόρα·
τέρμα δ' ἀμηχανῶ.

ΚΑΣΑΝΔΡΑ.

Καὶ μὴν ὁ χρησμὸς οὐκέτ' ἐκ καλυμμάτων
ἔσται δεδορκὼς νεογάμου νύμφης δίκην·
λαμπρὸς δ' ἔοικεν ἡλίου πρὸς ἀντολὰς   1180
πνέων ἐσᾷξειν, ὥστε κύματος δίκην

1165. δυταγγεῖ libri. Corr. Canter.
Deinde θρεομένας libri. Corr. Enger.
1166. θραύματ' FL. θαύματ' F.
recentt. Illud tuetur Enger., 'id
quod frangit'; sed nemini id pro-
babit. Ne forte dubites, θαύματ'
ἀκοῦσαι est ap. Hes. Th. 834.
1167. πόλεος ὀλωμένας Fl. πόλεως
ὀλουμένας V. Corr. Pors.

1171. ἔχειν FL ut videtur, corr.
in F.
1172. ἐγὼ libri. κἀγὼ quod sensus
postulat, metrum mavult, Heims.
ἐμπέδῳ βαλῶ libri. ἐμπελῶ Ahrens.,
πέδῳ ego. Jam vides cur ἐμπέδῳ
scriptum sit. βαλῶ est stolida interpretatio aut complementum. Quæ
autem corrigunt θερμὸν οὖς Canter.,

1165 sad, sad lot, while thou plaintively mournest woes,
   a strange tale to hear.

CASANDRA.

Alas, the woes, the woes of my country lost,
all-lost! alas, my sire's offerings before the walls,
when grass-pastured kine many were slain! and yet
1170   they served naught for cure,
   to save my country's ailing as she ailed;
   I too, brain-fevered, soon shall sink to earth.

CHORUS.

There thou spakest words following hard upon
the former *track*. Some ill-disposed
1175 daemon with ponderous weight falls on and makes thee chant
sufferings like a dirge, fraught with death; how 't will end
I am all in doubt.

CASANDRA.

But soon the augury will look out no more
like bride new-married from behind veil-folds:
1180 but to the sunrise blowing, clear of clouds,
   will hurtle forth, it seems, and wave-like wash

Herm., θερμὸν ῥοῦν Musgr., illud absurdum est, immane quantum; hoc vero comico poetæ convenit. Verto: 'Civitas mea, cui nulla medicina utilis fuit, morbo periit; et ego quoque, nunc morbo delirans, mox (quum furor quievit) humi procumbam'. πελῶ χθονὶ Prom. V. 284. Apparet, opinor, nihil aliud nisi θερμόνους verum esse posse.

1173. προτέροις libri. Corr. Pauw.
1174. καὶ τίς σε libri. καὶ τίς σε Butler., vulgo. σὲ τίς ego. κακοφρονεῖν libri. Corr. Schutz.
1176. θανατοφόρα Fl., corr. in F.
1179. νύμφας Fl., corr. in F.
1180. ἐξ ἥξειν Fl. ἐσήξειν V. Herm. vulgo. ἐσάξειν Bothe.

8*

κλύζειν πρὸς αὐγὰς τοῦδε πήματος πολὺ
μεῖζον. Φρενώσω δ' οὐκέτ' ἐξ αἰνιγμάτων.
Καὶ μαρτυρεῖτε συνδρόμως ἴχνος κακῶν
ῥινηλατούσῃ τῶν πάλαι πεπραγμένων.   1185
Τὴν γὰρ στέγην τήνδ' οὔποτ' ἐκλείπει χορὸς
σύμφθογγος οὐκ εὔφωνος, οὐ γὰρ εὖ λέγει.
Καὶ μὴν πεπωκώς γ', ὡς θρασύνεσθαι πλέον,
βρότειον αἷμα κῶμος ἐν δόμοις μένει
δύσπεμπτος ἔξω συγγόνων Ἐρινύων.   1190
Ὑμνοῦσι δ' ὕμνον δώμασιν προσήμεναι
πρώταρχον ἄτην· ἐν μέρει δ' ἀπέπτυσαν
εὐνὰς ἀδελφοῦ τῷ πατοῦντι δυσμενεῖς.
Ἥμαρτον; ἢ κυρῶ τι τοξότης τις ὥς;
ἢ ψευδόμαντίς εἰμι θυροκόπος φλέδων;   1195
ἐκμαρτύρησον προὐμόσας τό μ' εἰδέναι
λόγῳ παλαιὰς τῶνδ' ἁμαρτίας δόμων.

ΧΟΡΟΣ.

Καὶ πῶς ἂν ὅρκος, πῆμα γενναίως παγέν,
παιώνιον γένοιτο; θαυμάζω δέ σε
πόντου πέραν τραφεῖσαν ἀλλοθρῷ 'ν πόλει   1200
κυρεῖν λέγουσαν, ὥσπερ εἰ παρεστάτεις.

1182. κλύειν libri. Corr. Aur. Cf. Solon Frag. 5. 17. χρησμὸς est τίσεως patefactio s. τίσις ipsa; τόδε πῆμα est 'meum (Casandræ) malum', cujus se participem esse Chorus affirmavit; præterea ipsa cæsura demonstrat τοῦδε πήματος non cum αὐγὰς conjungendum esse, sed a voce μεῖζον i. e. μεῖζον πῆμα pendere. Sic et Herm. 1187. σύμφργγος Fl., corr. in F.

1192. πρώταρχος Fl., corr. in F. V. 1194. τηρῶ libri. θηρῶ Aur. κυρῶ Ahr. Et θηρῶ certe de sagittæ ictu dici nequit. Scilicet κ et η literæ eandem formam habent in M. 1196. Sic libri omnes: 'de me hucusque absente nunc testamini, quod ex verbis (λόγῳ) meis jam scitis, me scelerum gnaram esse'. Partem enim solum suæ significationis

up to the daybeams woe far worse than this
of mine. But I by riddles will instruct no more.
And bear me witness as I coursingly
1185 hunt down the track of crimes wrought long ago.
This roof a choir ne'er quits, well-matched in tune
but not well-toned, for it speaks no good words.
And having drunk men's blood, to dare the more,
this wassail-rout of kindred Furies still
1190 stays in the house, hard to be sent away.
Set firmly in its halls they chant a hymn,
the primal death-crime; and in turn they loathe
a brother's bed, its trampler's *ruthless* foe.
I missed? or do I, marksman-like, hit aught?
1195 am I a quack-seer? a door-pestering cheat?
first swear, then witness from my words that I
though absent know this household's ancient sins.

CHORUS.

How could an oath, a pain in good faith pledged,
be curative? yet I'm amazed that bred
1200 beyond sea in a strange-tongue-speaking land
you tell the truth, as if you stood close by.

---

vox ἰκμ. tenet; quod Chorus testa-
bitur de absente coram ea de qua
testatur.

1198. Sic libri. ὅρκου πῆγμα Aur.
ὅρκος, πῆγμα Pors. ab Herm., aliis
receptum. Sed Ὅρκος quater ap.
Hes. πῆμα dicitur, et πῆμα multo
meliorem sensum præbet. Spernen-
dum igitur est Hermanni, Porsoni,
ceterorum πῆγμα. Verte 'perjurii

poenæ, quas aliquis ex animi sententia jurejurando sibi confirmat'.
παιώνιον autem valet ἄκος.

1199. παιώνιος F. δὲ σου libri.
δὲ σε Aur., cet., præter Herm.

1200. ἀλλόθρουν πόλιν libri. ἀλλό-
θρῳ 'ν πόλει Enger. Res manifesta;
nam ἀλλόθρους nihil aliud est quam
βάρβαρος E. M., s. v.

ΚΑΣΑΝΔΡΑ.

Μάντις μ᾽ Ἀπόλλων τῷδ᾽ ἐπέστησεν τέλει.

ΧΟΡΟΣ.

Μῶν καὶ θεός περ ἱμέρῳ πεπληγμένος;

ΚΑΣΑΝΔΡΑ.

Προτοῦ μὲν αἰδὼς ἦν ἐμοὶ λέγειν τάδε.

ΧΟΡΟΣ.

Ἁβρύνεται γὰρ πᾶς τις εὖ πράσσων πλέον.   1205

ΚΑΣΑΝΔΡΑ.

Ἀλλ᾽ ἦν παλαιστὴς κάρτ᾽ ἐμοὶ πνέων χάριν.

ΧΟΡΟΣ.

Ἦ καὶ τέκνων εἰς ἔργον ἠλθέτην νόμῳ;

ΚΑΣΑΝΔΡΑ.

Ξυναινέσασα Λοξίαν ἐψευσάμην.

ΧΟΡΟΣ.

Ἤδη τέχναισιν ἐνθέοις ᾑρημένη;

ΚΑΣΑΝΔΡΑ.

Ἤδη πολίταις πάντ᾽ ἐθέσπιζον πάθη.   1210

1202—5. In libris leguntur ad hunc modum: Cas. 1202, 1204; Cho.
1203, 1205. Reposuit Herm.

CASANDRA.

This office seer Apollo laid on me.

CHORUS.

Not pierced with love of you, and he a god?

CASANDRA.

Ere now I was ashamed to speak of it.

CHORUS.

1205 True: every one when prosperous is more nice.

CASANDRA.

He sought the prize, much fired with love for me.

CHORUS.

Came ye to child-begetting by *love's* law?

CASANDRA.

After consenting I played Loxias false.

CHORUS.

When now possessed by god-implanted lore?

CASANDRA.

1210 I had foretold my people all their woes.

1205. βαρύνεται F.
1207. ἤλθετον libri. Corr. Elmsl. νόμῳ est 'amantium more'.

ΧΟΡΟΣ.

Πῶς δῆτ' ἄνακτος ἦσθα Λοξίου κότον;

ΚΑΣΑΝΔΡΑ.

Ἔπειθον οὐδέν' οὐδέν, ὡς τάδ' ἤμπλακον.

ΧΟΡΟΣ.

Ἡμῖν γε μὲν δὴ πιστὰ θεσπίζειν δοκεῖς.

ΚΑΣΑΝΔΡΑ.

Ἰοὺ ἰού.

Ὑπ' αὖ με δεινὸς ὀρθομαντείας πόνος   1215
στροβεῖ, ταράσσων φροιμίοις· ὢ ὢ κακά.
Ὁρᾶτε τούςδε τοὺς δόμοις ἐφημένους
νέους, ὀνείρων προσφερεῖς μορφώμασιν;
παῖδες θανόντες ὡσπερεὶ πρὸς τῶν φίλων,
χεῖρας κρεῶν πλήθοντες οἰκείας βορᾶς·   1220
σὺν ἐντέροις τὰ σπλάγχν', ἐποίκτιστον γέμος,
πρέπουσ' ἔχοντες, ὧν πατὴρ ἐγεύσατο.
Ἐκ τῶνδε ποινάς φημι βουλεύειν τινὰ
λέοντ' ἄναλκιν ἐν λέχει στρωφώμενον
οἰκουρόν, οἴμοι, τῷ μολόντι δεσπότῃ,   1225
ἐμῷ· φέρειν γὰρ χρὴ τὸ δούλιον ζυγόν.

1211. ἄνακτος ἦσθα Λοξίου κότῳ; libri. ἄνατος Canter., recentt. ἄνακτος ἦσθα Λοξίου κότον; Wieseler., probante Ahr. Canteri em. erit 'qui factum est, quæso, ut exitii expers evaseris per Loxiæ iram? Absurde dictum; et recte hæsit Blom. Sequi debebat non κότῳ sed οἴκτῳ vel simile quid; et sic tamen inepte respondetur. Weiseleri autem est: quonam modo Loxiæ iram cognovisti h. e. expertus es? πῶς δῆτ' non idem est quod καὶ πῶς, ut laudari possit Choeph. 532. καὶ πῶς ἄτρωτον οὖθαρ ἦν; 'illæ mammæ, opinor, non illæsæ erant'. ἦστε pro ἦδειτε citatur ex Soph. Colchis E. M. p. 439. 1. Schol. F. interpretatur πῶς ὀργῆς

CHORUS.

And how, pray, did you feel king Loxias' wrath?

CASANDRA.

I made none credit aught, since thus I sinned.

CHORUS.

To us you seem to prophecy the truth.

CASANDRA.

Ugh! ugh!
1215 again true divination's dread pain racks
and frets me with its boding words. Oh woe!
see ye these young ones, seated in the rooms,
like_forms that come in dreams? babes slain as if
by a kinsman, with hands full of flesh, meat made
1220 from their own carcases; they hold to view
the inwards with the bowels, most piteous meal
of which their father ate. For this, I say,
a craven lion couching in his bed,
a stay-at-home, is compassing revenge
1225 on him who has returned, the master, mine,
ah me! for one must bear the slavish yoke.

ἐπειράθης τοῦ 'Απόλλωνος;

1212. οὐδὲν οὐδὲν libri. Corr. Canter.

1214. ἰοὺ ἰοὺ, ὢ ὢ κακὰ libri, et φροιμίοις ἐφημένους v. 1216. Mirum est Engerum Weilii emendationem sprevisse, quæ ἰοὺ ἰοὺ. et mox φροιμίοις· ὢ ὢ κακά. reposuit.

1219. Casandra, ut quæ hariola

sit, id quoque dum pueros intuetur comperit.

1221. Dedi τὰ (libri τε); nam τε infirmius est quam ut hanc sedem occupet.

1226. ζυγὸν Fl. antea fuerat ζυγῷ.

1227. ἄπαρχος libri. ἔπαρχος Canter. Illud tuetur Ahr. ἀναστατήρ conj. Spanhem.

Νεῶν τ' ἔπαρχος Ἰλίου τ' ἀναστάτης
οὐκ οἶδεν οἷα γλῶσσα μισητῆς κυνὸς
λέξασα κἀκτείνασα φαιδρόνους, δίκην
ἄτης λαθραίου, τεύξεται κακῇ τύχῃ.   1230
Τοιάδε τόλμα· θῆλυς ἄρτενος φονεὺς
ἐστίν· τί νιν καλοῦσα δυσφιλὲς δάκος
τύχοιμ' ἄν; ἀμφίσβαιναν, ἢ Σκύλλαν τινὰ
οἰκοῦσαν ἐν πέτραισι, ναυτίλων βλάβην,
θύουσαν ἅδου λῆτορ', ἄσπονδόν τ' Ἄρη   1235
φίλοις πνέουσαν; Ὡς δ' ἐπωλολύξατο
ἡ παντότολμος, ὥσπερ ἐν μάχης τροπῇ,
ἔδοκει δὲ χαίρειν νοστίμῳ σωτηρίᾳ.
Καὶ τῶνδ' ὅμοιον εἴ τι μὴ πείθω· τί γάρ;
τὸ μέλλον ἥξει. Καὶ σύ μ' ἐν τάχει παρὼν   1240
ἄγαν ἀληθόμαντιν οἰκτείρας ἐρεῖς.

ΧΟΡΟΣ.

Τὴν μὲν Θυέστου δαῖτα παιδείων κρεῶν
ξυνῆκα καὶ πέφρικα, καὶ φόβος μ' ἔχει
κλύοντ' ἀληθῶς οὐδὲν ἐξῃκασμένα·
τὰ δ' ἄλλ' ἀκούσας ἐκ δρόμου πεσὼν τρέχω.   1245

ΚΑΣΑΝΔΡΑ.

Ἀγαμέμνονός σέ φημ' ἐπόψεσθαι μόρον.

ΧΟΡΟΣ.

Εὔφημον, ὦ τάλαινα, κοίμησον στόμα.

1229. καὶκτείνασα Fl. καὶ κτείνασα
F. V. Corr. Canter.
1230. Locus suspectus.
1231. τοιάδε τολμᾷ θῆλυς Fl. Ven.
τοιαῦτα τολμᾷ θῆλυς F. V. Corr.
Ahrens., et Enger.

1232. δυσφιλεὺς Fl.
1235. θύουσαν. ἅδου μητέρ' Fl.
Ahrentis λῆτορ' ceteris conjecturis
praestat, quam ex Hesychii glossa
λείτορες· ἱέρειαι, et schol. Lycophr.

And the ships' admiral, Ilion's ravager,

knows naught of what the brutal lewd one's tongue

spoke and enlarged on in mock-radiant mood,

1230 like lurking death, and by sad fate will win.

The plot is this: the female is the male's

assassin. What foul monster shall I best

surname her? amphisbaena? or the pest

of sailors, Scylla, housed in rocks? a mad

1235 priestess of Hades, breathing ruthless war

against her kin? and how she screamed for joy,

the all-daring, as in battle's rout, and seemed

joyed at his home-arriving safe-return!

'Tis all one should you credit naught: what else?

1240 what will, will come. You too shall soon stand by

and pitying say I was a seer too true.

CHORUS.

Thyestes' feast on children's flesh I knew

and shudder at; and fear takes hold of me

as I hear truly things not fancy-framed.

1265 Hearing the rest I lose scent and run wide.

CASANDRA.

I say you 'll look on Agamemnon's corse.

CHORUS.

Lull, hapless one, thy tongue to fairer words.

991 λήταρχος· ὁ δημόσιος ἱερεύς revo-
·cavit. Cf. ἱερεύς τις ἄτας supra.
Deinde ἀρὰν libri. Corr. Herm.
    1238. δοκεῖ libri. ἐδόκει ego.
    1240. καὶ σὺ μὴν libri. Corr. Aur.

1241. ἄγαν γ' libri. γ' deletum
est a Bl. et Bothio.
    1242. παιδίων libri. Corr. Schutz.
    1244. ἐξεικασμένα F. Cf. ἐξεικασ-
μένος· πεπλασμένος Suid. s. v.

ΚΑΣΑΝΔΡΑ.

Ἀλλ' οὔτι Παιὼν τῷδ' ἐπιστατεῖ λόγῳ.

ΧΟΡΟΣ.

Οὔκ, εἴπερ ἔσται γ'· ἀλλὰ μὴ γένοιτό πως.

ΚΑΣΑΝΔΡΑ.

Σὺ μὲν κατεύχει, τοῖς δ' ἀποκτείνειν μέλει.   1250

ΧΟΡΟΣ.

Τίνος πρὸς ἀνδρὸς τοῦτ' ἄγος πορσύνεται;

ΚΑΣΑΝΔΡΑ.

Ἦ κάρτα τἄρα παρεκόπης χρησμῶν ἐμῶν.

ΧΟΡΟΣ.

Τοὺς γὰρ τελοῦντας οὐ ξυνῆκα μηχανήν.

ΚΑΣΑΝΔΡΑ.

Καὶ μὴν ἄγαν γ' Ἕλλην' ἐπίσταμαι φάτιν.

ΧΟΡΟΣ.

Καὶ γὰρ τὰ πυθόκραντα· δυσμαθῆ δ' ὅμως.   1255

ΚΑΣΑΝΔΡΑ.

Παπαῖ παπαῖ.

1249. οὐκ εἰ παρέσται γ' libri.   εἰ scripto super ης. Fl. παρεσκόπεις V.
Corr. Schutz.   αὖ pro ἀν Herm., vulgo; ἀρὰν Aur.,
1251. ἄχος iibri. Corr. Aur.   Canter. Hartung. emendavit quem
1252. ἦ κάρτ' ἄρ' ἀν παρεσκόπης,   ad modum edidi. Corruptelæ origo

CASANDRA.

In naught does Paean superintend this tale.

CHORUS.

No; if it is to be: Heaven send it mayn't.

CASANDRA.

1250 You pray; their care is to assassinate.

CHORUS.

By what man is the impious deed performed?

CASANDRA.

You were much cheated of my augury's drift.

CHORUS.

Yes: for I don't see who fulfil the plot.

CASANDRA.

And yet I know full well the Hellenic tongue.

CHORUS.

1255 So do you Pythian verdicts; yet they're dark.

CASANDRA.

Oh misery!

non obscura est. παρεκόπης autem est 'fraudatus es'.

1253. τοῦ γὰρ τελοῦντο; libri. Corr. Heims.

1255. δυσπαθῆ libri. Corr. Canter.
1256. παπαῖ, οἷον τὸ πῦρ κτλ. libri. Recepi Weilii em. πῦρ est 'febris', cf. v. 1172.

Οἶον τόδ' ἕρπει πῦρ· ἐπέρχεται δέ μοι·
ὀτοτοῖ, Λύκει' Ἄπολλον, οἳ ἐγώ, ἐγώ·
αὕτη δίπους λέαινα συγκοιμωμένη
λύκῳ, λέοντος εὐγενοῦς ἀπουσίᾳ,
κτενεῖ με τὴν τάλαιναν· ὡς δὲ φάρμακον 　　　　1260
τεύχουσα κἀμοῦ μισθὸν ἐνθήσει ποτῷ.
Κἀπεύχεται θήγουσα φωτὶ φάσγανον
ἐμῆς ἀγωγῆς ἀντιτίσεσθαι φόνον.
Τί δῆτ' ἐμαυτῆς καταγέλωτ' ἔχω τάδε
καὶ σκῆπτρα καὶ μαντεῖα περὶ δέρῃ στέφη; 　　　　1265
σφὲ μὲν πρὸ μοίρας τῆς ἐμῆς διαφθερῶ·
ἴτ' ἐς φθόρον πεσόντ'· ἐγὼ δ' ἅμ' ἕψομαι·
ἄλλην τιν' ἄτης ἀντ' ἐμοῦ πλουτίζετε.
Ἰδοὺ δ' Ἀπόλλων αὐτὸς ἐκδύων ἐμὲ
χρηστηρίαν ἐσθῆτ', ἐποπτεύσας ἐμὲ 　　　　1270
κἀν τοῖσδε κόσμοις καταγελωμένην μέγα
φίλων ὑπ' ἐχθρῶν, οὐ διχορρόπως μάτην.
Καλουμένη δέ, φοιτὰς ὥς, ἀγύρτρια
πτωχός, τάλαινα λιμοθνὴς ἠνεσχόμην.
Καὶ νῦν ὁ μάντις μάντιν ἐκπράξας ἐμὲ 　　　　1275
ἀπήγαγ' ἐς τοιάςδε θανασίμους τύχας·
βωμοῦ πατρῴου δ' ἀντ' ἐπίξηνον μένει
θερμὸν κοπείσης φοινίῳ προσφάγματι.
Οὐ μὴν ἄτιμοί γ' ἐκ θεῶν τεθνήξομεν·

1258. δίπλους Fl. F., corr. in V.
1261. κότῳ libri. Corr. Aur. μισθὸς
est et hariolæ et scorti merces, illa
enim πέλανος dicebatur, teste Suida;
hæc μισθωμα. Hic utroque sensu ad-
hibetur. Mox addit 'naulum' ἀγωγῆς
μισθόν. ποτὸς autem est medicina quæ
Agamemnonis male factis medeatur.

1262. ἐπεύχεται libri. Corr. Dind.
1263. ἀντιτίσασθαι libri. Recepi
Blomfieldii conj.
1266. σὲ μὲν libri. Corr. Aur.
1267. ἀγαθὼ δ' ἀμείψομαι libri.
Præclare corr. Herm.
1268. τίν' Fl. ἄτην libri. Corr.
Stanl.

how fierce this fever grows! for me it comes!

alas, Lycean Apollo! alas, for me!

that biped lioness bedding with a wolf

in absence of the noble lion, *next*,

1260 will kill me hapless; and, as if she mixed

a medicine, to the draught will add my fee:

and, whetting for her lord the blade, will boast

that she 'll recoup herself my fare in blood.

Why do I keep these mockeries of myself,

1265 the wand, and prophet's garland round my neck?

I will destroy them ere my own decease.

Go! fall to ruin: I shall follow you:

enrich with woe some other in my stead.

Lo! here Apollo's self is stripping me

1270 of my diviner's garb; he who looked on

when in these trappings I was harshly mocked —

unjustly, the scale proves, — by friends unkind.

And I, as crazy, had to bear being called,

forlorn and famished, an alms-begging tramp.

1275 And now the seer, unmaking me a seer,

has brought me to this deadly pass: instead

of our domestic altar waits a block

warm with the crimson spurt when I am cleft.

Yet not by god unhonoured shall we die:

1270. δέ με Fl. ἐπωπτεύσας F.
1271. μέτα libri. μέγα Herm.
1272. Junge οὐ διχ. μάτην 'haud dubie falso irrisam'.
1274. λιμόθνης vulgo. Corr. Elberling.
1275. ἐκπράξας μάντιν est 'qui

exauguravit me vatem', et voci ἐκδύων alludit v. 1269.
1277. ἀντεπίξηνον Fl., priore acc. om. in cet. Corr. Aur. et Canter.
1278. θερμῷ libri. Corr. Schutz. πρόσφαγμα est profluvium sanguinis mactatæ victimæ.

ἥξει γὰρ ἡμῶν ἄλλος αὖ τιμάορος,   1280
μητροκτόνον φίτυμα, ποινάτωρ πατρός·
φυγὰς δ' ἀλήτης τῆςδε γῆς ἀπόξενος
κάτεισιν ἄτας τάςδε θριγκώσων φίλοις·
ὀμώμοται γὰρ ὅρκος ἐκ θεῶν μέγας
ἄξειν νιν, ὑπτίασμα κειμένου πατρός.   1285
Τί δῆτ' ἐγὼ κάτοικτος ὧδ' ἀναστένω,
ἐπεὶ τὸ πρῶτον εἶδον Ἰλίου πόλιν
πράξασαν ὡς ἔπραξεν· οἳ δ' εἷλον πόλιν
οὕτως ἀπαλλάσσουσιν ἐν θεῶν κρίσει;
ἰοῦσα πράξω, τλήσομαι τὸ κατθανεῖν·   1290
Ἅιδου πύλας δὲ τάςδ' ἐγὼ προςεννέπω,
ἐπεύχομαι δὲ καιρίας πληγῆς τυχεῖν,
ὡς ἀσφάδαστος, αἱμάτων εὐθνησίμων
ἀπορρυέντων, ὄμμα συμβαλῶ τόδε.

ΧΟΡΟΣ.

Ὦ πολλὰ μὲν τάλαινα, πολλὰ δ' αὖ σοφὴ   1295
γύναι, μακρὰν ἔτεινας. Εἰ δ' ἐτητύμως
μόρον τὸν αὑτῆς οἶσθα, πῶς θεηλάτου
βοὸς δίκην πρὸς βωμὸν εὐτόλμως πατεῖς;

ΚΑΣΑΝΔΡΑ.

Οὐκ ἔστ' ἄλυξις, οὔ, ξένοι· χρόνοι πλέῳ.

1284. Hunc versum qui post v. 1290 in libris legitur Herm. huc revocavit. Laudatur in Crameri Anec. I. p. 88 ἄραρε γὰρ ὅρκος. Inde Schneidew. ἄραρε μὲν γὰρ. Sed Engeri conj. tantum non certa est, v. 1290 olim ita se habere ἄραρ' ἰοῦσα cet., et inde errore grammatici vocem ἄραρε esse sumptam. ὑπτίασμα est 'id quod quis precatur manibus supinis'.

1285. ἄξειν νῦν Fl. ἄξει νιν F., corr. in V.

1286. κάτοικος libri, corrupte. Corr. Scaliger.

1288. εἶχον libri. Corr. Musgr.

1280 one will again, as our avenger, come,

a mother-slaying, sire's-blood-price-levying son;

an exile, wanderer, outcast from this land,

will come to raise the top-stone for his race

of death-crimes: by the gods a mighty oath

1285 is sworn to bring him, as his fallen sire

will pray with hands upturned. Why wail I then,

thus doleful? since I first beheld Troy's town

fare as she fared; and those who sacked the town

come off thus by the judgement of the gods?

1290 I'll go and take my lot, endure the death:

but I address these gates of death and pray

to get a mortal stroke, that so I may

without a struggle, when with easy death

the blood has flowed away, shut-to these eyes.

CHORUS.

1295 O woman much unblest, in much, too, wise,

thou hast stretched far thy words. But if in truth

thou know'st thy doom, how dost thou, heifer-like

god-driven, to the altar boldly tread?

CASANDRA.

There's no escape, friends, none: the times are full.

1289. ἐκ θεῶν Fl.

1290. Recipienda erat Engeri conjectura si ille ostendisset unde vox πράξω orta sit.

1291. τὰς λέγω libri. Corr. Aur. et Canter.

1295. δὲ σοφὴ Fl. Corr. in F. V.

1299. οὐ, ξένοι Fl. οὐ F. V. χρόνῳ

πλέω omnes. Et equidem non video quid displiceat in repetita negatione. Weil. conj. οὐ, ξένοι, χρόνοι πλέῳ. Sic illud ξένοι frigide interponitur. Sed χρόνοι πλέῳ recte dicitur, et partim ex Theogn. 817 sumitur, partim ex Hes. Op. 790 πλέῳ ἤματι. Interpunxi igitur post ξένοι.

9

ΧΟΡΟΣ.

Ὁ δ' ὕστατός γε τοῦ χρόνου πρεσβεύεται.   1300

ΚΑΣΑΝΔΡΑ.

Ἥκει τόδ' ἦμαρ· σμικρὰ κερδανῶ φυγῇ.

ΧΑΡΟΣ.

Ἀλλ' ἴσθι τλήμων οὖσ' ἀπ' εὐτόλμου Φρενός.

ΚΑΣΑΝΔΡΑ.

Οὐδεὶς ἀκούει ταῦτα τῶν εὐδαιμόνων.

ΧΟΡΟΣ.

Ἀλλ' εὐκλεῶς τοι κατθανεῖν χάρις βροτῷ.

ΚΑΣΑΝΔΡΑ.

Ἰὼ πάτερ σοῦ σῶν τε γενναίων τέκνων.   1305
Ἀλλ' εἶμι κἀν δόμοισι κωκύσουσ' ἐμὴν   1313
Ἀγαμέμνονός τε μοῖραν. Ἀρκείτω βίος.   1314

ΧΟΡΟΣ.

Τί δ' ἐστὶ χρῆμα; τίς σ' ἀποστρέφει Φόβος;

ΚΑΣΑΝΔΡΑ.

Φεῦ Φεῦ.

1300. In eo lusus est quod et Κρόνου et χρόνου ad aures venire possit: quorum illud erit, 'Ζεὺς minimus ille natu e Κρόνου natis principatum tenet'; hoc autem, 'vi morituro novissima quæque vitæ momenta, (i. e., quam longissima mora) maximi æstimantur'.

1303, 1304. Hos versus inverso ordine posuit Heath., quem omnes edd. secuti sunt, exceptis Coningtono et Paleio. Scilicet Chorus id agit

CHORUS.

1300 At least Time's latest birth takes foremost rank.

CASANDRA.

This day is come: I little gain by flight.

CHORUS.

Know thou art firm from an intrepid soul.

CASANDRA.

None of the happy has this said to him.

CHORUS.

But to die bravely has a charm for man.

CASANDRA.

1305 Alas, my sire, for thee and thy brave brood!
1313 But I'll go wail even in the house my fate
1314 and Agamemnon's. Let past life suffice.

CHORUS.

Why, what is this? what terror makes thee start?

CASANDRA.

Faugh! faugh!

ut soletur Casandram; illa tamen fovet querelas. Res manifesta est.
1305. τῶν τε libri. σῶν τε Aur.
1306, 1307. Hi duo versus vulgo post v. 1312 leguntur; sed quum illic inepti essent, hic autem Casandram aliquid loqui oporteret unde intelligeretur eam in aedes introituram esse, huc revocandos censuit Enger.

ΧΟΡΟΣ.

Τί τοῦτ᾽ ἔφευξας; εἴ τι μὴ φρενῶν στύγος.

ΚΑΣΑΝΔΡΑ.

Φόνον δόμοι πνέουσιν αἱματοσταγῆ.

ΧΟΡΟΣ.

Καὶ πῶς; τόδ᾽ ὄζει θυμάτων ἐφεστίων.　　　　　　　　1310

ΚΑΣΑΝΔΡΑ.

Ὅμοιος ἀτμὸς ὥςπερ ἐκ τάφου πρέπει.

ΧΟΡΟΣ.

Οὐ Σύριον ἀγλάϊσμα δωμάτων λέγεις.

ΚΑΣΑΝΔΡΑ.

Ἰὼ ξένοι.　　　　　　　　　　　　　　　　　　　1315
Οὗτοι δυςοίζω θάμνον ὡς ὄρνις φόβῳ
ἄλλως· θανούσῃ μαρτυρεῖτέ μοι τόδε,
ὅταν γυνὴ γυναικὸς ἀντ᾽ ἐμοῦ θάνῃ,
ἀνήρ τε δυσδάμαρτος ἀντ᾽ ἀνδρὸς πέσῃ·
ἐπιξενοῦμαι ταῦτα δ᾽ ὡς θανουμένη.　　　　　　　1320

ΧΟΡΟΣ.

Ὦ τλῆμον, οἰκτείρω σε θεσφάτου μόρου.

1309. φόβον libri. ν super β scripto in F. Corr. Aur. et Canter.
1310. Interrogandi sign. primus Pauw. posuit.

1317. ἀλλ᾽ ὡς θανούσῃ libri. Corr. Herm. Et sane sensus postulat ἄλλως. At, inquit, avis non frustra timet. Immo vero nostrates quidem aves

CHORUS.

Why 'faugh'? unless it be the mind's disgust.

CASANDRA.

These rooms breathe horrid fumes from dripping blood.

CHORUS.

1310 Why 'horrid'? the hearth's victims yield the smell.

CASANDRA.

As from a grave a *ghostly* mist appears.

CHORUS.

You name no Syrian luxury for the house.

CASANDRA.

1315 Ah friends! I scream
for fear not idly, as at a *shaking* bush
a bird: and when I'm dead attest me this:
when woman has for me a woman died,
and man for man ill-wived has fallen; this
1320 I, as one dying, charge you with, as friends.

CHORUS.

Brave heart, I pity thee for thy god-taught doom.

non magis intrepidæ sunt quam Ho-
ratii hinnuleus si mobilibus veris
inhorruit adventus foliis. Hic enim
neque visci neque serpentium, quorum neutrum est inane periculum,
ulla ratio habetur.
　1320. 'Hoc ego ut moritura com-
mendo vobis ut amicis',

ΚΑΣΑΝΔΡΑ.

Ἅπαξ ἔτ᾽ εἰπεῖν χρὴ πρὶν ἢ θρῆνον λέγω
ἐμὸν τὸν αὑτῆς· ἡλίῳ δ᾽ ἐπεύχομαι,
πρὸς ὕστατον φῶς, δεσποτῶν τιμαόρους
ἐχθροῖς φονεῦσι τοῖς ἐμοῖς τίνειν ὁμοῦ   1325
δούλης θανούσης, εὐμαροῦς χειρώματος.

• ΧΟΡΟΣ.

Ἰὼ βρότεια πράγματ᾽· εὐτυχοῦντα μὲν
σκιᾷ τις ἂν πρέψειεν· εἰ δὲ δυστυχεῖ
βολαῖς ὑγρώσσων σπόγγος ὤλεσεν γραφήν·
καὶ ταῦτ᾽ ἐκείνων μᾶλλον οἰκτείρω πολύ.   1330

Τὸ μὲν εὖ πράσσειν ἀκόρεστον ἔφυ
πᾶσι βροτοῖσιν· δακτυλοδείκτων δ᾽
οὔτις ἀπειπὼν εἴργει μελάθρων,
μηκέτ᾽ ἐσέλθῃς, τάδε φωνῶν.
Καὶ τῷδε πόλιν μὲν ἑλεῖν ἔδοσαν   1335
μάκαρες Πριάμου·
θεοτίμητος δ᾽ οἴκαδ᾽ ἱκάνει·
νῦν δ᾽ εἰ προτέρων αἷμ᾽ ἀποτίσει

1322. εἰπεῖν ῥῆσιν ἢ θρῆνον θέλω libri. ῥῆσιν quod nemo tolerare potuit ex χρῆσιν depravatum est, quod et ipsum pro χρη ᾽ν prave correctum erat. Correxi χρὴ πρὶν. Sed χρῆσιν ansam dedit corruptioni vocis λέγω quam restitui. Quid autem χρῆσις et ῥῆσις significent omnibus notum est, et neutrum hic dici posse.

1324. τοῖς ἐμοῖς τιμαόροις libri. Scribæ enim oculi ad proximum versum aberraverunt. δεσποτῶν ego,

nam nihil aliud hic stare potuit; non utique βασιλέως, κοιράνου, similia.

1326. His dictis Casandra ædes ingreditur. Id Weilius solus omnium vidit; ἡμεῖς γὰρ πατέρων. Et pro certo habeo Casaudram non potuisse ea dicere quæ sequuntur. Quid si Chorus solet prius quatuor versus iambicos loqui quam cantilenam canit.

1328. σκιά τις ἀντρέψειεν libri. ἂν τρέψειεν Pors. πρέψειεν Boissonad.,

CASANDRA.

Yet must I speak once ere I sing my dirge,
my own. I pray to Helios, the last light
I see, that the avengers of my lord
1325 may likewise pay my hated murderers, *mine*,
the slave's who died, an easy victory.

CHORUS.

Alas the state of man! if good betide,
one might compare it to a sketch; if ill,
a wet sponge by its touch wipes out the lines:
1330 I pity each, but this far more than that.

Success is for all men a thing without cloy;
and from halls at whose splendour the finger is raised
no one, contented, repels it and says this:
"do not enter here more".
1335 To this hero the blessed gods granted to sack
Priam's metropolis,
and with honour from heaven he returns to his home.
But now if he pays back their blood who before

Herm., e Photii glossa πρέψαι· τὸ ὁμοιῶσαι: Αἰσχύλος, et Hesychii πρέ-ψας· εἰκασμένος, εἰκασθείς. Sed illud requirit σκιᾷ quod Wieseler et Conington corr., hoc autem σκιᾷ ut sit: εἰ εὐτυχοίη, σκιᾷ τις εἰκασμένη ἂν εἴη. Id agitur, utrum horum sit rectum, nam constat de voce πρέψειεν. Et, me quidem judice, σκιᾷ præstat; et Photius locum aliquem male interpretatus est. Ceterum in hac similitudine nihil omnino est de co-loribus inditis: hoc dicit 'res secundæ imaginem delineant, quam res adversæ detergent'. id est: hominum vita, si optime se habet, vanitas est; sed hac vanitate pejus quiddam est, siquando ex rebus secundis in adversas migrandum est.

1331. πράττειν libri. Corr. Pors.
1332. βροτοῖς libri. Corr. Pauw. δακτυλοδεικτῶν libri. Corr. Schutz.
1334. μηκέτι δ' εἰςέλθῃς libri. Corr. Herm.

καὶ τοῖσι κανοῦσι θανὼν ἄλλων
ποινὰς θανάτων ἐπικραίνει,   1340
τίς ποτ᾽ ἂν εὔξαιτο βροτῶν ἀσινεῖ
δαίμονι φῦναι, τάδ᾽ ἀκούων;

ΑΓΑΜΕΜΝΩΝ.

῍Ωμοι, πέπληγμαι καιρίαν πληγὴν ἔσω.

ΚΟΛΤΦΑΙΟΣ.

Σῖγα· τίς πληγὴν ἀϋτεῖ καιρίως οὐτασμένος;

ΑΓΑΜΕΜΝΩΝ.

῍Ωμοι μάλ᾽ αὖθις, δευτέραν πεπληγμένος.   1345

ΚΟΡΤΦΑΙΟΣ.

Τοὔργον εἰργάσθαι δοκεῖ μοι βασιλέως οἰμώγματι·
ἀλλὰ κοινωσώμεθ᾽ ἄν πως ἀσφαλῆ βουλεύματ᾽ ᾖ.

ΧΟΡΕΤΤΗΣ ά.

Ἐγὼ μὲν ὑμῖν τὴν ἐμὴν γνώμην λέγω,
πρὸς δῶμα δεῦρ᾽ ἀστοῖσι κηρύσσειν βοήν.

ΧΟΡΕΤΤΗΣ β'.

Ἐμοὶ δ᾽ ὅπως τάχιστά γ᾽ ἐμπεσεῖν δοκεῖ   1350
καὶ πρᾶγμ᾽ ἐλέγχειν ξὺν νεορρύτῳ ξίφει.

1339. θανοῦσι libri. κτανοῦσι Canter., qui κανοῦσι voluit. Insolentius illud 'moriendo mortuis' conciliare mihi non potui.
1340. ἐπικρανεῖ libri, ἄγαν praeeunte in F. Corr. Herm. ἄγαν intulit Tricl. ut versum acatalecticum, more suo, efficeret.
1341. τίς ἂν εὔξαιτο libri. Dedi Hermanni et Ahrentis correctionem. τίς ἂν ἐξεύξαιτο Schneid.
1343. ἔσω non tam ineptum est

perished, and, dying, ordains for his slayers
1340   additional deaths' retribution,
what mortal ever will boast, when he hears it,
that he lives with a lot that is painless?

AGAMEMNON.

Ah me! I'm struck a mortal stroke; struck home!

CORYPHAEUS.

Hush! who cries that he is stricken with a home-thrust mortally?

AGAMEMNON.

1345 Ah me! again ah me! struck yet again!

CORYPHAEUS.

Done, it seems to me, the deed is, from the monarch's groaning cry.
But let us in common counsel, what, if any, plans are safe.

CHORISTER 1.

I give you my advice: to raise a cry
and call the townsmen to the palace here.

CHORISTER 2.

1350 To rush in with all speed seems best to me,
and with its reeking blade convict the deed.

ut ineptius quiddam corrigi non possit, e. gr. πλευρῶν ἔσω. Verti 'ictu valido'; sed nescio an melius esset 'intus'. Sic enim recte Jebb. Soph. Ai. 235 ἔσω σφάζε 'intus ju-gulabat'; ubi Schneid. 'ictu valido'. Moriens enim admonere videtur intro ire auxilio oportere.

1347. ἄν πῶς libri. Corr. Herm. βουλεύματα libri. Corr. Enger.

ΧΟΡΕΥΤΗΣ γ΄.

Κἀγὼ τοιούτου γνώματος κοινωνὸς ὢν
ψηφίζομαί τι δρᾶν· τὸ μὴ μέλλειν δ᾽ ἀκμή.

ΧΟΡΕΥΤΗΣ δ΄.

Τὸ δρᾶν πάρεστι· φροιμιάζονται γὰρ ὡς
τυραννίδος σημεῖ᾽ ἀράσσοντες πόλει.   1355

ΧΟΡΕΥΤΗΣ έ.

Χρονίζομεν γάρ· οἱ δὲ τῆς μελλοῦς κλέος
πέδοι πατοῦντες οὐ καθεύδουσιν χερί.

ΧΟΡΕΥΤΗΣ ς΄.

Οὐκ οἶδα βουλῆς ἧςτινος τυχὼν λέγω·
τοῦ δρῶντος ἔστι καὶ τὸ βουλεῦσαι πέρι.

ΧΟΡΕΥΤΗΣ ζ΄.

Κἀγὼ τοιοῦτός εἰμ᾽, ἐπεὶ δυσμηχανῶ   1360
λόγοισι τὸν θανόντ᾽ ἀνιστάναι πάλιν.

ΧΟΡΕΥΤΗΣ ή.

Ἦ καὶ βίον τείνοντες ὧδ᾽ ὑπείξομεν
δόμων καταισχυντῆρσι τοῖςδ᾽ ἡγουμένοις;

1354. δραν πάρεστι libri, quod mirum est edd. tamdiu ferre posse. Non sic Æschylus. τὸ δρᾶν ego, ut sit 'agendi sententia adest', breviter dictum pro 'licet tibi, per meam sententiam, agere, τὸ δρᾶν πάρεστί σοι ἐξ ἐμοῦ'. Cf. Eum. 867 τοιαῦθ'

ἐλέσθαι σοι πάρεστιν ἐξ ἐμοῦ. 1355. σημεία πράσσοντες libri. Et hic indignor exstitisse qui id Æschylo inscriberent, quod si puer in ludo literario admisisset infortunium haberet. σημεῖ᾽ ἀράσσοντες ego; jamque adeo, si Atticismum vulgati solœ-

CHORISTER 3.

I, too, partaking in this judgement, vote
to act; the moment's need is — no delay.

CHORISTER 4.

Here is a vote to act. They start the tune
1355 and strike the notes of tyranny for the town.

CHORISTER 5.

Because we dally: they, trampling to earth
the praise of caution, sleep not with their hands.

CHORISTER 6.

I doubt which counsel I shall rightly give;
a doer should also ponder well *his deed*.

CHORISTER 7.

1360 I too am of that mind, since I've no plan
by words to raise the dead to life again.

CHORISTER 8.

But shall we to our lives' end thus succumb
to these king's-house-defilers as our chiefs?

---

cismi loco recipias, lusum in voce
'ferire' habebis; et, fortasse, σημεῖα
sunt 'notæ tonorum musicorum'.
 1356. τῆς μελλούσης κλέος libri.
Herm. corr. ex Tryphone Grammatico. Idem parum scite affirmat vocem χάριν hic non male lectum iri;

nam locutio sumpta est ex Sol. Fr.
27. 4 μιάνας καὶ καταισχύνας κλέος.
 1357. πέδον libri. Corr. Herm.
 1359. Cf. Eur. Hec. 504 Ἀγαμέμνονος πέμψαντος, ὦ γύναι, μέτα.
 1362. κτείνοντες libri. Corr. Canter.

ΧΟΡΕΤΤΗΣ θ'

Ἀλλ' οὐκ ἀνεκτόν, ἀλλὰ κατθανεῖν κρατεῖ·
πεπαιτέρα γὰρ μοῖρα τῆς τυραννίδος.   1365

ΧΟΡΕΤΤΗΣ ί.

Ἢ γὰρ τεκμηρίοισιν ἐξ οἰμωγμάτων
μαντευσόμεσθα τἀνδρὸς ὡς ὀλωλότος;

ΧΟΡΕΤΤΗΣ ιά.

Σάφ' εἰδότας χρὴ τῶνδε θυμοῦσθαι πέρι·
τὸ γὰρ τοπάζειν τοῦ σάφ' εἰδέναι δίχα.

ΚΟΡΤΦΑΙΟΣ.

Ταύτην ἐπαινεῖν πάντοθεν πληθύνομαι,   1370
τρανῶς Ἀτρείδην εἰδέναι κυροῦνθ' ὅπως.

ΚΛΤΤΑΙΜΝΗΣΤΡΑ.

Πολλῶν πάροιθεν καιρίως εἰρημένων
τἀναντί' εἰπεῖν οὐκ ἐπαισχυνθήσομαι.
Πῶς γάρ τις ἐχθροῖς ἐχθρὰ πορσύνων φίλοις
δοκοῦσιν εἶναι πημονῆς ἀρκύστατ' ἂν   1375
φράξειεν ὕψος κρεῖσσον ἐκπηδήματος;
Ἐμοὶ δ' ἀγὼν ὅδ' οὐκ ἀφρόντιστος πάλαι
νείκης παλαιᾶς ἦλθε, σὺν χρόνῳ γε μήν.
Ἕστηκα δ' ἔνθ' ἔπαισ' ἐπ' ἐξειργασμένοις.
Οὕτω δ' ἔπραξα, καὶ τάδ' οὐκ ἀρνήσομαι·   1380
ὡς μήτε φεύγειν μήτ' ἀμύνεσθαι μόρον,

1364. κράτει libri. Corr. Casaubon.
1368. μυθοῦσθαι libri. Corr. E.

Ahrens et Herm.
1375. πημονὴν ἀρκύστατον libri. πημονῆς Aur. ἀρκύστατ' ἂν Elmsl.

CHORISTER 9.

Intolerable! nay, death's advice is best;
1365 it is a milder lot than tyranny.

CHORISTER 10.

But shall we thus on proofs derived from groans
forecast as if the hero were destroyed?

CHORISTER 11.

We must, quite certain of it, rouse our ire;
conjecture's far removed from certainty.

CORYPHAEUS.

1370 On all grounds I go with the stream to approve
this — to see clearly how Atreides fares.

CLYTEMNESTRA.

I will not blush to say the opposite
of many words fitly pronounced before.
How else could one, when scheming hostile deeds
1375 for foes who look like friends, fence the net-stakes
of sorrow to a height too great for a leap?
This bout came off for me at last, and not
without long brooding on a long-lived feud.
I stand where I did strike, with all achieved.
1380 'Twas thus I managed, and I'll not deny 't:
against his flight or parrying of his doom,

1378. νίκης libri. Corr. Heath.   1381. ἀμίνασθαι codices. ἀμίνε-
1379. ἔπεσ' Fl. V. Corr. in Ven. F.   σθαι V.

ἄπειρον ἀμφίβληστρον, ὥςπερ ἰχθύων,
περιστιχίζω, πλοῦτον εἵματος κακόν·
παίω δέ νιν δίς· κἀν δυοῖν οἰμωγμάτοιν
μεθῆκεν αὐτοῦ κῶλα· καὶ πεπτωκότι   1385
τρίτην ἐπενδίδωμι, τοῦ κατὰ χθονὸς
Διὸς νεκρῶν σωτῆρος εὐκταίαν χάριν.
Οὕτω τὸν αὑτοῦ θυμὸν ὁρυγάνει πεσών,
κἀκφυσιῶν ὀξεῖαν αἵματος σφαγὴν
βάλλει μ' ἐρεμνῇ ψακάδι φοινίας δρόσου   1390
χαίρουσαν οὐδὲν ἧσσον ἢ διοςδότῳ
γάνει σπορητὸς κάλυκος ἐν λοχεύμασιν.
Ὡς ὧδ' ἐχόντων, πρέσβος Ἀργείων τόδε,
χαίροιτ' ἄν, εἰ χαίροιτ', ἐγὼ δ' ἐπεύχομαι·
εἰ δ' ἦν πρεπόντων ὥςτ' ἐπισπένδειν νεκρῷ· 1395
τάδ' ἂν δικαίως ἦν· ὑπερδίκως μὲν οὖν·
τοσόνδε κρατῆρ' ἐν δόμοις κακῶν ὅδε
πλήσας ἀραίων αὐτὸς ἐκπίνει μολών.

ΧΟΡΟΣ.

Θαυμάζομέν σου γλῶσσαν, ὡς θρασύστομος,
ἥτις τοιόνδ' ἐπ' ἀνδρὶ κομπάζεις λόγον.   1400

ΚΛΥΤΑΙΜΝΗΣΤΡΑ.

Πειρᾶσθέ μου γυναικὸς ὡς ἀφράσμονος·
ἐγὼ δ' ἀτρέστῳ καρδίᾳ πρὸς εἰδότας
λέγω· σὺ δ' αἰνεῖν εἴτε με ψέγειν θέλεις,

1383. περιστοιχίζων Fl. περιστοι-
χίζω V. περιστιχίζω F.
1384. οἰμώγμασιν libri. οἰμωγμάτοιν Elmsl., cui invitus obtemperavi;
nam displicet dualis ille vehemens,
ut si dicas 'par gemituum'.
1387. Αἶσαυνεκρῶν libri. Διὸς Enger.

1388. αὐτοῦ libri. Corr. Schutz.
ὁρμαίνει libri. ὀρυγάνει corr. Herm.
et sententia ductus et Hesychii glossa
ὀρυγάνει· ἐρεύγεται.
1391, 1392. διὸς νότῳ γᾶν. εἰ Fl.
γᾶν εἰ Ven. Corr. Porsonus. σπό-
ρητος codices. Corr. in V.

I with a sort of fish-net hedge him round,
with no way out — ill treasure of a dress.
I hit him twice; and with two groans he there
1385 did let his limbs collapse. When he is down
I give a third to boot, a votive gift
to the underground Zeus who keeps dead men safe.
So fallen he doth ruckle forth his breath;
and puffing out a nimble jet of blood
1390 smites with a dark-red shower of murder-dew
me greeting it not less than corn-field doth
the god-sent rain-joy at the wheat-ear's birth.
Things being so, if you, those Argive lords,
rejoice, why, you 'll rejoice; but I exult:
1395 would we had liquors fit to drench his corpse!
it would be right, nay, more than right; so great
a bowl of cursed woes he mixed within
the house — and came and drank it off himself.

CHORUS.

We marvel at thy tongue, how bold thou art
1400 in speech, who vauntest o'er thy lord such words.

CLYTEMNESTRA.

You sound me as some woman without plan:
but I with dauntless soul tell you who know —
and should you choose to praise me or upbraid

1395. Hæc est εὐχὴ ἐπὶ ῥθιμένῳ.
'utinam adessent idonei liquores quos
in mortuum libarem; nam indigemus
eorum quos decet; ipse enim post-
quam crateram malorum in his ædi-
bus impleverat, domum reversus,
ad fæcem hausit': hoc est 'utinam

plus mali ei inferre possem'. εἴθ'
pro εἰ δ' conjici potest, et τῷδ' pro
τάδ' cum Tyrwhitt. in prox. v., sed
non prorsus necessario.
1397. τοσῶνδε libri. τοσόνδε conj.
Bl., quod mihi necessarium videtur.

ὅμοιον. Οὗτός ἐστιν Ἀγαμέμνων, ἐμὸς
πόσις, νεκρὸς δὲ τῆςδε δεξιᾶς χερός,
ἔργον δικαίας τέκτονος. Τάδ'. ὧδ' ἔχει. 1405

ΧΟΡΟΣ.

στρ. Τί κακόν, ὦ γύναι.
χθονοτρεφὲς ἐδανὸν ἢ ποτὸν
πασαμένα ρυτᾶς ἐξ ἁλὸς ὅρμενον
τόδ' ἐπέθου θύος δημοθρόους τ' ἀρὰς
ἀπέδικες; Ἀπετάμης· ἀπόπολις δ' ἔσει, 1410
μῖσος ὄβριμον ἀστοῖς.

ΚΛΥΤΑΙΜΝΗΣΤΡΑ.

Νῦν μὲν δικάζεις ἐκ πόλεως φυγὴν ἐμοὶ
καὶ μῖσος ἀστῶν δημόθρους τ' ἔχειν ἀράς,
οὐδὲν τότ' ἀνδρὶ τῷδ' ἐναντίον φέρων·
ὃς οὐ προτιμῶν, ὡςπερεὶ βοτοῦ μόρον, 1415
μήλων φλεόντων εὐπόκοις νομεύμασιν,
ἔθυσεν αὐτοῦ παῖδα, φιλτάτην ἐμοὶ
ὠδῖν', ἐπωδὸν Θρηκίων ἀημάτων.
Οὐ τοῦτον ἐκ γῆς τῆςδε χρῆν σ' ἀνδρηλάτειν,
μιασμάτων ἄποιν'; ἐπήκοος δ' ἐμῶν 1420
ἔργων δικαστὴς τραχὺς εἶ. Λέγω δέ σοι
τοιαῦτ' ἀπειλεῖν, ὡς παρεσκευασμένης

1405. Præstat interpunctio post
χερός, ut vulgo; post ἔργον V., Canter., Tyrwhitt., Enger.
1406. δικαία τέκτων duplici sensu
usurpatur; quæ meritas pœnas ex-
petit, et, quæ opus locanti probat,
par lanificæ illius Homericæ quæ
fuit χερνῆτις ἀληθής.
1408. ρύσας FL ρυσᾶς F. V. Corr.
Stanl. ὁρώμενον Fl. Corr. Abresch.

1409. Post ἀρὰς interrogandi signum vulgo ponitur.
1410. ἀπέδικες ἀπέταμες ἄπολις δ'
ἔσῃ, in ἀπέταμες ad alterum α super-
scripto ε in Fl. Weilium secutus interpunxi post ἀπέδικες et scripsi ἀπε-
τάμης. ἀπόπολις corr. Seidler. 'ex-
cussisti exsecrationes et induisti
insaniam'.
1411. ὄμβριμον Ven. F. Herm.

'tis all the same — here's Agamemnon, here!

1405 my husband and this right hand's victim dead,

a right good craftsman's work. That's how it stands.

CHORUS.

Woman, what poison-food

earth-grown or from the flowing sea

sprung hast eaten? and put on this frenzied mind,

and hast cast away *fear of* the people's curse?

1410 thou art *sheer* cut off, and shalt an outcast be,

monstrous hate of the people.

CLYTEMNESTRA.

Now you adjudge me exile from this land,

to bear the townsmen's hate, the people's curse,

though then you voted this man naught untoward

1415 who, reckoning it a brute beast's death, no more,

when his flocks teemed with fleecy pasturers,

butchered his own child, and my best-beloved

birth-pain, as charm against the Thracian blasts.

Should you not as his foul deeds' penalty

1420 have driven him from this land? but of my deeds

when arbiter you are an angry judge.

I bid you threaten thus — I being prepared

1414. οὐδὲν τόδ' libri. Corr. Voss.
1416. εὐτόκοις Ven. Schneidewin.
1418. θρηκίων τε (vel τὲ) λημμάτων libri. Corr. Canter.
1419. χρὴ libri. χρῆν Pors.
1422. Hunc versum ejecit Enger. Equidem non video quid hic sit quod offendat; omittitur ἐμοῦ, sed facile potest subintelligi. Ceterum hic et alibi particula ὡς dubitatio-

nem excludit num principalis verbi subjectum dum agat, id revera intelligat, vel (si futuri temporis participium sequitur) id ipsum sibi propositum habeat, quod hac particula subjungatur. Qua formula usus ubique explicare poteris haec et similia, ὡς (πρὸς omisso) βασιλέα, ὡς ἐλέγξων, ὡς εἰδότων, ὡς (πρὸς vel νομίζων omisso) εἰδότας, ὡς πλείστους·

10

ἐκ τῶν ὁμοίων, χειρὶ νικήσαντ' ἐμοῦ
ἄρχειν· ἐὰν δὲ τοὔμπαλιν κραίνῃ θεός,
γνώσει διδαχθεὶς ὀψὲ γοῦν τὸ σωφρονεῖν. 1425

ΧΟΡΟΣ.

ἀντ. Μεγαλόμητις εἶ,
περίφρονα δ' ἔλακες, ὥσπερ οὖν
φονολιβεῖ τύχᾳ φρὴν ἐπιμαίνεται·
λίπος ἐπ' ὀμμάτων αἵματος ἐμπρέπει.
Ἀτίετον ἔτι σε χρὴ στερομέναν φίλων
τύμμα τύμματι τῖσαι. 1430

ΚΛΥΤΑΙΜΝΗΣΤΡΑ.

Καὶ τήνδ' ἀκούεις ὁρκίων ἐμῶν θέμιν·
μὰ τὴν τέλειον τῆς ἐμῆς παιδὸς δίκην,
Ἄτην Ἐρινύν θ' αἶσι τόνδ' ἔσφαξ' ἐγώ,
οὔ μοι φόβου μέλαθρον ἐλπὶς ἐμπατεῖν
ἕως ἂν αἴθῃ πῦρ ἐφ' ἑστίας ἐμῆς 1435
Αἴγισθος, ὡς τὸ πρόσθεν εὖ φρονῶν ἐμοί·
οὗτος γὰρ ἡμῖν ἀσπὶς οὐ μικρὰ θράσους.
Κεῖται γυναικὸς τῆσδε λυμαντήριος,
Χρυσηΐδων μείλιγμα τῶν ὑπ' Ἰλίῳ·
ἥ τ' αἰχμάλωτος ἥδε καὶ τερασκόπος, 1440
καὶ κοινόλεκτρος τοῦδε θεσφατηλόγος,
πιστὴ ξύνευνος, ναυτίλων δὲ σελμάτων
ἰσοτριβής. Ἄτιμα δ' οὐκ ἐπραξάτην·

1427. περίφρονα hic fere idem valet quod παράφρονα, ut proximo versu ostenditur.
1428. λίπος libri. Corr. Pors. Deinde εὖ πρέπει ἀντίετον ἔτι σε χρὴ Fl. εὐπρέπεια τίετον Ven. V. εὖ πρέπει ἀτίετον F. Corr. Aur. et Canter.
1430. τύμμα τύμμα τίσαι. Corr. illud Voss., hoc Pors.
1433. ἐρινύν libri.
1434. ἐμπατεῖν V. ἐμπατεῖ codices.

with similar threats — to rule me when by force
you 've conquered. Should god grant the alternative
1425 you 'll know, though taught it late, what good sense is.

CHORUS.

An arch-schemer thou!
and declaimest in raving words:
and what wonder? thy mind is distracted by
thy gore-blotted state: blots of blood glare on thy
visage. Yet must thou, spurned and bereft of friends,
1430 stricken pay for this striking.

CLYTEMNESTRA.

This solemn form, too, of my words on oath
thou hearest; by my child's full Recompense,
by Ate and Erinnys, those to whom
I slew that man, I have no hope to tread
1435 Fear's house, while on my hearth Ægisthus lights
the fire, love-loyal as before to me;
for he's my shield of trust and that not small.
Here lies this wife's insulter, and the pet
of the Chryseides at Troy: here too
1440 the captive portent-scanner and this man's
couch-sharing utterer of words inspired;
a faithful bed-mate, now, as when she pressed
the same ship's-deck-boards. Not unsuitably

Illud recepi: 'quamdiu' inquit 'Ægisthus domi meæ versatur, non est
exspectandum fore ut Timoris domum frequentem'.
1435. ἑστίας ἐμάς libri. Corr.
Pors.

1438. γυναικὸς τῆςδε idem est quod
ἐμοῦ ut ἀνδρὸς τοῦδε passim. Sio et
μητρὸς τῆςδε (Clyt.) Eum. 122.
1441. ἡ pro καὶ Karsten., Enger.
1443. ἱστοτριβής libri. Corr. Pauw.

ὁ μὲν γὰρ οὕτως· ἡ δέ τοι κύκνου δίκην
τὸν ὕστατον μέλψασα θανάσιμον γόον   1445
κεῖται φιλήτωρ τοῦδ᾽· ἐμοὶ δ᾽ ἐπήγαγεν
εὐνῆς παροψώνημα τῆς ἐμῆς χλιδῆς.

ΧΟΡΟΣ.

στρ ά. Φεῦ τίς ἂν ἐν τάχει μὴ περιώδυνος
          μηδὲ δεμνιοτήρης,
          μόλοι τὸν ἀεὶ φέρουσ᾽ ἐν ἡμῖν   1450
          μοῖρ᾽ ἀτέλευτον ὕπνον, δαμέντος
          Φύλακος εὐμενεστάτου;
          πολέα τλάντος γυναικὸς διαί,
          πρὸς γυναικὸς δ᾽ ἀπέφθισεν βίον.

σύστ.ά. Ἰὼ ἰώ, παράνους Ἑλένα   1455
          μία τὰς πολλάς, τὰς πάνυ πολλὰς
          ψυχὰς ὀλέσασ᾽ ὑπὸ Τροίᾳ.

στρ.β'. Νῦν δὲ τέλειον ἐπήνθισεν αἷμ᾽ ἄνιπτον,

1446. φιλήτως Fl.
1447. παροψόνημα libri. Corr. Casaubon. Nihil hic dicitur de paropside nihil de paropsemate, quorum hoc obsonium est vel bellaria, illa autem obsonii plena patella, extra ordinem apposita. παροψώνημα est obsonium clam paratum ut clam edatur. Sic Casandra Agamemnoni erat quasi libidinis pulpamentum subsecundarium quod cupediæ ejus clam inserviret, si quando legitimi concubitus eum tæderet. Hoc igitur dicit Clyt. 'quantam illi clandestinam voluptatem præbitura erat, tantum gaudii advectitii et additilii lætitiæ meæ præbuit'. παρόψημα est hujus interpretationis quod derisor illa et ipsa jamdiu probe callebat

quidnam esset concubitus παροψώνημα. Cf. Ar. Eccl. 226 et Schol. Soph. Tr. 360. Æsch. Supp. 296. Simonid. περὶ γυναικῶν v. 46.
1448. A numeratione harum stropharum et systematum quam Herm. statuit intra certos fines declinavi; quod ubique systemata propriis numeris a strophis distinxi; et hoc quidem simplicitati concedendum erat. Præterea, lacunis antiquatis, in duobus locis systemata inter se inæqualem versuum numerum habentia exhibui; hoc enim sententiæ dare æquum videbatur. Nam ut se habent versus nihil omnino refert ubi lacunam ponas, adeo nulla esset lacunæ suspicio nisi responsionem præstare in animum induxisset Her-

they 've fared: for he — the way I told you; she,

1445 having swan-like trilled her last death-wail, lies down

his own sweet love; and for my transport's zest

brought a love-dalliance-dainty-on-the-sly.

CHORUS.

O that some destiny joined with no pain extreme,

no bed-keeping confinement,

1450 would quickly come bringing o'er us slumber

ever-unending, for our most loving

guardian hath been overcome:

who for one woman bore many toils,

and hath now lost his life by woman's hands.

1455 Alas, alas, Helen infatuate!

of that number, that very great number, of lives

in the Troad the single destroyer!

now she hath poured out a crowning indelible blood-stream,

mannus. Neque ille quidem, me judice, sine aliqua ratione; sed non ut operæ pretium sit bonum sensum importunis illis asteriscis interrumpere. Quo autem modo choristæ hæc inter se partiti sint res admodum dubia est. Probabile tamen videtur medium quatuor choristarum ζυγὸν octo illas strophas antistrophasque γ', δ', et systemata antisystemataque γ', δ' sortitum esse; et ceteras duodecim strophas antistrophasque α', β', ἐ et systemata antisystemataque α', β', ἐ inter octo primanos et tertianos choristas quoquo ordine esse distributa.

1450. Sic libri. ἐφ' ἡμῖν Herm.

1453. καὶ πολλὰ libri. καὶ ejecit Franz. πολέα corr. Wieseler. et Enger.

1454. ἀπέφθισεν βίον ut quod maxime corruptum est. Vide Comm.

1455. ἰὼ παρανόμους libri. Alterum ἰὼ addidit Bl. παράνους corr. Herm.

1457. ὀλέσας Fl.

1458, 1459. νῦν δὲ τελείαν πολύμνηστον ἐπηνθίσω δι' αἷμ' ἄνιπτον libri. Hæc Heimsoethius in formam quam maxime probabilem redegit, quam exhibui. Hermannus, qui satis multos asseclas habuit, lacunæ signa post τελείαν posuit et versum 1459 ad hunc modum ordinavit: ἢ πολύμναστον ἐπηνθίσω αἷμ' ἄνιπτον. Sed Hermanni auctoritas non tanta est ut credam v. πολύμναστον voci ἐπιτύμβιος respondere. Lacunæ signa, si lacuna est ubi sensus integer

ἥτις ἄρ' ἐν δόμοις ἦν   1460
ἐριμνάστευτος ἀνδρὸς οἰζύς.

ΚΛΤΤΑΙΜΝΗΣΤΡΑ.

σύστ β'.   Μηδὲν θανάτου μοῖραν ἐπεύχου
τοῖςδε βαρυνθείς,
μηδ' εἰς Ἑλένην κότον ἐκτρέψῃς,
ὡς ἀνδρολέτειρ', ὡς μία πολλῶν   1465
ἀνδρῶν ψυχὰς Δαναῶν ὀλέσασ'
ἀξύστατον ἄλγος ἔπραξεν.

ΧΟΡΟΣ.

ἀντ.ά.   Δαῖμον, ὃς ἐμπίτνεις δώμασι καὶ διφυίοισι Τανταλίδαισιν,
κράτος τ' ἰσόψυχον ἐκ γυναικὸς   1470
καρδιόδηκτον ἐμοὶ κρατύνεις·
ἐπὶ δὲ σώματος δίκαν
κόρακος ἐχθροῦ σταθεὶς ἐννόμως
ὕμνον ὑμνεῖς ἀπεύχετον μόρου.

ΚΛΤΤΑΙΜΝΗΣΤΡΑ

ἀντισύστ.β'. Νῦν δ' ὤρθωσας στόματος γνώμην   1475
τὸν τριπάχυντον

mansit, ponenda sunt post Τροίᾳ. δι' est ant literarum αι repetitio aut cerrectoris cujusdam additamentum. πολύμναστον vero manifesto est glossa ad ἐριμνάστευτος adscripta, quæ vox reginæ nomini aperte alludit, κλυτὴ μνηστείᾳ. Deinde ἐπηνθίσω est peccatum librarii qui hoc verbo Helenam compellari somniavit. Hæc Heimsoeth., qui lacunam non agnoscit nedum sex versuum.

1460, 1461. ἥτις ἦν τότ' ἐν δόμοις ἔρις ἐρίδματος ἀνδρὸς ἀίξύς libri. Versum 1460 hoc modo corr. Heims. ἥτε τότ' ἐν δόμοις ἦν. Sed τότ' est metri complementum, et pro ea ἄρ' scripsi quod ansam dedisse videtur ei qui ἔρις scripsit, nam αρ et ιρ eandem fere formam habent in M.
1464. ἐκτρέχῃς Fl. Corr. in V.
1466. ὀλέσαν Fl. ὀλέσασ' F.
1468. ἐμπίπτεις libri. Corr. Can-

1460 she, who at home was staying
      her husband's much-wooed tribulation.

CLYTEMNESTRA.

      Pray not at all for the portion of death,
          weighed down by these deeds,
          nor against Helena turn your resentment,
1465 *saying* that she the manslayer, the single
          destroyer of many Greek warriors' lives,
          wrought out ineffaceable sorrow.

CHORUS.

      Daemon, who savagely crushest this house and the
          two sons, Tantalus' offspring,
1470 and dost impose, swayed by equal rancour,
          rule by a woman, that stings my bosom;
          and now like a raven fell
          by the corpse perched dost hymn, well attuned
      to the deed, execrable hymns of death!

CLYTEMNESTRA.

1475 Now thou hast righted the sense of thy language
          by thus invoking this

---

ter. διφυέίσι libri. διφυίαισι corr.
Herm., quæ vox formatur ex δὶς et
φυιὸς filius. Mox τανταλίδεσιν Fl.
    1470. τ' inscruit Herm. κράτος
ἰσόψυχον est 'imperium quod tui si-
milem animum gerit'. Deinde ἐκ
γυναικῶν libri. ἐκ γυναικὸς conjecit
Schutz., recepit Enger., nam de
Ægistho non agitur.
    1471. καρδία δηκτὸν libri. Corr.
Abresch.

    1473. μοι κόραχος libri. Corr.
Franz. ἐκνόμως F. V. perperam.
    1474. ὕμνον ὑμνεῖν ἐπεύχεται libri.
Deest unus pes. Scripsi ὑμνεῖς ἀπεύχετον μόρου ut probabilem sensum
extunderem. Prædicatio autem fit
per invocationem.
    1475. νῦν γ' Aur. 'sed δὲ refertur
ad suppressum πρόσθεν μὲν οὐκ' Herm.
    1476. τριπάχυιον libri. Corr. Bam-
berger.

δαίμονα γέννης τῆςδε κικλήσκων·
ἐκ τοῦ γὰρ ἔρως αἱματολοιχὸς
νείρει τρέφεται, πρὶν καταλῆξαι
τὸ παλαιὸν ἄχος, νέος ἰχώρ.   1480

ΧΟΡΟΣ.

στρ.γ'. Ἦ μεγάροισι μέγαν
δαίμονα καὶ βαρύμηνιν αἰνεῖς·
Φεῦ φεῦ, κακὸν αἶνον ἀτη-
ρᾶς τύχας ἀκορέστου·
ἰώ, ἰή, διαὶ Διὸς   1485
παναιτίου πανεργέτα·
τί γὰρ βροτοῖς ἄνευ Διὸς τελεῖται;
τί τῶνδ' οὐ θεόκραντόν ἐστιν;

σύστ.γ'. Ἰὼ ἰὼ βασιλεῦ, βασιλεῦ,
πῶς σε δακρύσω;   1490
Φρενὸς ἐκ φιλίας τί ποτ' εἴπω;
κεῖσαι δ' ἀράχνης ἐν ὑφάσματι τῷδ'
ἀσεβεῖ θανάτῳ βίον ἐκπνέων.

στρ.δ'. Ὤμοι μοι, κοίταν τάνδ' ἀνελεύθερον·
δολίῳ μόρῳ δαμείς·   1495
ἐκ χερὸς ἀμφιτόμῳ βελέμνῳ.

ΚΛΥΤΑΙΜΝΗΣΤΡΑ.

σύστ.δ'. Αὐχεῖς εἶναι τόδε τοὔργον ἐμόν,
μὴ δ' ἐπιλέξῃς

1479. νείρει dativum esse ignoti vocabuli νείρος intimum locum significantis statuit Herm. Cf. Suidas s. v. νείαρα· τόπος ἔσχατος τῆς γαστρός et s. v. νῆστις· τὸ μεταξὺ τῆς κοιλίας καὶ τοῦ στομάχου ἔντερον, 'intestinum jejunum'. Suspicor νείρει ex glossa νειάρᾳ, ad νήστει adscripta, ortum esse.

1481. ἦ μέγαν οἴκοις τοῖςδε libri, quae v. antistr. non respondent. Probabile mihi videtur οἴκοις τοῖςδε esse interpr. Itaque μεγάροισι scripsi, vocabulum alioqui tragicis ignotum.

family's trebly-gorged daemon of evil.

For from him is this blood-lapping appetite nursed

in its bowels; before the old sore has surceased,

1480   lo, fresh blood *already is flowing*.

CHORUS.

Truly thou fablest a dire

fiend for this house, and with hate full-laden.

Oh! oh! the calamitous uncloyed

fortune's ruinous story!

1485 alas! alas! by means of Zeus,

the cause of all, the doer of all!

for what's achieved by mortals Zeus-unaided?

of this, what is not god-determined?

alas! alas! O my king! O my king!

1490   how shall I mourn thee?

from my loving heart what shall I utter?

for there in that spider-spun web thou dost lie,

by unholy death breathing thy life out.

Ah me! me! this couch base and inglorious!

1495 by a wily death subdued!

death from her hand by that two-edged weapon!

CLYTEMNESTRA.

You fancy this deed to be mine; but append

not the name, and declare

1485. πανεργέταν Fl. Ven. Corr. in F. V.

1489. ἰὼ semel Fl. Ven. bis F. V. et sic v. 1513.

1494. τᾶνδ' Fl.

1498. μηδ' ἐπιλέχθης Fl. Ven. μὴ δ' ἐπιλεχθῆς F. μὴ δ' ἐπιλέξης Vossius et Franz. 'dæmon' inquit 'meam formam indutus hoc facinus patravit; ne ei Clytemnestræ nomen indideris' itaque non concedit suum esse facinus.

Ἀγαμεμνονίαν εἶναί μ' ἄλοχον·

Φανταζόμενος δὲ γυναικὶ νεκροῦ   1500

τοῦδ' ὁ παλαιὸς δριμὺς ἀλάστωρ

Ἀτρέως χαλεποῦ θοινατῆρος

τόνδ' ἀπέτισεν

τέλεον νεαροῖς ἐπιθύσας.

ΧΟΡΟΣ.

ἀντ.γ΄. Ὡς μὲν ἀναίτιος εἶ   1505

τοῦδε φόνου, τίς ὁ μαρτυρήσων;

πῶ, πῶ; πατρόθεν δὲ συλλή-

πτωρ γένοιτ' ἂν ἀλάστωρ.

Βιάζεται δ' ὁμοσπόροις

ἐπιρροαῖσιν αἱμάτων   1510

μέλας Ἄρης, ὅποι δίκαν προβαίνων

πάχνᾳ κουροβόρῳ παρέξει.

ἀντισύστ.γ΄. Ἰὼ ἰὼ βασιλεῦ, βασιλεῦ,

πῶς σε δακρύσω;

Φρενὸς ἐκ φιλίας τί ποτ' εἴπω;   1515

κεῖσαι δ' ἀράχνης ἐν ὑφάσματι τῷδ'

ἀσεβεῖ θανάτῳ βίον ἐκπνέων.

ἀντ.δ΄. Ὤμοι μοι, κοίταν τάνδ' ἀνελεύθερον·

δολίῳ μόρῳ δαμείς·

ἐκ χερὸς ἀμφιτόμῳ βελέμνῳ.   1520

ΚΛΤΤΑΙΜΝΗΣΤΡΑ.

ἀντισύστ.δ΄· Οὐδὲ γὰρ οὗτος δολίαν ἄτην

1511. δὲ καὶ libri. δίκαν corr.   1512. πάχνα libri. Corr. Herm.
Butler. προςβαίνων libri. Correxit   1517. εὐσεβεῖ FL
Canter.   1521. οὔτ' ἀνελεύθερον οἶμαι θάνατον

САabetic

that I'm the wife of *king* Agamemnon:
1500 for likened in form to the wife of this corse
the former time's guilt-unforgiving fierce fiend,
roused by the merciless banqueter Atreus,
served the debt upon him
and has slain him full-grown for the children.

CHORUS.

1505 Who is the man who will bear
witness that thou of this death art guiltless?
whence? whence? but a fiend his father
roused might be thine abettor:
for dreadful Ares presses on
1510 with frequent streams of kindred blood
to the goal to which advancing he 'll avenge the
clotted gore of the eaten children.
Alas! alas! O my king! O my king!
how shall I mourn thee?
1515 from my loving heart what shall I utter?
for there in that spider-spun web thou dost lie,
by unholy death breathing thy life out.
Ah me! me! this couch base and inglorious!
by a wily death subdued!
1520 *death* from her hand by that two-edged weapon.

CLYTEMNESTRA.

And did not he also bring on the family

τῷδε γενέσθαι, quæ auto οὐδὲ γὰρ sententia et hiatu motus; et sic
οὗτος in libris leguntur, Æschylo omnes rece.
abjudicavit Seidler., frigida ineptaque

οἴκοισιν ἔθηκ';
ἀλλ' ἐμὸν ἐκ τοῦδ' ἔρνος ἀερθὲν   1525
τὴν πολύκλαυτον ἀνάξια δράσας
'Ιφιγένειαν, ἀνάξια πάσχων
μηδὲν ἐν Ἅιδου μεγαλαυχείτω,
ξιφοδηλήτῳ
θανάτῳ τίσας ἅπερ ἔρξεν.   1530

ΧΟΡΟΣ.

στρ. έ.   Ἀμηχανῶ, φροντίδος στερηθεὶς
εὐπαλάμων μεριμνᾶν,
ὅπᾳ τράπωμαι, πίτνοντος οἴκου.
Δέδοικα δ' ὄμβρου κτύπον δομοσφαλῆ
τὸν αἱματηρόν· ψακὰς δὲ λήγει.
Δίκην δ' ἐπ' ἄλλο πρᾶγμα θηγάνει βλάβης   1535
πρὸς ἄλλαις θηγάναισι Μοῖρα.
ἀντισύστ. ά.   Ἰὼ γᾶ, γᾶ, εἴθε μ' ἐδέξω
πρὶν τόνδ' ἐπιδεῖν ἀργυροτοίχου
δροίτας κατέχοντα χαμεύναν.   1540
Τίς ὁ θάψων νιν; τίς ὁ θρηνήσων;
ἢ σὺ τόδ' ἔρξαι
τλήσει, κτείνασ' ἄνδρα τὸν αὑτῆς
ἀποκωκῦσαι ψυχῇ τ' ἄχαριν
χάριν ἀντ' ἔργων   1545

1524. Interrogandi signum addidit Schutz.
1526. τὴν πολύκλαυτον τ' Ἰφιγένειαν
ἀνάξια δράσας ἄξια πάσχων libri. Correxit C. H. Weise. Quod ad diae-
resin attinet, cf. vv. 1555 et 1557.
Sic et sensus pulchrior exit. Ἰφιγένειαν τὴν πολυκλαύτην Karsten. τὴν

πολύκλαυτον παῖδ' Ἰριγόνην Ahrens. In-
credulus odi tam πολυκλαύτην quam
Ἰριγενείαν, quae Dind. corr.
1527. ἄξια δράσας ἄξια πάσχων
Herm., alii.
1530. ἅπερ ἥρξεν libri. ἔρξεν Eu-
ger., alii.
1531. φροντίδων F. V.

treacherous murder?

1525   Well: having treated unfairly my blossom

raised from him, much-mourned Iphigenia,

let him too treated unfairly not boast

loud in the chambers of Hades; in his death

by the mischievous sword

1530   having paid us back that he inflicted.

CHORUS.

I am perplexed — spoiled of deftly-working

counsel's *adroit* conclusion —

which way to turn now the house is falling.

I fear the shower's palace-overturning splash,

the bloody *splash*, for the sprinkle ceases:

1535 and Fate on other whetstones whets *the sword of Right*

for yet one deed of mischief-dealing.

O earth! O earth! would thou hadst taken me

ere I had seen him tenant that lowly bed

1540   on the floor of the silver-walled laver!

Who shall his burier be? who his lamenter?

wilt thou dare to perform

this task, who didst slay him, thine own wedded lord?

to bewail, and in face of these heinous deeds

1545   insincerely present

1532. εὐπάλαμνον μέριμναν libri.
Quæ dedi, ea Karsten. et Enger.
invenerunt; recte, me judice. Nam
etsi syntaxis patitur μέριμναν, tamen
εὐπάλαμος est subjecti epitheton, ut
φροντίδα corrigere deberemus si et
genitivus hic stare non posset. Constructio est ἀμηχανῶ ὅπᾳ τράπωμαι,
itaque comma post ἀμ. posui.

1534. ψεκάς libri. Corr. Bl.

1535. δίκη FL δίκα superscr. η
Ven. δίκᾳ superscr. η F. δίκην Aur.
Deinde θήγει libri. θηγάνει Herm.

1536. θηγάναις libri. Corr. Pauw.

1537. Sic F. εἶθ' ἔμ' cet.

1544. ἀποκωκῦσαι libri.

μεγάλων ἀδίκως ἐπικρᾶναι;

ἀντ β'. Τίς δ' ἐπιτύμβιος αἶνος ἐπ' ἀνδρὶ θείῳ
σὺν δακρύοις ἰάπτων
ἀληθείᾳ φρενῶν πονήσει;   1550

ΚΛΤΤΑΙΜΝΗΣΤΡΑ.

σύστ ἑ   Οὐ σὲ προσήκει τὸ μέλημ' ἀλέγειν
τοῦτο· πρὸς ἡμῶν
κάππεσε, κάτθανε, καὶ καταθάψομεν·
οὐχ ὑπὸ κλαυθμῶν τῶν ἐξ οἴκων,
ἀλλ' Ἰφιγένειά νιν ἀσπασίως   1555
θυγατήρ, ὡς χρή,
πατέρ' ἀντιάσασα πρὸς ὠκύπορον
πόρθμευμ' ἀχέων
περὶ χεῖρα βαλοῦσα φιλήσει.

ΧΟΡΟΣ.

ἀντ.ἑ. Ὄνειδος ἥκει τόδ' ἀντ' ὀνείδους·   1560
δύσμαχα δ' ἐστὶ κρῖναι.
Φέρει φέροντ', ἐκτίνει δ' ὁ καίνων.
Μίμνει δὲ μίμνοντος ἐν θρόνῳ Διὸς
παθεῖν τὸν ἔρξαντα· θέσμιον γάρ.
Τίς ἂν γονὰν ἀραῖον ἐκβάλοι δόμων;   1565
κεκόλληται γένος προσάψαι.

1549. δακρύοιν Fl. V. Corr. in Ven. F.
1551. μέλημα λέγειν libri. Corr. Karsten. et Schneid.
1555. ἰφιγένειαν· ἰν' libri. Corr. Jacob. Ante hunc v. lacunam ponunt.

1559. χεῖρε Pors. sine idonea causa. φιλήσῃ libri. Corr. Jacob.
1563. χρόνῳ libri. θρόνῳ corr. Schutz. Et ne forte dubites cf.· Orph. Fr. 1 οὗτος γὰρ (Ζεὺς) χάλκειον ἐς οὐρανὸν ἐστήρικται χρυσέῳ εἰνὶ θρόνῳ.

to his shade an unthankworthy tribute?

What panegyric pronounced on the godlike hero,

aiming *its words* with weeping,

1550   shall do its work with true emotion?

CLYTEMNESTRA.

It belongs not to thee to harbour the thought

    of this care: by my hand

    as he fell, *as* he died, so will I bury him:

    with no escort of wailings *in pomp* from his home,

1555   but lovingly Iphigenia his child,

    as it behoves her,

    shall come to the swift-flowing channel of woes

    and, meeting her sire,

    shall throw her arms round him and kiss him.

CHORUS.

1560   Here comes a charge th' other charge rebutting:

    hard is the strife to judge them.

    One robs a thief; he who killed takes ransom.

    Yet it abides, long as Zeus enthroned abides,

    that 'he who does, suffers': 'tis an ord'nance.

1565   Who shall drive out a curse's seed from families?

    'tis fixed so as to bind the offspring.

1564. Interpunctionem post γάρ
recte posuerunt edd. recentt.
    1565. γονὰν ῥάον libri. Corr. Herm.
    1566. Sic libri. πρὸς ἄτᾳ Bl.
'agglutinata est gens exitio', justo
vehementius. Hoc dicitur: 'dirarum
semen ita genti agglutinatum est ut
sobolem quoque sibi connectat'. Itaque
vulgatum retinui.

ΚΛΥΤΑΙΜΝΗΣΤΡΑ.

ἀντισύστ.έ. Ἐς τόνδ' ἐνέβης ξὺν ἀληθείᾳ
χρησμόν· ἐγὼ δ' οὖν
ἐθέλω δαίμονι τῷ Πλεισθενιδᾶν
ὅρκους θεμένη τάδε μὲν στέργειν   1570
δύστλητά περ ὄνθ'· ὃ δὲ λοιπόν, ἰόντ'
ἐκ τῶνδε δόμων ἄλλην γενεὰν
τρίβειν θανάτοις αὐθένταισιν.
Κτεάνων δὲ μέρος
βαιὸν ἐχούσῃ πᾶν ἀπόχρη μοι   1575
μανίας μελάθρων
ἀλληλοφόνους ἀφελούσῃ.

ΑΙΓΙΣΘΟΣ.

Ὦ φέγγος εὖφρον ἡμέρας δικηφόρου.
Φαίην ἂν ἤδη νῦν βροτῶν τιμαόρους;
θεοὺς ἄνωθεν γῆς ἐποπτεύειν ἄγη,
ἰδὼν ὑφαντοῖς ἐν πέπλοις Ἐρινύων   1580
τὸν ἄνδρα τόνδε κείμενον φίλως ἐμοί,
χερὸς πατρῴας ἐκτίνοντα μηχανάς.
Ἀτρεὺς γὰρ ἄρχων τῆσδε γῆς, τούτου πατήρ,
πατέρα Θυέστην τὸν ἐμόν, ὡς τορῶς φράσαι,
αὑτοῦ τ' ἀδελφόν, ἀμφίλεκτος ὢν κράτει,   1585
ἠνδρηλάτησεν ἐκ πόλεώς τε καὶ δόμων.
Καὶ προστρόπαιος ἑστίας μολὼν πάλιν
τλήμων Θυέστης μοῖραν εὗρετ' ἀσφαλῆ,

1567. ἐνέβη libri. Corr. Canter.   Ἀθηναίοις καὶ περισπωμένως σὺν τῷ ι
1571. ὄυσπλητά περ Fl.   γράφεται Ε. Μ. s. v.
1574. τε μέρος libri. Corr. Aur.   1576, 1577. μοι δ' ἀλληλοφόνους;
1575. ἀπόχρη· παρὰ τοῖς παλαιοῖς   μανίας μελάθρων. Transposuit Er-

CLYTEMNESTRA.

You advert with good reason to that divine law:
 I then am willing
 to take oath to the Pleisthenids' daemon of ill
1570 that with things as they are I will be satisfied,
 hard to bear though they be: and for what yet remains,
 that he go from this house, and with murderous deaths
 waste *in* some other age *its descendants.*
 And, though scanty the share
1575 of the wealth that I own, it suffices me quite,
 if I sweep from the house
 these mad-fits of mutual slaughter.

ÆGISTHUS.

O joyful light of the vengeance-bringing day!
 now will I grant that gods above as man's
 right-vindicators scan the crimes of earth;
1580 now that I see there, grateful sight to me,
 that man lie in the Furies' own-spun robes,
 atoning for his father's hand's device.
 For Atreus, this land's king and that man's sire,
 having his rule disputed, drove my sire
1585 Thyestes, mine, to speak explicitly,
 and his own brother, from his state and home.
 Then coming back, as suppliant at the hearth,
 Thyestes sad got safe conditions, not

furdt, ejecto δὲ, quod ad vitandum
hiatum additum est.
 /1579. ἄχη libri. ἄγη corr. Aur.

1585. αὐτοῦ libri. αὑτοῦ Elmsl.,
Dind.

1588. ηὖρετ' Dind.

τὸ μὴ θανὼν πατρῷον αἱμάξαι πέδον
ʼαὐτός. Ξένια δὲ τοῦδε δύσθεος πατὴρ   1590
τὠμῷ, κρεουργὸν ἦμαρ εὐθύμως ἄγειν
δοκῶν, παρέσχε δαῖτα παιδείων κρεῶν.

Τὰ μὲν ποδήρη καὶ χερῶν ἄκρους κτένας
ἔκρυπτ᾽, ἄνωθεν ἀδρὰ κρέα καὶ θέρμ᾽ ἐνεὶς   1595
ἄσημ᾽· ὁ δ᾽ αὐτῶν αὐτίκ᾽ ἀγνοίᾳ λαβὼν
ἔσθει βορὰν ἄσωτον, ὡς ὁρᾷς, γένει.

Κᾆπειτ᾽ ἐπιγνοῦσ᾽ ἔργον οὐ καταίσιον
ᾤμωξεν, ἀμπίπτει δ᾽ ἀπὸ σφαγὴν ἐρῶν,
μόρον δ᾽ ἄφερτον Πελοπίδαις ἐπεύχεται,   1600
λάκτισμα δείπνου ξυνδίκως τιθεὶς ἀρᾷ.

Ἐκ τῶνδέ σοι πεσόντα τόνδ᾽ ἰδεῖν πάρα.

Κἀγὼ δίκαιος τοῦδε τοῦ φόνου ῥαφεύς·
τρίτον γὰρ οὖν με παῖδ᾽ ἔτ᾽ ἀθλίῳ πατρὶ   1605
συνεξελαύνει τυτθὸν ὄντ᾽ ἐν σπαργάνοις·
τραφέντα δ᾽ αὖθις ἡ δίκη κατήγαγεν.

1590. αὐτοῦ· ξένια δὲ libri. αὐτός.,
corr. Bl. In vulg. sequitur: Ἀτρεὺς·
προθύμως μᾶλλον ἢ φίλως, πατρὶ quem
versum, ex glossis ad πατήρ et εὐθύμως
adscriptis concinnatum, recte ejece-
runt Schutz. et Enger.
1595, 1596. ἔθρυπτ᾽ ἄνωθεν ἀνδρακὰς καθήμενος. ἄσημα δ᾽ αὐτῶν libri.
ἔκρυπτ᾽ corr. Tyrwhitt., et ut de
intrito taceam, hæc verba θρύπτειν
et κρύπτειν in codd. non semel per-
mutata sunt. Non minus certe ἄσημ᾽·
ὁ δ᾽ αὐτῶν Dind. Restat ἀνδρακὰς
καθήμενος nam ἄνωθεν integrum est.
Illud 'viritim sedens' significat; quod
prorsus absurdum est. Nec multum
lucraris recepta Herm. corr. καθη-
μένοις, nam nonnisi comici poetæ
esset et ceteros convivas Thyestæ
puerorum carnibus farcire. Videamus

igitur quid fecerit nefarius Atreus.
Quum heroicæ ætatis more singulæ
singulis convivis mensæ (τράπεζαι)
appositæ essent, bovinam scilicet
ceteris, Thyestæ vero cæsorum puerorum carnem subministrandam curavit; hanc autem in satis alta pa-
tina ita disposuit, ut crudi pedum
et manuum digiti imam sedem te-
nerent, et mollibus accurateque coctis
carnibus superimpositis tegerentur;
quibus comesis, Thyestes digitos
offendit et rem comperit. Hunc ego
sensum secutus correxi ἀδρὰ κρέα
καὶ θέρμ᾽ ἐνεὶς, nam digiti erant
ἰσχνοὶ et ψυχροί, carnes vero superim-
positæ ἀδραὶ et θερμαί. Vox ἐνεὶς
duplici sensu usurpatur; quorum
alter est 'injiciens', ut quum Helena φάρμακον ἐνῆκε ποτῷ Od. 4. 232;

to die and stain with blood his native ground
1590 himself. In token, this man's impious sire
pretending festively to spend a day
of fresh-meat-food, gave mine a feast on flesh
of children; hid foot-joints and palm's end-combs,
1595 setting above them plump hot bits that gave
no sign: he forthwith ignorantly partook
and ate food costly to the race, you see.
Then when he knew th' inhuman deed, he groaned,
fell back, threw off the murder-flesh, called down
1600 a fatal doom on Pelops' line; and couched
in his curse the spurn he gave the food, and Right
concurred. For this you may behold this man
lie there. I also was this murder's right
1605 concocter: me the third child yet, a babe
in swaddling clothes, with my unhappy sire
he banished — and, when grown, the Right restored.

alter, 'immittens', hoc est fallaci specie (ἄτημα) ad aliquam rem illiciens, et hic quidem ad edendum. Origo corruptelæ erat satis probabilis literarum evanidarum αδρακακαθιμενις correctio; et certe quum primum ανδρα pro αδρα correctum erat, cetera prona erant. ἄσημα dicitur ut ἄσημος ἐργάτης, 'quem nullo signo argueres' Soph. Ant. 252.

1599. ᾤμωξεν ἄν. πίπτει δ' ἀπὸ σφαγῆς ἐρῶν libri. ἀμπίπτει corr. Canter. Deinde ἐμῶν conj. Aur., recte sprevit Karsten., σφαγῆς in σφαγὴν mutato cum Hartung.

1601. ἀρᾷ Fl. ἀρᾷ F. V. ἱρᾷ Ven. Deinde in libris sequuntur οὕτως ὀλέσθαι πᾶν τὸ Πλεισθένους γένος, quas ineptias Schutzius primus intellexit ab Æsch. non esse profectas.

1605. τρίτον γὰρ ὄντα μ' ἐπὶ δέκ' ἀθλίῳ πατρὶ libri. ἐπὶ δέκ' corruptum esse docuit Emper., id quod monitore vix egebat; nam nihil absurdius sonare potuit quam ea quæ leguntur. Hermannus ἐπίδειχ' ostendit tantum, nemini enim probavit. Melius ἐπὶ δὶ' ἀθλίοιν Ahr., ἔτι δυσαθλίῳ G. C. W. Schneider. Sed verissime statuit Enger. neque ἐπὶ neque ἔτι ap. Æsch. in trimetris sub ictu cadere. Præterea ὄντα corruptum esse repetitum ὄντα in proximo v. ostendit. Inde ego τρίτον γὰρ οὖν με παῖδ' ἔτ'. Quod autem Herm. statuit exquisitius aliquod vocabulum hic latere, id nihili est; nam is locus est ut omnia præter simplicissima quæque prorsus respuat.

11*

Καὶ τοῦδε τἀνδρὸς ἡψάμην θυραῖος ὤν,
πᾶσαν συνάψας μηχανὴν δυσβουλίας.
Οὕτω καλὸν δὴ καὶ τὸ κατθανεῖν ἐμοί,   1610
ἰδόντα τοῦτον τῆς δίκης ἐν ἔρκεσιν.

ΧΟΡΟΣ.

Αἴγισθ᾽, ὑβρίζειν ἐν κακοῖσιν οὐ σέβω·
σὺ δ᾽ ἄνδρα τόνδε φὴς ἑκὼν κατακτανεῖν,
μόνος δ᾽ ἔποικτον τόνδε βουλεῦσαι φόνον·
οὔ φημ᾽ ἀλύξειν ἐν δίκῃ τὸ σὸν κάρα   1615
δημορριφεῖς, σάφ᾽ ἴσθι, λευσίμους ἀράς.

ΑΙΓΙΣΘΟΣ.

Σὺ ταῦτα φωνεῖς νερτέρᾳ προσήμενος
κώπῃ, κρατούντων τῶν ἐπὶ ζυγῷ δορός;
γνώσει γέρων ὢν ὡς διδάσκεσθαι βαρὺ
τῷ τηλικούτῳ σωφρονεῖν εἰρημένον.   1620
Δεσμὸς δὲ καὶ τὸ γῆρας αἵ τε νήστιδες
δύαι διδάσκειν ἐξοχώταται φρενῶν
ἰατρομάντεις. Οὐχ ὁρᾷς ὁρῶν τάδε;
πρὸς κέντρα μὴ λάκτιζε, μὴ παίσας μογῇς.

ΧΟΡΟΣ.

Γύναι σύ, τοὺς ἥκοντας ἐκ μάχης μένων   1625
οἰκουρός, εὐνὴν ἀνδρὸς αἰσχύνας ἅμα,
ἀνδρὶ στρατηγῷ τόνδ᾽ ἐβούλευσας μόρον;

1612. Post hunc versum lacunæ
signa posuit Herm.
1620. Comma post τηλικούτῳ su-
stulit Karsten.

1621. δεσμὸν δὲ Fl. Ven. Corr.
in F. V.
1624. πήσας libri. παίσας Schol.
Pind. ad finem Pyth. 2. quod Herm.

And I, though absent, laid my hands on him,
and patched up all the fatal plot's design.
1610 This done, for me 'twere glorious even to die,
having seen him *lie* in Retribution's nets.

CHORUS.

Ægisthus, I dont hold with scorn in woe:
you say you killed this man designedly
and planned this piteous murder all alone:
1615 I say your head will not escape when tried,
know 't well, the people's curses hurled with stones.

ÆGISTHUS.

You say this sitting at the lower-deck oar
though the ship's main-deck men have mastery?
greybeard, you 'll know how hard it is to learn
1620 when one so old is bidden to be wise.
But chains, age, hunger-pangs, for teaching this
are the mind's most expert physician-seers.
Seeing this, do you yet not see 't? Dont kick
against the goads; lest, striking them, you smart.

CHORUS.

1625 You woman, who for men returned from fight
stayed housewife-like; shamed, too, a true man's bed,
you planned this host-commanding hero's death?

---

recte recepit. Alii Butleri conj. Deinde νέον libri. μένων corr. Wie-
πταίσας probarunt, cui verbo nihil seler.
negotii est cum stimulis. 1626. αἰσχύνουσ' libri. Corr. Herm.
  1625. γύναις σύ conj. Meineke.

ΑΙΓΙΣΘΟΣ.

Καὶ ταῦτα τἄπη κλαυμάτων ἀρχηγενῆ.
Ὀρφεῖ δὲ γλῶσσαν τὴν ἐναντίαν ἔχεις·
ὁ μὲν γὰρ ἦγε πάντ' ἀπὸ φθογγῆς χαρᾷ,   1630
σὺ δ' ἐξορίνας νηπίοις ὑλάγμασιν
ἄξει· κρατηθεὶς δ' ἡμερώτερος φανεῖ.

ΧΟΡΟΣ.

Ὡς δὴ σύ μοι τύραννος Ἀργείων ἔσει,
ὃς οὐκ, ἐπειδὴ τῷδ' ἐβούλευσας μόρον,
δρᾶσαι τόδ' ἔργον οὐκ ἔτλης αὐτοκτόνως.   1635

ΑΙΓΙΣΘΟΣ.

Τὸ γὰρ δολῶσαι πρὸς γυναικὸς ἦν σαφῶς·
ἐγὼ δ' ὕποπτος ἐχθρὸς ἦ παλαιγενής.
Ἐκ τῶν δὲ τοῦδε χρημάτων πειράσομαι
ἄρχειν πολιτῶν· τὸν δὲ μὴ πειθάνορα
ζεύξω βαρείαις, οὔτι μὴ σειραφόρον   1640
κριθῶντα πῶλον· ἀλλ' ὁ δυσφιλὴς σκότῳ
λιμὸς ξύνοικος μαλθακόν σφ' ἐπόψεται.

ΧΟΡΟΣ.

Τί δὴ τὸν ἄνδρα τόνδ' ἀπὸ ψυχῆς κακῆς
οὐκ αὐτὸς ἠνάριζες; ἀλλά νιν γυνή,
χώρας μίασμα καὶ θεῶν ἐγχωρίων,   1645

1631. ἡπίοις libri. νηπίοις corr.
Jacob., recentt.
1634. τῶδε βουλεύσας; Fl. Ven.
Corr. in V. F.
1637. ἦ libri. ἦ corr. Pors. Post

hunc versum lacunam notavit Herm.;
sed ingratum lacunarum exquiren-
darum laborem aversati sunt Meineke
et Heimsoeth.
1637. ἐκ τῶνδε libri. Corr. Jacob.

ÆGISTHUS.

These words are also harbingers of tears.
You have the contrary of Orpheus' tongue:
1630 he by his voice led all things with delight;
you by your silly howls will drive them wild
and lead them so. Mastered, you 'll look more tame.

CHORUS.

That you, my god! should be the Argives' king!
who, when you 'd planned his doom, dared not perform
1635 the killing act in person, no, not you.

ÆGISTHUS.

Enveigling clearly was a woman's part;
I was a foe from ancient date suspect.
But with his treasures I will try to rule
the people; and will yoke with heavy bands
1640 him who won't heed the driver; not as some
gay grain-fed prancer; no, unlovely Fast
that dwells with Darkness shall behold him meek.

CHORUS.

Why, with your craven soul, did you not kill
this man yourself? no, but a woman did —
1645 stain of her country and the tutelar gods —

Et equidem scire velim quomodo etiam lacunæ ope illud explicare possint.

1640. σειρασφόρον Fl. Corr. in

F. Ven., et sic Pollux 7. 24.

1641. νότῳ libri. σκότῳ Auratus.

1644. ἀλλὰ σὺν γυνή libri. Corr. Spanhem.

ἔκτειν'. Ὀρέστης ἆρά που βλέπει φάος,
ὅπως κατελθὼν δεῦρο πρευμενεῖ τύχῃ
ἀμφοῖν γένηται τοῖνδε παγκρατὴς φονεύς.

ΑΙΓΙΣΘΟΣ.

'Αλλ' ἐπεὶ δοκεῖς τάδ' ἔρδειν καὶ λέγειν γνώσει τάχα.

ΧΟΡΟΣ.

* * * * * * *

ΑΙΓΙΣΘΟΣ.

Εἶα δή, φίλοι λοχῖται, τοὔργον οὐχ ἑκὰς τόδε.   1650

ΧΟΡΟΣ.

Εἶα δή, ξίφος πρόκωπον πᾶς τις εὐτρεπιζέτω.

ΑΙΓΙΣΘΟΣ.

'Αλλὰ μὴν κἀγὼ πρόκωπος οὐκ ἀναίνομαι θανεῖν.

ΧΟΡΟΣ.

Δεχομένοις λέγεις θανεῖν σε· τὴν τύχην δ' αἱρούμεθα.

ΚΛΥΤΑΙΜΝΗΣΤΡΑ.

Μηδαμῶς, ὦ φίλτατ' ἀνδρῶν, ἄλλα δράσωμεν κακά·

1648. Interrogandi signum post φονεύς Franzius delevit. Hos sex versus post v. 1632 posuit Engerus, huc transpositis vv. 1633—5, quod sic nexus melius procedat et systematum responsio fiat simplicior. Sed hæc 'Ορέστης ἆρά που κτλ sunt ultima ea verba quæ aperte declarent Chorum omnimodis et non verbis tantum ab Oreste stare propositum habere. Et de convicio illo inertiam suam tangente Ægisthus cavillari potuit; hoc tamen de Oreste ad vim et arma instigat. Hæc et similia reputans nihil mutavi, et prox. v. incolumem reliqui.

she slew him. 'Tis for this Orestes lives,
that he by favouring fortune here restored
may be the all-conquering slayer of them both.

ÆGISTHUS.

Well, since you think fit to act thus and to speak you soon shall know.

CHORUS.

* * * * * * *

ÆGISTHUS.

1650 Come on now, my trusty guardsmen, this affair is not remote.

CHORUS.

Yes, come on; let each one fairly hold prepared his unsheathed sword.

ÆGISTHUS.

I too, with my sword unsheathed, I do not refuse to die.

CHORUS.

'Die' you say; we take the omen; for ourselves we take our lot.

CLYTEMNESTRA.

Nay, my dearest husband, let us do no further deeds of harm:

1649. Sic libri, nisi quod γνώσῃ ut solent. κοὐ λέγειν Herm. ἀλλ' ἐμ' εἰ δοκῶ τάδ' ἐρδειν κοὐ λέγειν Enger., omnibus nominibus, ut mihi videtur, sine idonea causa.

1650. Signa personarum in libris confusa in ordinem redegit Herm.

Idem unius versus lacunam ante hunc versum recte posuit.

1652. ἀλλὰ κἀγὼ μὴν libri. Corr. Pors. πρόκοπος Fl. Corr. in Ven. V.

1653. ἐρούμεθα libri. αἱρούμεθα Auratus. Certa est emendatio.

1654. δράσομεν codices. Corr. in V.

ἀλλὰ καὶ τάδ᾽ ἐξαμῆσαι πολλὰ δύστηνον θέρος·   1655
πημονῆς ἅλις δ᾽ ὑπάρχει· μηδ᾽ ἔθ᾽ αἱματώμεθα·
σώφρονος γνώμης δ᾽ ἁμαρτεῖν τὸν κρατοῦντ᾽ αἶσχος μέγα.
Στεῖχε καὶ σὺ χοὶ γέροντες πρὸς δόμους πεπρωμένους,
πρὶν παθεῖν ἄρξαι τ᾽ ἀκαίρων· χρῆν τάδ᾽ ὡς ἐπράξαμεν.
Εἰ δέ τοι μόχθων γένοιτο τῶνδ᾽ ἅλις, δεχοίμεθ᾽ ἄν,
δαίμονος χηλῇ βαρείᾳ δυστυχῶς πεπληγμένοι.   1660
Ὧδ᾽ ἔχει λόγος γυναικός, εἴ τις ἀξιοῖ μαθεῖν.

ΑΙΓΙΣΘΟΣ.

Ἀλλὰ τούσδε μοι ματαίαν γλῶσσαν ὧδ᾽ ἀπανθίσαι,
κἀκβαλεῖν ἔπη τοιαῦτα δαίμονος πειρωμένους.

ΧΟΡΟΣ.

Οὐκ ἂν Ἀργείων τόδ᾽ εἴη φῶτα προσσαίνειν κακόν.   1665

ΑΙΓΙΣΘΟΣ.

Ἀλλ᾽ ἐγώ σ᾽ ἐν ὑστέραισιν ἡμέραις μέτειμ᾽ ἔτι.

ΧΟΡΟΣ.

Οὐκ, ἐὰν δαίμων Ὀρέστην δεῦρ᾽ ἀπευθύνῃ μολεῖν.

1655. ὁ ἔρος libri. θέρος est Schutzii correctio, ab omnibus recepta.

1656. πημονῆς δ᾽ ἅλις γ᾽ ὑπάρχε· μηδὲν ἡματώμεθα libri. πημονῆς ἅλις δ᾽ Herm. ὑπάρχει et αἱματώμεθα Auratus ille, quem nemo digne laudare potuit. μηδ᾽ ἔθ᾽ Bl.

1657. Hic versus qui post v. 1663 in libris legitur, huc ab Herm. repositus est. ἁμαρτῆτον κρατοῦντα libri. ἁμαρτεῖν τὸν κρατοῦντα corr. Casaubon. Desunt verba sex mora-

rum mensuram habentia, quæ fortasse, ut in prælongo versu, supra scribebantur. Versionis meæ causa in textum recepi αἶσχος μέγα, quæ Æschylo digna suppeditavit Herm.

1658. στείχετε δ᾽ οἱ γέροντες πρὸς δόμους πεπρωμένους τούσδε libri. Quæ dedi, Franzio debentur; sed hujus correctionis rationes equidem perspectas nondum habeo. Apta est; sed veram esse nego. τούσδε delevit Scaliger; incertum an recte. Cf. Soph.

1655 to have reaped ev'n these, so many, yields a miserable crop.

There is suffering in abundance: let us spill no further blood.

For a prince to miss the prudent counsel is a great disgrace.

Go, both you and these the elders, to the homes assigned by Fate,

ere they rue, and broach untimely deeds: 'twas fated as we fared.

Sure, if this might be enough of trouble we would acquiesce,

1660 by the daemon's painful talon sadly torn as we have been.

If 'tis worth one's while to listen, thus a woman's word directs.

ÆGISTHUS.

Shall I brook it that they scatter on me silly talk like leaves,

and give vent to speech of this sort, braving what the god may send?

CHORUS.

1665 It would not be like the Argives at a coward's feet to cringe.

ÆGISTHUS.

On some future day I'll bring you yet to your account for this·

CHORUS.

No, if fortune guide Orestes hither to return again.

O. R. 637.

1659. πρὶν παθεῖν. ἔρξαντες καιρὸν
Fl. πρὶν παθεῖν. ἔρξαντα καιρὸν Ven.
V. F., qui meliorem lectionem præbent. Inde ego, fere nulla mutati-
one, ἄρξαι τ' ἀκαίρων, quod dicitur
ut ἄρχειν ἀδίκων χειρῶν. Sed totus
hic locus adeo corruptus est ut
desperatus jure dicatur. Non amo
insolens illud πεπρωμένους quod glossam corruptam olet ad χρῆν τάδ'

adscriptam. Deinde ἐπραξάμην Ven.
Proximo autem versu ἅλις γ' ἐχοίμεθ'
ἄν libri. Corr. Martin. Ceterum et
τοι in τῳ mutandum esse videtur.
1660. χολῇ Fl. V. χηλῇ Ven. F.;
nihil enim ineptius voce χολῇ, 'bile
petiti', quod Paleius notavit.
1663. ὁ̃αίμονας libri. Corr. Casaubon.
1665. προσαίνειν Fl. V. Corr. in
Ven. F.

ΑΙΓΙΣΘΟΣ.

Οἶδ' ἐγὼ φεύγοντας ἄνδρας ἐλπίδας σιτουμένους.

ΧΟΡΟΣ.

Πρᾶσσε, πιαίνου, μιαίνων τὴν δίκην, ἐπεὶ πάρα.

ΑΙΓΙΣΘΟΣ.

Ἴσθι μοι δώσων ἄποινα τῆςδε μωρίας χάριν.   1670

ΧΟΡΟΣ.

Κόμπασον θαρσῶν, ἀλέκτωρ ὥςτε θηλείας πέλας.

ΚΛΥΤΑΙΜΝΗΣΤΡΑ.

Μὴ προτιμήσῃς ματαίων τῶνδ' ὑλάγμαθ', ὡς ἐγὼ
καὶ σὺ θήσομεν κρατοῦντε τῶνδε δωμάτων καλῶς.

1671. θαρρῶν libri. Corr. Pors. ὥσπερ libri. Corr. Scaliger et Canter. 1672. ὑλαγμάτων libri, ceteris omissis; sed Heathius satis probabiliter voc. ἐγὼ ex schol. F. revocavit, et ὑλάγμαθ' ὡς corr. Rauchenstein, ut

ÆGISTHUS.

I know well that men in exile on their hopes are wont to feed.

CHORUS.

Thrive on, feed thee fat, defiling justice, since thou hast the chance.

ÆGISTHUS.

1670 Be assured that you shall pay me reckoning for this foolishness.

CHORUS.

Crow *and chuckle* fearing nothing, like a cock that's near the hen.

CLYTEMNESTRA.

Dont regard these silly creatures' yelpings past their worth, for I,
I and thou will fairly settle, as its sovereigns, this domain.

---

verbo προτιμήσης constructio sua
servaretur.
  1673. Et huic versui pes unus

deest; cujus vestigia Heathius et
Canterus in schol. F., ut ipsis vi-
sum est, consecuti, καλῶς addiderunt.

COMMENTARY.

1—39. Prologue. Time: night. The scene probably represented moon and stars, the belvedere of the palace of the Atreidæ at Argos, and the watchman, armed, standing by a watch-fire. At v. 22 a new light is seen somewhere to the right, on Mt. Arachnæum. The watchman makes his exit by stairs leading to the interior of the house, and this scene is changed at v. 39.

1. ἀπαλλαγήν. The first word which indicates the ἦθος, 'discharge', 'relief'.

2. φρουρᾶς. Genitive after μῆκος, which word of time gives αἰτῶ the force of a perfect; so ἦν to κάτοιδα v. 4. The Gramm. distinguish ἔτειος 'lasting a year' from ἐπέτειος 'occurring once a year' See v. 1016. ἄγκαθεν = ἀνέκαθεν is 'away on the top'; They wrong the poet who construe 'head on hand, like a dog' and Herm. did not intend this; but 'with the body raised and propped on the arm bent at the elbow, the forearm lying on the ground'. Even so, the simile of the dog is ludicrous. κυνὸς δίκην is correctly explained by the Sch. 'because of its watchfulness and fidelity'.

4. The soldier speaks: 'a host of constellations who marshal themselves by night'. The distinction ἄστρον, 'sidus', and ἀστήρ, 'stella' is always observed in correct writers.

6. All the ancient Greeks from Orpheus to Aristotle, not excepting Epicharm. acc. to Menand. Mein. p. 196, believed the sun moon and stars to be divine persons, 'animales deos' Apul. De Dogm. Plat. I. 11; Plut. de Pl. Phil. passim. Lucretius l. 5 proves that they are not. More literally 'showing themselves conspicuously in æther'.

10 κρατεῖ = νικᾷ = vincit = 'proves'; so v. 1364, κατθανεῖν
κρατεῖ 'death carries the day', like μολεῖν ἐνίκησεν, the
φύλαξ Soph. Ant. 233. ἀνδρόβουλον is 'giving her opinion (βουλὴ v. 1358) with masculine assurance and force
of reasoning'.

14. Literally: 'for fear (of falling asleep) is my comrade (next
man to the right or left) so that my eyelids do not re-
solutely fall-to with sleep'. Here we have the soldier
again: if θάρσος (about falling asleep) were his comrade,
then he would come to an engagement at once; but with
only fear to support him he avoids it. ὑπνομαχῶ in
Aristoph. is 'fight against sleep'. But for the word φόβος
it might be proposed to take συμβαλεῖν in another of its
meanings 'come to a league or covenant with'. But this
is peculiarly the part of a general.

17. Of all the possible meanings of ἀντίμολπον it seems best to
take it as formed on the analogy of ἀντίρροπος 'which
opposes song to sleep' with an allusion to ἀντίτομον wich
appears to mean 'a medicinal herb either cut out of the
ground or chopped up as a remedy against'. But μνήμην
ἀντίμισθον Suppl. 270 is 'memory in place of fee' and
according to this we should expect μολπῆς ἀνθύπνου.
ἀντίμηλον, formed (by the Ed.) like ἀντίφερνον v. 406,
would mean 'slipping in this probe-like cure for sleep'.
But we want a cutting instrument used as if he were in
a swoon or a lethargy. Ἐντέμνων. The meaning 'chop-
ping up herbs or roots upon', given by Stanley and all
editors, seems to be without any support whatsoever
except their authority. It should have been ἐπιπάσσων,
see Suid. s. v. πόλιον. τέμνειν is 'to lance' Arist. Probl.
1. 32 etc. ἐντομαὶ are 'incisions' or 'punctures' Hie-
rocles (p. 280 Dacier.) ἄκη τομαῖα Supp. 268, Choëph.
537 are 'effectual cures by amputation'; cf. ἰατρὸς ἀπο-
τομος in Plut. Apophth. Catonis 'a surgeon fond of
desperate remedies'. τομαὶ Pind. P. 3. 53 are punctures'
or 'amputations'. ἐντέμνειν σφάγιον is 'to make an in-
cision in a victim for the purpose of examining the inwards'.
ἄκος itself is κυρίως ἡ διὰ σιδήρου θεραπεία E. M. s. v.
ἀκεύμενος. Hierocl., Iambl., Porphyr. often allude to the
surgeon's knife, seldom to medicines. Add that the watchman ought here to say nothing about song, which is fully

expressed before. A few trials will soon convince that it
is impossible to translate the line fairly and not absurdly,
and that it is incredible that it should have proceeded from
the poet in its present form.

22. Lit. 'hail, Lamp, son of Night'; the salutation is couched
in the usual form, e. gr. Eur. Med. 665 ὦ χαῖρε, παῖ
Πανδίονος. Αἰγεῦ.

23. χορῶν κατάστασιν. Instead of the present φυλακῶν κατά-
στασις.

26. σημαίνειν τοξῶς is the usual military phrase. See Suid. s. v.
τοξόν.

30. Lit. 'is clearly seen reporting'; 'beams' in the Trans. is a
verb.

32. The meaning is: 'I will take the master's lucky throws as
my own' i. e. lay my money on them, and be quite sure
that such as are good for him will bring me luck. The
allusion is to some game at dice, perhaps like backgammon.

35. βαστάσαι. See Suid. s. v. διασηκῶσαι. But here it is simply
a soldier's word, which he usually applied to the bearing
of arms, his spear or shield.

36. Besides the passages cited by Schutz and Blomf. there is
βοῦν ἀφωνίας ἐπὶ τὴν γλῶσσαν βεβλημένοι Philost. V. S.,
Scopelianus; and οὐδ' εἰ βοῦς μοι, τὸ λεγόμενον, φθέγ-
ξαιτο Alciphr. 2. 4. 3. The Spartans (Plut. Instt. Lac.
25) sacrificed an ox to Ares after a victory gained by
artifice, and the noisy cock when victorious by open force.
It is evident, therefore, that the ox was an emblem of
silence. Compare παχὺς γὰρ ὗς ἔκειτ' ἐπὶ στόμα Menand.
Fr. p. 10 Mein. which is only a variation to express the
swinish gluttony, not the bovine silence, of Dionysius.

38. ἑκὼν is correctly explained by Paley.

40. Parodos. Time: morning. Scene: the front of the palace
of the Atreidæ at Argos.

42. This line, in apposition with μέγας ἀντίδικος, expresses
the Athenian view of the paradox that two kings at
Sparta should be the μόναρχος of the state; a monarchical
form with two kings.

44. Hes. Op. 427. Since the adoption of words and phrases
from Hesiod is so remarkable a feature of this play, the
reader will be reminded of it even in the less important
instances.

48. ὥςτ' αἰγυπιοὶ μεγάλα κλάζοντε μαχέσθην — ὡς οἱ (Hercules and Cycnus) κεκλήγοντες ἐπ' ἀλλήλοισιν ὄρουσαν Hes. Sc. 405. 412.

50. ἐκπατίοις 'which make them leave their ordinary path of flight'. So Bellerophontes in his frenzy πάτον ἀνθρώπων ἀλεείνων Il. ζ. 202.

51. ὕπατοι takes the gen. through its positive ὑπέρ. Cf. 'propius montem' Sall. J. 49 etc. 'Le Vaillant saw at an *immense height* a flock of Vultures (the Oricou) gradually descending in *concentric circles* (curves?) and seeming to come *out of the vault of heaven*'. Bree's History of the Birds of Europe. περιφερὲς δὲ ἦν τὸ πτῆμα τῶν οἰωνῶν Suid. s. v. πτῆμα. The parallelism is very close in the words ἐκπατίοις. λεχέων, ἐρ. ἐρεσσόμενοι. δεμνιοτήρη. The Greeks sail far away from home because the partner of Menelaus' bed is lost.

55. Lit. 'some *one who goes by the name of* Apollo etc.' Observe the caution of a Pythagorean in mentioning the name of a god.

57. τῶνδε μετοίκων are, of course, the young birds which have been carried away from home, like Helen. So the Schol. It is gen. after Ἐρινύν.

63. γυῖα—πόδας καὶ χεῖρας Il. 5. 122. So the Scholl. passim.

64. Alluding to the Homeric description γνὺξ δ' ἔριπ' οἰμώξας Il. 5. 68, 309, etc.

65. and here to passages like Il. 13. 162. ἐν καυλῷ ἐάγη δολιχὸν δόρυ.

69. ὑποκαίων. ὑπὸ has the force of ὕστερον. Weil compares Hdt. 3. 159 ἵνα σφι γένεα ὑπεγίνηται.

70. The best interpretation hitherto current is based on Soph. Ant. 1007 where the unwillingness of the fire of a sacrifice to burn is an omen of evil. But this is only a sign of displeasure at something which has been done before; assuredly the sacrifice itself is no cause of intense wrath. That interpretation, therefore, is false. ἄπυρα ἱερὰ are acts in which the gods and their laws are disregarded, as they would be when a sacrifice was offered and no θυηλαὶ, ἀπαρχαὶ or κατάργματα burnt in their honour. The Orphic code was promulgated under divine sanction, and every infraction was an act of irreligion. ἄπυρα ἱερὰ are the same as ἄθυτα ἱερὰ Soph. Fr. 601. Suid. s. v.

COMMENTARY. 179

ἀθύτους. In the case of Paris there are no sacrifices at all, good or bad, but an act in defiance of the law of Zeus, the rape of Helen. Clytemnestra is δύσθεος γυνὴ Cho. 46, the unjust man is ἄθεος Eum. 540. So Virg. in the often-quoted line 'discite justitiam moniti et non temnere divos' 'learn not to defy the gods by injustice'. In Æsch. all unjust acts are ἄπυρα ἱερά.

71. ἀτενεῖ τε νόῳ Hes. Th. 661. ἀ in ἀτενὴς represents ἄγαν acc. to Donaldson.

72. ἀτίτης is 'which does not pay' and here 'which pays no military service' as being ὑπὲρ τὸν κατάλογον which phrase was παροιμία ἐπὶ τῶν γεγηρακότων Suid. s. v. ἀτίτας Eum. 257 is 'without paying for his crime'.

75. Paraphrase of Hes. Op. 113 in so far as he describes old age with reference to the feet and arms. Comp. Anth. 6. 25 γηραλέον νῦν ἀντὶ πανοπλίης βάκτρον ἀμειψάμενος. The warriors, on the other hand, apply full-grown strength to the spear.

76. μυελὸς is 'the blood'. In Hom. Od. β. 290 ἄλφιτα is μυελὸς ἀνδρῶν because it makes the blood.

78. 'Ares is not an indigenous god in a child's breast' οὐκ ἔνι χώρᾳ is for ἐπιχώριος. ἐγχώριος. or ἔγχωρος· ὁ ἐν τῇ χώρᾳ ὤν E. M. s. v. So Schol. M. τῷ τόπῳ ἐκείνῳ.

80. From Hes. Op. 531 τρίποδι βροτῷ ἶσοι.

82. The Homeric Ὄνειρος makes easy the comparison of a person to a dream. Hopes, the fancies of poets, and the musings of lovers are ἐγρηγορότων ἐνύπνια.

95. ἀδόλοισι implies a fear of δόλος in the mind of the speakers. παρ. 'blanditiæ' Prop. 5. 6. 72. See Soph. Fr. 340.

96. πελάνῳ. λέγεται δὲ πέλανος καὶ το πεπηγὸς καὶ ἐξηραμμένον ὁπῶδες δάκρυον οἷον λιβανωτός, κόμμι Suid. s. v. For the torches compare Aristæn. 1. 10 fin. ἐκάοντο δὲ κατὰ δώματα δαΐδες ἐκ λιβανωτοῦ συγκείμεναι, ὥστε ἅμα κάεσθαι καὶ θυμιᾶσθαι καὶ παρέχειν τὸ φῶς μετ' εὐωδίας.

103. From Hes. Op. 795. See Crit. Notes. θυμοβόρος· ἡ τὴν ψυχὴν διαφθείρουσα Suid. s. v. is very like a scholium on this passage written when the text was as yet uncorrupted.

105. ἐκτελὴς Hes. Op. 464 is 'having arrived at full growth and mature strength', the τέλος of ib. 472. οἱ τέλειοι at Sparta were married men in the flower of their age

12*

180 COMMENTARY.

Plut. Apoph. Leon. 15. See alo Plut. Instt. Lac. 15.
θεόθεν. From. Hes. Op. 660.

106. μολπᾶν ἀλκᾷ is the ἀκάματος αὐδὴ of Hes. Th. 39.
107. σύμφυτος is the αὐτοφυής of Hes. Th. 813 'grown in one
piece'; αἰὼν σημαίνει τὸν τῆς ζώης χρόνον E. M. s. v. δήν.
Literally, then, poetic power is here said to be one being
with their term of life, so that the might of song abides
with them in their old age. Soph. makes the poetic
faculty and the term of life foster-children Fr. 768 οὐκ
ἔστι γῆρας τῶν σοφῶν ἐν οἷς ὁ νοῦς θείᾳ ξύνεστιν ἡμέρᾳ
τεθραμμένος which seems to mean:
those gifted ones have no old age in whom
dwells genius nursed with days ordained by god.
And so Æsch. at 67 years of age is now exhibiting the
Agamemnon.
110. Hes. Sc. 50 οὐκέθ' ἅμα φρονέοντε· κασιγνήτω γε μὲν ἤστην.
111. πράκτωρ is properly 'a collector of taxes' Suid. s. v. πράκτωρ and φορολόγος.
113. Pythagoras recognised divination from dreams as previsions
of the soul, from fortuitous words (κληδόνες), from birds,
and the smoke of incense, Diog. L. V. Pyth., not from
sacrifices Plut. de Pl. Phil. 5. 1. This latter fact seems
to explain Æsch. Sept. 24 ἐν ὠσὶ νωμῶν καὶ φρεσὶν
πυρὸς δίχα.
115. πρὸς δὲ τὴν διαφορὰν τῶν ἀετῶν νομίζειν χρὴ καὶ τὰ ἀπο-
τελέσματα γίνεσθαι Artemidorus 2. 20. The white-tailed
eagle is the representative of Agamemnon; and the white
tail seems to forebode death to him at the end of this
successful expedition; see ib. 2. 3 τὸ δὲ μέλαν ἱμάτιον
σωτηρίαν προσημαίνει, and for the passage generally ib.
2. 20 ἀετὸν ἰδεῖν ἐπὶ ὑψηλοτάτῳ τόπῳ ἀγαθὸν τοῖς ἐπὶ
πρᾶξιν ὁρμῶσι.
116. ἵκταρ Hes. Th. 691 where the Schol. ἐκ τοῦ σύνεγγυς. ὡς
ἀπὸ τοῦ ἱκνοῦμαι—χρῶνται δὲ οἱ τραγικοὶ τῇ λέξει.
120. βλάπτειν with gen. occurs three times in Theognis, vv.
223, 705, 938, in this sense of 'debarring'. βλαβέντα
is, of course, the mother-hare and her φέρμα (Æsch.
Supp. 690) 'the young she is still carrying'.
122. First Stasimon. κενός· συνετός, σώφρων ἢ φρόνιμος Suid.
s. v. Ἴσοι in the end of a line Hes. Op. 531. In Homer
Menelaus is more merciful than Agam. but not less brave:

how readily he accepts the challenge of Paris, and is
the only one of all the bravest to close without hesitation
with Hector's, Il. 7. 96. It is suggested in the critical
note that δέ, in such a position, was pronounced ἰδέ.
δέ, ἰδέ and ἠδέ seem to be different forms of the same
word as its pronunciation was varied in an age when
there was little or no writing. (So ἔην, ἤην, ἦα. ἔα, ἔον, ἦ,
for the first person imperfect of εἰμί, preceded ἦν, the
form fixed by writing.) The meaning of each was 'likewise' Latin 'item'. The ι in ἰδέ, and i in 'item'
and 'idem' are probably the neuter of ἵ the nominative
(in E. M. and a Fragment of Sophocles) of the so-
called reflexive pronoun, which is not reflexive in the
early Greek language. The fixed form δέ cannot stand
first, probably because the ι in order to be lost in pronunciation required a word to be pronounced before it
without a pause. Perhaps a similar reason may be given
for the fact that que (itque, idque) quidem (iquidem,
equidem), and the rest, cannot stand first. So 'nam'
had an original form 'enim' which was pronounced 'nim'
in conversation, but was used to complete a dactyl in
poetry. μέν must not stand first for the same reason;
it had a vowel sound before it, as in ἠμέν. 'et' is probably the first part of an original form of which 'que'
is the last; thus 'i', the pronoun and 'que', which seems
to be the Sanscrit 'cha', would form ique, idque, itque
or etque 'it too'; and so 'et' lost 'que' by collision
with the following word, and 'que' loses 'et' through a
preceding word. Nevertheless 'et' is sometimes second
word in poetry. So there seems to be no reason why
ἰδέ should not be sounded in some places where we now
read δέ. But in twenty-four instances of its occurrence
in the Homeric poems, and the four in Hesiod none (in
'The Works and Days) it is always first word. Now
ἠδέ, a much more artificial form, occurs too often for
the instances to be all given in Seber: and the ὲ suffers
elision probably because it does not belong to the root,
and is only a sound, with no meaning, added to help
the metre like the Sanscrit 'hi'. The ἠ in ἠδέ arose
through hyperthesis of the ε in ἰδέ, and ἰδέ cannot suffer
elision because δέ is the root, possibly the same as

Sanscrit 'tu'. In Soph. Ant. 969 we must either read
ἰδὲ Θρηκῶν, or pronounce ἰδ' ὁ corrupt. ἰδ' requires correction also in some very recent imitations of Homeric
verse. This rare occurrence of ἰδὲ as compared with
ἠδὲ the less likely form, the frequent occurrence of
δέ τε in epic poetry in places where the τε is so hard
to explain, and the existence of passages like μουνογενὴς
δὲ πάις εἴη Hes. Op. 374 (for the ις in πάις is repeatedly
short in Homer, and is long in only one peculiar passage Il. χ 492, 497) lead to the conclusion that the
Alexandrine editors or their predecessors removed ἰδὲ
from every place in which the metre allowed δὲ to stand,
from such as Hes. Op. 510, for example, ὄηρες δὲ φρίσ-
σουσι and a hundred like it. The result is that ἰδὲ
occurs only as first word, for of course they could not
substitute δὲ where ἰδὲ stood first in a clause. The pe-
culiarities of ἰδὲ besides that already mentioned, that its
ὲ is not elided, are (1) that it has the digamma (the
readily evanescing ν and ς being sometimes placed before
it), and this digamma was derived from ἰ, as before
suggested; (2) that it makes the two short syllables of
a dactyl seven times out of twenty-eight instances in
which the particle occurs in Homer and Hesiod, so that
the statement in Liddell and Scott's lexicon requires cor-
correction, and (3) in the remaining twenty one (in six
after τε) it is used to complete a dactyl and take the
arsis before two consonants or a liquid; and it is so
used in the present passage, if the Editor's suspicion
be correct.   ·

The apparent anomaly involved in the elision of ε in
δὲ whereas ἰδὲ does not suffer elision is, perhaps, capable
of explanation in the following way. Ϝιδ' would represent
only the pronoun Ϝι, as in the Latin; but δ' with the
slight vowel-sound which remains after elision, or by a
synizesis with the following vowel, would be a sufficient
representative of the conjunction. It is still easier to
account for 'nam' standing first; but this subject is
interminable. Enough has been said to explain the Editor's reasons, and to show that as there is no reason
in the nature of things why ἰδὲ should not stand second,
so there are several reasons why it should be replaced

as second word in many passages where we now read
δέ, and this will have been learnt from a consideration
of this passage, because of the exact correspondence of
the choral odes of Æschylus.

123. ἐδάη = οἰωνοὺς ἔκρινεν Hes. Op. 799 and 826. To intrude
a little on the province of philologists, the roots δα
'divide' and κριν 'separate' appear to approach very
closely in meaning. So ἐδάη means 'was made to see
them distinct from everything which they were not' and
this is to leard what a thing really is so far as it can
be known.

126. ἀγρεῖ. 'bindeth' in the Trans. is the hawker's word for
'seizes'.

129. κτήνη is a fit word for property which consisted chiefly in
cattle; (that of Augeas is κτῆσις Theocr. 25. 57. and
κτέανα v. 109) especially at a time when the value of
a thing was estimated in cattle. In Hesiod the men of
the golden age are ἀφνειοὶ μήλοισι, and the ἀνδρῶν ἡρώων
θεῖον γένος fight μήλων ἕνεκ' Οἰδιποδάο Op. 119, 162.

135. The syntax is: 'for Artemis disliking these eagles as much
as she loves their young victims prays (Zeus) to fulfil
the omens which please the latter' i. e. please by avenging them. For ὅσσον—τόσσον, compare Il. χ. 42 εἴθε
θεοῖσι φίλος τοσσόνδε γένοιτο ὅσσον ἐμοί. οἴκῳ of the Mss.
was first condemned by Scaligen.

137. αὐτότοκον. It is impossible to preserve the parellelism in
the English version. All of these words apply also to
Iphigenia, when αὐτότοκον will mean 'begotten by himself', i. e. by Agam.

144. αἰτεῖ 'begs of Zeus', like the gods in Homer.

145. Hes. Op. 12 τὴν μέν κεν ἐπαινήσειε νοήσας, ἡ δ' ἐπιμωμητή.
κατὰ in κατάμομφα in its distributive sense. φήνη, properly the lammer-geier, is εἶδος ὀρνέου ἴσον ἀετῷ Suid. s. v.

151. All these epithets are by contrast; neither could be said
of the hare.

152. σύμφυτον is as before, v. 107. οὐ δεισήνορα applies to Clytemnestra.

155. μῆνις δέ ἐστιν ὀργή τις πεπαλαιωμένη, ἐπίκοτος καὶ ἐπιτη-
ρητική. Diog. L. 7. 113.

156. ἀπέκλαγξεν κλάζω, Lat. 'clango', is properly said of birds
of omen, and here of Calchas as if he were one.

160. Ζεὺς is nominative by a sort of inverse attraction to ὅςτις, for the thought to be expressed is 'Zeus, and not Artemis, nor any of these vulgar gods, none, in truth, but the one living god, is he whom if man worships from the heart, he (man) will hit the sum of wisdom'. His real name is known only to the immortals, Orph. Fr. 3.

163. προςεικάσαι is 'compare either alternative to a preponderating scale'.

164. σταθμᾶσθαι is to put weights σταθμία, σταθμά into a scale πλάστιγξ. here 'to put opposite arguments into the opposite scales, philosophy and priestcraft'. χωρὶς γὰρ τὰ τῶν Φιλοσόφων καὶ τῶν ἱερέων ὁρίσματα Damasc. cited by Suidas.

167. Οὐρανός, as in Hesiod and Orph. Fr. Ined. 20. (C. Tauchnitz.)

168. βρύειν takes a dat by preference; a gen. pretty frequently; and an acc. of a neuter adj. as βρύειν ἀγαθά Hes.

171. Κρόνος, as in Hes. and Orph. Fr. l. c. With τριακτῆρος compare Orph. F. 7 καὶ κρατεροί περ ἐόντες ἀμείνονος ἀντιάσαντες, the Titans and Zeus. πρὶν ὢν in the line above is 'as being the Zeus (from ζῆν, Plato) of that time'.

178. κυρίως, properly of a law or a judicial decision.

179. We are made eye-witnesses, as it were, of a dream of the Eum. v. 94 foll. This prophetic faculty of the soul in sleep seems to have been universally believed by Greek philosophers, except perhaps Democritus who refers them to εἴδωλα and κινήσεις. For the Pythagorean view see Phot. Ex. V. Pyth. 5, Iambl. V. Pyth. p. 51 Artemid. 4. 2. With Aristotle (de Div. in Somno) dreams are not θεόπεμπτα because οἱ τυχόντες, καὶ τὰ ἄλλα ζῷα have them; rather they are δαιμόνια, from dæmons. So with the Pythagoreans they came from dæmons and heroes. "During the Algerian campaigns it was observed that privation of food, thirst, and fatigue singularly predisposed the soldier to have the most extraordinary dreams; the soul was gifted with a power of clairvoyance which would be incredible if not attested by facts". All the Year Round; Aug. 24. 1861. Epicurus, acc. to Lucr. 5. 1161 foll., thought that men got their notion of the

existence of gods from seeing their real forms in dreams. This belief in gods is the strangest thing in that philosophy; for by parity of reason there are centaurs and chimæras. Diog. L. p. 235 V. Epic. puts it rather differently ἐναργὴς γὰρ αὐτῶν ἡ γνῶσις 'men's knowledge of gods and their nature is a manifest fact'. στάζει seems to allude to the first drops of a shower. πρὸ καρδίας is πρὸ ὀμμάτων (Cho. 817) τῆς καρδίας, or rather the heart is the eye of the soul in sleep. Comp. ὃν λόγον ἔχει ὄψις ἐν ὀφθαλμοῖς τοῦτον ἔχειν νοῦν ἐν ψυχῇ a paraphrase from Aristotle Top. by Alex. Aphrod. ap. Suid.

180. See Macrob. S. S. p. 11 (Gron.) 'somnium proprium est quum se quis patientem aliquid somniat'; ibid. p. 31 'hanc habere legem omnia somnia ut de adversis oblique aut denuntient, *aut minentur*, aut moneant'.

182. Dæmons in Æsch. are the dæmons described by Hesiod, as left by Zeus as his representatives and agents when he and the other divinities were compelled by the sins of the iron age to leave the world. So Plato in Apul. de D. Pl. 1. 12 'dæmonas vero ministros deorum arbitratur (et) hominum interpretes si quid a deis velint'; They were the spirits of the men of the golden age.

183. Lit. 'by right of power seated', on the vice-regal thrones in which they were installed by Zeus.

186. Blaming not the seer when called upon to slay his child, but he did blame the seer when he was told to send back Chryseis.

187. 'Conspiring with *the winds of* chances as they struck upon *his course*'.

190. E. M. s. vv. ἁμαρτῇ and δηρὸν· ἡ πέρα, τῆς πέρας, τῇ πέρᾳ, τὴν πέραν.

191. Hes. Op. 649, and for the next line ib. 505. With δύσορμος comp. λιμὴν εὔορμος Hes. Sc. 207.

196. παλιμμήκη. See Suid. s. v. παλινοσκίῳ· τὸ γὰρ πάλιν ἐπίτασιν δηλοῖ. Rather 'long time and then long time again'.

208. ἄγαλμα· ἐφ' ᾧ τις ἀγάλλεται καὶ χαίρει E. M. s. v. Ajax is ἀ. πολέμου, Socrates ἀ. σοφίας, Athens ἀ. δαιμόνων, Helen ἀ. πλούτου. 'what one claims as one's own with pride and joy'.

210. The three wrong things are sufficiently indicated in the Trans. Comp. Cho. 338 where three evils are expressed

in τάφος, ἱκέτας, φυγάδας and there is a play in ἀτρί-
ακτος 'not without the complete number three'. τῶν
τριῶν κακῶν ἓν was a proverb Suid. s. v.

216. περιοργῶς (fr. περιοργὴς Suid. where the acc. is rightly
given) means 'with yearning which transcends every other,
even that to save the maiden'.

217. Hes. Sc. 447.

218. He puts on the collar of necessity when he persuades himself that it is god's will, θέμις, that he should slay his
child. This line is based on Theognis 195 ἐπεὶ κρατερή
μιν ἀνάγκη ἐντύει. ἥ τ' ἀνδρὸς τλήμονα θῆκε νόον. ἀνάγκας
ἔντεα .Pind. P. 4. 418.

219. τροπαία in Arist. Probl. 26. 5 is the reverse of a wind
blowing off land. Here it is a change of feeling, the
desire to save his child, into the opposite, the desire
to kill her.

220. ἄναγνος is the 'improbus' of Hor. Sat. 2. 3. 200.

221. Lit. 'he thereupon adopted in its stead the all-daring spirit'.

223. παρακοπὰ is 'religious fanaticism' which ever leads men
into the greatest absurdities and violations of the plainest
natural laws; exactly as it is put by Lucretius 1. init.
πρωτοπήμων 'harbinger of suffering' is an unusual cpd.
πρωτοπαγὴς Il. 5. 194 is an epithet of a chariot whose
new-made parts, νευτευχῆ, would be put together for
the first time or near the first, if it were used.

224. The preposterous thing is the killing an innocent woman
as a help in taking vengeance for the abduction of one
still alive who was not innocent.

231. θεμιστοπόλοι βασιλῆες Hes. Fr. p. 314 Heins.

232. The words *father, priestly-slayers, after prayer* are a triplet
like that at v. 209. ἀόζοις, from the same root as
ἀοσσητήρ, is explained by μάγειροι in Suid., and ὑπη-
ρέται in E. M.

233. The χίμαιρα was the proper offering to Artemis ἀγροτέρα
Ael. V. H. 2., 25, and the well-known passage in Xen.
Anab. 'vitula' Hor.

237. ἀρχία οἴκοις Eur. Med. 608.

238. Lit. 'by force and mute energy of bridles'. See Suid. s.v. φιμοῖ.

239. ἀπέδυ τὰς τῶν ἐφεστρίδων βαφάς. Philost. V. Sap. Isaeus.

241. I. e. 'a look of loving welcome to pity if it would come'.

242. 'as in painted forms' i. e. with mute expression.

244. But now might not speak. ἀταύρωτος follows up the common comparison of a maiden to a heifer.

245. φίλος is 'loving', φίλιος 'loved'; with exceptions. The third libation was to Zeus Σωτήρ, the Life-preserver.

246. πα.ὼν γὰρ ὕμνος εὐχαριστήριος Suid. τιμᾶν, τίειν v. 706, and σεβίζειν often mean 'to honour a thing by performing it'. Comp. Hes. Op. 16 ἔριν τιμῶσι.

247. This reads as if the old men had gone to Aulis; but the opposition is only between relating and not relating, none of the things described having been actually seen by the Chorus, except the start from Argos.

250. Δίκα. 'scire nefas', 'nec scire fas est', 'si mortalis ultra fas trepidat' Hor.

254. ''t will come' i. e. the knowledge of to-morrow's events will come with to-morrow's light. The nom. is τὸ μέλλον.

355. πέλοιτο ὡς θέλει seems to be a variation of the common form 'may you have all you desire' which the Pythagoreans changed to ὅσα ἂν θεὸς θέλῃ.

256. ἄγχιστον is translated by the Ed. as being nearly equal to ·ἐπιφανές. Agam. is the supreme ruler, but he is absent, and his power is not felt. Clyt. is the regent, and her power is displayed by acts which are seen and felt. So Suppl. 1036 δύναται γὰρ Διὸς ἄγχιστα σὺν Ἥρᾳ.

257. ἔλεγε δὲ οὗτος τείχη εἶναι τῆς Σπάρτης τοὺς νέους Plut. Apoph. Lac. Antalc. 7. χώρας λέλειπται μοῦνος ἀντὶ σοῦ φύλαξ Chorus, of Creon Soph. O. T. 1418.

265. εὐφρόνης. The euphemistic name of Night. So in Hes. Op. 558 'the long festive nights of winter'.

267. Comp. Lysander's despatch ἑαλώκαντι ταὶ Ἀθᾶναι.

271. 'accuses you' of being well pleased.

275. The irreligious soul, from a Pythagorean point of view.

276. 'unfledged' 'inflated'; quite different metaphors, which is a sign of excited feeling.

280. Lit. 'and who of messengers could attain this speed'. But Prof. Karsten's correction should be adopted, ἀγγέλλων.

281. There were three torch-races at Athens, Προμήθεια, Ἡφαί-στεια, Παναθήναια. Suid. s. v. λαμπάδος.

283. Juno's stages, Il. 14, 225, are Olympus, Athos, Lemnos, Imbros, Ida.

286. From Hes. Th. 781. ἀγγελίη πωλεῖται ἐπ' εὐρέα νῶτα

θαλάσσης. νωτίζειν seems to be formed like κελητίζειν. Comp. νῶθ᾽ ἵππων ἐπιβάντες Hes. Sc. 286. ἵππων νώτοισιν ἐφήμενος Theogn. 249. Several of the words in this celebrated passage are chosen for their suggestiveness: Ἴδη. ἰδεῖν; Ἑρμαῖον v. 283, ἕρμα, the string of lights; Ἀθῷον v. 285, without damage; Μακίστου v. 289 the stage of greatest length, μάκιστον σέλας Æsch. Fr. 283 Did.; Εὐρίπου v. 292, ῥιπὴ fair beam; Γοργῶπιν v. 302, Αἰγίπλαγκτον v. 303, αἰγὶς and perhaps αἴγλη; μεγαίρειν v. 304 Megaris, which country the light is then traversing; πώγωνα v. 306, Τροιζήνιος λιμὴν οὕτω καλούμενος Suid. s. v.; πρῶν᾽ v. 307, Πρῶν was the hill on the side of which Hermione stood Paus. 2. 34. No doubt there are others which the Ed. has been unable to detect.

288. This passage is a direct imitation of the following: ὁ δ᾽ ἄρ᾽ ἐκ δίνης ἀνορούσας, ἤϊξεν πεδίοιο ποσὶ κραιπνοῖσι πέτεσθαι Hom. Il. 21. 245, where ἤϊξεν stand first in a verse. Compare also ibid. 302 τοῦ δ᾽ ὑψόσε γούνατ᾽ ἐπήϊα ἀίσσοντος, and ἐμμανεῖ σκίρτηματι ᾇσσον Prom. V. 676, where ᾇσσον is again first word. In Persæ 470 ᾔσ᾽ is the reading of M., most of the other Mss. have ἤϊξ᾽.

295. Heath must grow to a much larger size in Greece than with us, as is evident from Theocr. 5. 64 δρυτόμος ξυλοχίσδεται τὰς ἐρείκας. E. M. s. v. ἐρείκω. ἐρείκη εἶδος δένδρου εὐχερῶς σχιζομένου· γέντο δ᾽ ἐρείκης σκηπάνιον Suid. s. v. ὀγκή.

301. Perhaps there is an allusion in φρουρὰ to a block-house guarded by περίπολοι.

304. ὤτρυνε θεσμὸν is from ὀτρύνειν πομπὴν Hom. Od. 7. 151; 8. 30; Il. 10. 158. 'the edict' i. e. those who were to execute it. Perhaps the earliest instance of the verb μεγαίρειν is Sol. Fr. 1. 2 μηδὲ μέγαιρε. ἀμέγαρτος is found in Hom., Hes., and at least twice in Æsch.

314. Lit. 'they win first and last alike, fulfilling the course by taking up the running one from another'.

322. ἄλειφαρ is liquid fat, oil; στέαρ hard fat, dripping; πιμελὴ soft fat, like lard. Suid. s. v. πιμελή.

323. προςεννέπειν is 'to say with reference to' and so equals 'speak to' when you expect a reply, and 'speak of' when you do not.

COMMENTARY. 189

327. Editors object without reason to the vulgate. The poet
wishes to remind us of such scenes as the death of
Priam. In the F. Scholia correct γίνεται φυτλάμιος (sic).
Compare φυτχλμίῳ πατρὶ Soph. Fr, 538.
328. 'Heretofore' i. e. as before their slavery they used to do.
332. Seems to allude to some arrangement by drawing lots for
securing order at the ἑστιάσεις. Compare Ar. Eccl. 681
foll. κληρώσω πάντας ἕως ἂν εἰδὼς ὁ λαχὼν ἀπίῃ
χαίρων ἐν ὁποίῳ γράμματι δειπνεῖ κτλ.
335. αἰθρία is ἀὴρ ἀννέφελος in which μᾶλλον ψῦχος γίνεται
Arist. Prob. 25. 18.
336. Comp. Menand. p. 96 Meineke. ᾤμην ἐγὼ τοὺς πλουσίους
οὐ στένειν τὰς νύκτας. οὐδὲ στρεφομένους ἄνω κάτω οἴμοι
λέγειν. ἡδὺν δὲ καὶ πρᾶόν τινα ὕπνον καθεύδειν, ἀλλὰ τῶν
πτωχῶν τινα.
344. As if the whole course were a straight piece of wire which
the runner bends at the middle making the two halves
parallel to one another. The two strings of a sling were
called κῶλα Suid. s. v.
345. ἀναίτιος ἀθανάτοισι Hes. Op. 118. Clyt. is stating all the
chances against the victors: let them be as pious as they
will, they have shed much blood; and the spirits of the
dead will not rest until their slayers have paid the
penalties of homicide.
350. Lit. 'for I have chosen the enjoyment of many blessings'.
σὺν ἐσθλοῖσιν πολέεσσιν Hes. Op. 118.
351. εὐφρόνως 'cheerfully' because hopefully. The last two lines
of the queen's speech have two meanings. The Chorus
understand them to signify a sincere desire for the welfare of the Greeks; or they speak insincerely and praise
her for that in which her speech was deficient. εὔφρων
in Æsch. always means 'cheerful'. The gnome that a
sensible man will hold fast to good hope is of common
occurrence in Greek.
352. τεκμήριον is ἀληθινὸν σημεῖον, for σημεῖον may be false.
Suid. s. v.
354. Lit. 'not unworthy of our pains' in the following ode.
355. 'Ω Ζεῦ — παναλώτου. The predication is blended with the
invocation. Thus βασιλεῦ equals 'assuredly thou art
king' and so on; and often elsewhere. Νὺξ · ἐστὶ γὰρ
ἡ νὺξ θεὸς ὑπὲρ κόσμον Procl. on Hes. Op. 17. Her

peculiar γέρας is μαντοσύνη ἀψευδής Orph. Fr. p. 168
C. Tauch.
358. στεγανὸν is 'holding fast whatever is enclosed in it'. So of
a water-tight ship Supp. 134. Suid. s. v. τὸ Μηλιακὸν
πλοῖον; of a tower which keeps out the enemy Theb.
797; of a roof that keeps out wet, Diodorus cited by
Suid. s. v.
367. See Critical notes.
374. νοῦς ἐγγενής Soph. El. 1328; πόνος ἐγγενής Æsch. Cho. 466;
κῆδὶς ἐγγενές Æsch. Supp. 336; ἐγγενῆ κηλῖδα τῆς κακίας
Plut. De Sera N. V. 20. ἔγγονος is 'produced in' not
necessarily from birth; ἔκγονος is 'born from'; ἐγγενὴς
is 'born in', inherent from birth.
375. As this passage relating to the Trojans is directly taken
from Il. 13. 620 foll., the student will do well to read
over the whole of Menelaus' speech. δῆρις ῥυσίων Supp.
412. θάρσος δὲ πρὸς ὄλβῳ Hes. Op. 317.
376. Compare the phrase πολὺς πνεῖν.
378. ὄλβιος ὃς ναίει ἀπήμαντος Hes. Th. 955. οὐκ ἔραμαι πλουτεῖν, οὐδ' εὔχομαι, ἀλλ' ἐμοὶ εἴη ζῆν ἀπὸ τῶν ὀλίγων
μηδὲν ἔχοντι πόνον Theogn. 1155.
379. τόσσον κράτος, ὅσσον ἐπαρκεῖν Sol. Fr. 20. 1. ἀπαρκεῖν is
retained in deference to the Codex Fl. It should be
clearly understood by the reader that these quotations
from Hesiod Theognis and Solon are not given as il-
lustrations but as the actual source from which the ideas
and phrase of Æschylus were immediately derived.
380. This is directly from Theogn. 353 εἰ γνώμης ἔλαχες μέρος
and μέτρον ἔχων σοφίης v. 876, and remotely from Hom.
Od. 8. 547 ὀλίγον περ ἐπιψαύσῃ πραπίδεσσιν 'who has
even a slight touch of sense'. It may be observed in
passing that Theocr. 21. 4 κἂν ὀλίγον νυκτός τις ἐπι-
ψαύσῃσι is taken directly from the latter passage; so
that 'and if he does get a little touch of night' will be
the poetic form of μικρὸν δ' ὕπνου λαχὼν Xen. Anab. 3.
1. 4, and will approximate to Tennyson's 'and ever
failed to draw the quiet night into her veins'. Here
you may contrast the ancient and modern from of expression; and observe how florid the latter is even in our
most chaste of poets. It should be added that the editors
wish to *correct* the passage in Theocr.; for which see Paley.

385. καί με βιᾶται οἶνος Theogn. 503; μή σε βιάσθω γαστήρ
     ibid. 486; πενίης δέ μιν ἔργα βιᾶται Sol. Fr. 5. 41.
386. 'fatal child of Ruin'. ἄφερτος in Æsch. is applied only
     to what is in the highest degree pernicious. Ἄτη is
     here the goddess of death and destruction; Temptation,
     her daughter and coadjutor by quasi-Hesiodic genealogy.
387. οὐδὲ καθάρσιον εὑρήσει τᾶς ἀμπλακίας ταύτας ἄκος. ἐπὶ γὰρ
     ταύτᾳ τᾷ ἀδικίᾳ καὶ τὸ δαιμόνιον ἀσυγγνωμότατον γίνεται.
     Stob. 74, 61.
396. οὐ γὰρ τοίγε κλύουσιν, ἀποπτύουσι δέ τ᾽ ἀράς Hes. Op. 724.
     ἀθέριξε λιτάων Apoll. Rh. 2. 477. νῦν ἔχων παλίντροπον
     ὄψιν ἐν λιτᾱῖσιν Æsch. Supp. 173.
397. 'each' is taken out of οὔτις, as always in this sort of
     sentence. The meaning required for ἐπίστροφον is clear,
     but it is a singular fact that it only occurs in Gram-
     marians in this sense of 'worshipper, one who turns
     towards a god in prayer'. Prof. Weil cites Eustathius
     Opuscula 2. 48; 247. 10. There is besides Moschop.
     Hes. Op. 725 where also ἐπιστροφὴ is 'worship', and
     τοῦ Διὸς ἐπιστροφὴ E. M. s. v. βείομαι. For this use of
     δὴ compare δοκεῖτε δὴ Prom. V. 955, τὰς ἑταιρίδας δὴ
     Xen. Hell. 4. 56, φίλους δὴ ὄντας Thuc. 6. 80 and often.
407. ῥίμφα is partly like κοῦφα βιβᾶς Hes. Sc. 223 and partly
     like ῥαδίως = 'temere'. It occurs Hes. Sc. 342, 378.
     Compare 'domo levis exsilit' Hor. Sat. 2. 6. 98.
408. Lit. 'daring things not to be dared'. ἄτλητα πεπονθὼς
     Theogn. 1029; Theocr. 25. 203.
411. στίβοι. 'form' as in the phrase 'a hare's form'.
412. ἀτίμως is from τιμὴ in the sense of 'penalty' as in the
     verb ἐπιτιμᾶν. In fact τιμὴ appears to be radically a
     neutral word like 'pretium' 'cum et recte et perperam
     facto pretium deberetur' Livy. 5. 47. If ἀγάομαι comes
     from a root of neutral signification, e. gr. ἄγαν, it can
     mean (1) 'regard as in excess', and so, of a good thing,
     'admire', or (2) of a bad thing 'disparage'. With the latter
     interpretation Hom. Il. 3. 224 is sound, though rejected
     by all the editors, οὐ τότε γ᾽ ὧδ᾽ Ὀδυσῆος ἀγασσάμεθ᾽
     εἶδος ἰδόντες. Odyss. 10. 249 is like it, ἀλλ᾽ ὅτε δή μιν
     πάντες ἀγασσάμεθ᾽ ἐξερέοντες 'regarded him as overdoing
     his sorrow and silence' 'surprised at him', with a
     mixture of contempt.

413. ἄδιστα ἰδεῖν. So λευκῶν ἰδεῖν at the extremities of a verse
Supp. 720. κάλλιστον εἰςιδεῖν infra v. 900. ἀδημονῶν
has a neuter acc. like δαιμονῶν ἄχη Ar. Thesm. 1054.
Contrast a woman's frantic grief at the sight of the marriage bed in the case of Jocasta Soph. O. R. 1242, of
Deianira Trach. 913, of Halcyone Ov. Met. 11. 471
foll. The grief of Menelaus is silent σιγᾷς, which is
the exact meaning of ἀδημονῶν. ἄπας γὰρ δι' ὁτιοῦν
ἀχθόμενος τὴν ψυχὴν τὸ λυποῦν ἐκλαλῶν ἐπικουφίζει τῆς
ἀδημονίας τὸ βάρος Aristæn. 1. 17. By this word Suid.
and E. M. explain ἀλύειν. ἀλυσθαίνειν, ἀλύσσειν, ἀσχάλ-
λειν, ἀπορεῖν. ἀμηχανεῖν.

416. τοῖς τροπαίοις καὶ τοῖς κολοσσοῖς Plut. de Her. M. p. 225.
where it *may* mean merely 'statues'. For the custom comp.
(in addition to Eur. Alc. 248. 356) 'imagines defuncti,
quas ad habitum dei Liberi formaverat, divinis percolens
honoribus *ipso sese solatio cruciabat*' Apul. Met. 8. 7.

417. 'χάρις verbum Venereum est, et Attici χαρίεντα καὶ ἰταμὰ
κοράσια vocant puellas *in quarum oculis apparet* μαχλο-
συνη' D. Heins. Hes. p. 127. χάρις γὰρ οὖν ἡ τοῦ
θήλεως ὕπειξις τῷ ἄρρενι κέκληται πρὸς τῶν παλαιῶν
Plut. Amat. 5. This is the meaning also infra v. 421.

418. ἀχηνίαις is, in this passage, from ἀ and κέχηνα, i. e. Æsch.
uses it in that sense, and his is the only derivation of
any importance for the interpretation of his poems. Love
is an affection which flows (ῥεῖ and so ἔρως) from the
eyes of the loved one through the eyes of the lover into
his soul. This derivation may seem absurd, but, for the
student of Greek Literature, it is the only right one.
Eur. proposed πτέρως but only playfully.

426. τάχα γάρ σε παρέρχεται, ὡς ὄναρ, ἥβη Theoc. 27. 8. So
Prof. Conington makes 'volucri Somno Virg. Æn. 2. 794
equal to Somnio and at ib. 6. 282 the 'somnia vana' are
in the form of *birds*.

430. τλησικάρδιος is formed like ταλακάρδιος Hes. Sc. 429, and
has the meaning indicated in the Critical note.

432. χωρεῖ πρὸς ἧπαρ δύη Soph. Ai. 938. ἐςεμάσσατο θυμὸν 'laid
his hand on my soul' Hom. Il. 20. 425.

435. From Hom. Il. 7 333 ἄταρ κατακήομεν αὐτούς, τυτθὸν
ἀποπρὸ νεῶν, ὥς κ' ὀστέα παισὶν ἕκαστος οἴκαδ' ἄγῃ, ὅτ'
ἂν αὖτε νεώμεθα πατρίδα γαῖαν.

437. Ares is like a money-changer who gives gold for small coin, little gold for much inferior metal; since he takes the corpse and gives back a few precious ashes.

441. βαρύ. The gold is heavy, and the ashes are the cause of much grief.

443. εὑθέτους. The specific gravity is great but the quantity of the gold (i. e. ashes) is small, so that the vessel containing it may be called light. εὔθετον σάκος Sept. 642. εὐθέτοις ἐν ἀρβύλαις Æsch. Fr. 255.

454. εὔμορφοι Mss. Paley's interpretation 'unburnt', which Herm. would accept if the reading were ἔμμορφοι, is untenable for the following reasons. The custom at Troy l. c. is for the Greek bodies to be burnt and the ashes brought home; the Trojans burn their dead and then bury them; for it is the native land of the deceased. Some Greek heroes, as Patroclus, *seem* to have had their bones, after burning, enclosed in cinerary urns and then buried in the Troad Il. 23. 244. Apparently, there is no other mode of burial. Ajax, Soph. Ai. 1403, died by suicide, and in such a case the form of burial was certainly different in some respects, and probably in this, that he was buried entire. Without doubt the full rites included burning both in the time of Homer and of Thucydides (2. 52 end; 2. 34). In the case of an enemy burial without burning appears to be the custom; it was the more careless and unceremonious mode. Thus the body of Astyanax has an ὀρυκτὸς τάφος Eur. Tro. 1153; but the Seven are burnt, Eur. Supp. 349. Rhesus is burnt, Eur. Rh. 960. Alcestis was intended to be burnt, Eur. Alc. 739. Polyxena's pyre is raised by the Greeks themselves, for she is the bride of Achilles, Eur. Hec. 574, 575. But even if some corpses *were* buried entire εὔμορφοι could not express so much. We want a word which will express the difference between resting at Troy in the polyandrion heaped over their ashes, and being carried home across the sea. The objections, then, to this interpretation are, (1) the Homeric account; (2) the indignity to brave men; (3) the custom of the time of Æsch. (4) the inadequateness of the word εὔμορφοι to express it. Εὔμορφοι is a gloss written to εὔκαλοι, the Doric form of εὔκηλοι. Which of these two forms

13

is to be chosen is uncertain, but εὔκαλοι is the cause of the gloss. Compare εὖδον δ᾽ εὔκηλοι Hom. Od. 14. 479; and εὔκηλοι διάγουσιν ἐνὶ σφετέροισι δόμοισιν Hom. H. Heph. 7 from which this passage seems to be derived. It is not clear that the Spartans buried the corpse without burning, Dict. Ant. p. 555, for Pausanias was a criminal, Thuc. 1. 134, and the passage in Plut. proves nothing. εὔκηλοι occurs Hes. Op. 669.

458. Lit. 'and exacts the debt imposed by a curse which the people sanctions'.

463—467. Ἐρινύες. τοὺς δὲ πάμπαν ἀνιάτους ἀπωσαμένης τῆς Δίκης. ἡ τρίτη καὶ ἀγριωτάτη τῶν Ἀδραστείας ὑπουργῶν Ἐρινὺς εἰκτρῶς τε καὶ χαλεπῶς ἅπαντας ἠφάνισε καὶ κατέδυσεν εἰς τὸ ἄρρητον καὶ ἀόρατον Plut. de Sera N. V. 22, who here lays down the Orphic doctrine more clearly than Plato Phæd. 70. By ἄϊστοι, then, Æsch. means the spirits of unjust men undergoing punishment after their existence on earth is closed. It is the νώνυμνοι of Hes. Op. 153. Ἄνευ δίκας ἀμαυρὸν is from Hes. Op. 819 εἰ γάρ τις καὶ χερσὶ βίῃ μέγαν ὄλβον ἄρηται ῥεῖα δέ μιν μαυρῶσι θεοί. Οὔτις ἀλκά. κακοῦ δ᾽ οὐκ ἔσσεται ἀλκά Hes. Th. 876. τελέθωσι Op. 199. μηδὲ φανεῖσθαι τοῖς ἐν ᾅδου πρὸς βοήθειαν οὐδὲ τὴν τρυφήν, οὐδὲ τὰς πολυαράτους τιμάς, Damascius ap. Suid. s. v. χρηματισμός. The unjust man after death is in the hands of Adrasteia from whom there is no escape. Ἀΐστοις. Theog. 152 ἀνδρὶ ᾧ μέλλει (Ζεὺς) χώρην οὐδεμίαν θέμεναι. Linus Fr. 1. 3 Κῆρας. αἵ τε βεβήλων ὄχλον ἀϊστῶσαι ἄταις περὶ πάντα πεδῶσι.

469. βαρύ—ὄγκοις. ἡ μήτηρ ὑφεωρᾶτο τὸ βάρος τοῦ οἴκου καὶ τὸν ὄγκον Plut. Amat. 2. ἐν ὄγκοις γάρ εἰσι τό τε ὀξὺ καὶ τὸ βαρὺ Philop. ap. Suid. s. v. ὀξύ. τὸν ὄγκον τῆς τυραννίδος ib. s. v. Τιβέριος. κατά τε προγόνων ὄγκον Dion. H. ib. s. v. Ποστόμιος. εἰ τοιοῦτον ἦν ὄγκῳ τὸ ζῶον Babr. 28.

481. πυρωθέντα καρδίαν — καμεῖν. The metaphor is given in the Trans. The heart's 'catching fire from the fever-poison' is probably in strict conformity with medical science in the time of Æsch. καμεῖν alludes to the languor and prostration which follow upon febrile excitement. See also vv. 1172, 1255.

483. αἰχμή in at least three places in Æsch. is equal to θυμός. P. V. 405, Cho. 630 and here. They are from synonymous roots ἄϊσσω and θύω.

484. πρὸ τοῦ φανέντος is πρὸ τινὸς φανέντος just as you write πρὸ σοῦ and not πρό σου. The grammarians confine this rule to personal pronouns; if they are right we must read πρό του. Lit. 'before the appearance of anything'. 'In preference to what is clearly seen' is absurd, and thoroughly untrue.

485. πιθανοὶ δὲ οὕτως εἰσί τινες ὥστε πρὶν εἰδέναι τὸ πραττόμενον πρότερον πείθεσθαι Xen. ap. Suid. s. v. This is precisely what the poet says 'women are prone to credit what is pleasing, before it is actually proved to be true'. There is a double meaning in ὅρος (1) 'axiom, or, admitted truth' (2) 'boundary land'. The right interpretation of this passage was discovered by Donaldson to whose genius and genuine scholarship we are so greatly indebted.

492. φηλῶσαι· παρὰ τὸ σφάλλω E. M. s. v. ἀσύφηλος.

494. κάσις πηλοῦ κόνις. This relationship was probably so defined by Pythagoras; else it is a poetic expansion of one of his ipse-dixits. From him no doubt Plato derived that which is ascribed to him by Apuleius De Dogm. Pl. 1. 8 'et sicut ignis acri *cognatione* conjungitur ita *humor terrenæ affinitati* jugatur'. They mean, 'a proof from something of an opposite nature to fire, and of a more substantial character'. With ἄναυδος cp. ἄγγελος ἄφθογγος of a fire signal, Theogn. 549.

500. Lit. 'may an adjunct to fair appearances turn out fairly'.

501. This is a demonstrative proof that they understood the queen's prayer at v. 349 τὸ δ' εὖ κρατοίη to mean 'that which is favourable to me'.

505. ῥαγεισῶν lit. 'snapped'; but when the cable snaps the ship is wrecked. τυχὸν seems to be from a different metaphor, or it is used in its unfigurative use.

507. 'grave-land share' is opposed to a share of land for cultivation during life.

511. εἶσβα ll. 10. 450, 'ibis'. It has not yet been clearly put by any editor that in Soph. Ai. 172 foll. Ἄρτεμις Ταυροπόλα and Ἐνυάλιος are proposed by the Chorus as the probable agents of the madness of Ajax *because*

13*

they were indigenous divinities; that is Soph. with imperfect knowledge of the localities regards the Artemis of the Taurian peninsula (this is all that Ταυροπόλα means) and Ἄρης the Thracian war-god, as gods of the land; and they pray that Phœbus of the Argive land, v. 187, may put forth a more powerful influence in favour of Ajax.

520. If he said φαιδροῖς ἰδόντες ὄμμασιν (Voss, Weil) it would imply that that they were not *then* looking with glad eyes.

526. The time for sharpening the share χαρασσομένοιο σιδήρου and turning up the soil was at the setting of the Pleiads, so that for this reason alone we could not be very much offended with line 826 of this play. See Hes. Op. 382, 608. — μακέλλην τὸ παρὰ τοῖς κοινοῖς τζάπιον Moschop. l. c. The philologists must decide whether τζάπιον has anything to do with 'spade'.

528. The metaphor is taken from clearing land.

532. συντελεῖς οὖν οἱ συνδαπανῶντες καὶ συνεισφέροντες Suid. s. v.

535. ῥύσια δόντες Sol. Fr. 19. 3 is said of unjust men punished by the gods. Here it seems to be 'the property seized by Paris and claimed back by the Atreidæ.

537. διπλᾶ acc. to Hes. Op. 709 δὶς τόσα τίνυσθαι μεμνημένος. ἁμάρτιον is rightly explained by Sch. F. ὁ μισθὸς τῆς ἁμαρτίας.

539. Non jam mortem deprecor. Sall. J. 24 end. In Soph. Fr. 494 Did. ἀνταίρουσιν· ἀντιλέγουσιν, read ἀντεροῦσιν.

542. νόσημ' ἔρωτος τοῦτ' ἐφίμερον κακόν Soph. Fr. 646.

543. δεσπόσω, not 'master the meaning of' but 'make the statement my own; own to it'; so δεσπόζειν φόβης Choeph. 188.

546. 'latere petitus imo spiritus'; a sign of love.

548. βλάβη is Lat. 'malum' the punishment of slaves. τυράννων Fl. V. and κοιράνων F. in the next line are glosses on δεσποτῶν written by some one who took offence at the comparison.

550. Nunc est profecto interfici cum perpeti me possem Ter. Eun. 3. 5. 3.

554. παναπήμων Hes. Op. 809.

555. οὐδέ ποτ' ἦμαρ παύσονται καμάτου καὶ ὀϊζύος. οὐδέ τι νύκτωρ φθειρόμενοι — ἀλλ' ἔμπης καὶ τοῖσι μεμίξεται ἐσθλὰ κακοῖσιν Hes. Op. 174. The herald complains in

v. 557 that they had only κακὰ without the admixture
of ἐσθλά.

556. πάρηξις seems to be the same as πάροδος 'a passage from
one end of the deck to the other by the side of the
rowers, Lat. 'agea',' L. and S. πάροδον καὶ ἐπιβάθραν
Artemid. III. proem. 'gang-way' in both senses.

560. The generation of dew is accurately described Arist. Meteor.
1. 10; Apul. de Mundo 8.

562. The common interpretation of ἔνθηρον 'like that of wild
beasts' having been at length deservedly exploded, some
editors have fallen back on Stanley's conj. ἀνθηρὸν which
is even worse. Something might be said, in despair,
for ἔνθηρον but ἀνθηρὸν is a blunder without any redeeming
feature. For it means 'like a flower' in glossiness, luxu-
riance, richness of colour, and curliness: compare, for
example, ἐπανθεῖν· ὃ σημαίνει μᾶλλον τὸ δασὺ E. M. s. v.
ἐπενήνοθε, — πλόκαμοι ἀνθηροὶ καὶ ἔναυλοι Callist. Ecphr.
p. 524 Aldine Ed. τριχὸς ἄνθησιν ibid. 'Like the hyacinth'
in the Odyssey is rightly referred by Hayman to the curl
of the petals. Again, if Stanley's conj. be said to mean
'grey', ἄνθος has in itself no notion of whiteness. In a
word like φάλανθος, ἀνθ signified 'sprouting', and φαλ
the whiteness; so φαλακρὸς is 'white at top' and Suid.
s. v. is mistaken. λευκανθὲς κάρα Soph. O. T. is another
place where ἀνθ has no shade of white in it, and ἠν-
θισμένον Soph. El. 43 is wrongly rendered by Jebb 'with
this silver hair'; it should be 'thus tricked out', as
Wunder and others. That nothing may be left unsaid
in vindication of that impossible reading ἄνθηρον, there
is Hes. Fr. p. 312 D. Heyne καὶ γάρ σφιν κεφαλῆσι
κατὰ κρύος αἰνὸν ἔχευεν, ἄλφος γὰρ χρόα πάντα κατέ-
σχεθεν· ἐν δέ νυ χαῖται ἔρρεον ἐκ κεφαλέων· ψιλῶτο δὲ
καλὰ κάρηνα. and Plut. Quæst. Nat. 6. where dew is
said to have a septic property, τὸ δηκτικόν. Hes. Op.
537 ἵνα τοι τρίχες ἀτρεμέωσι μηδ' ὀρθαὶ φρίσσωσιν ἀει-
ρόμεναι κατὰ σῶμα. The last is of hair standing erect
through cold, and if the Ed. is right it was not this
passage which Æsch. had in mind but ibid. 553, 554.
The considerations in support of ἔμπεδον σίνος τιθέντες
ἐν θηρῶν τριχὶ ἐσθημάτων are the following. Hesiod re-
commends for winter clothing (and Æsch. is speaking of

cold weather) undergarments of wool, ox-leather boots
with linings of compressed wool, a kid-skin cloak, and
a felt cap covering the ears, ἵνα (ὑετὸς) οὔατα μὴ κατα-
δεύῃ v. 552, and μήποτέ σ' οὐρανόθεν σκοτόεν νέφος
ἀμφικαλύψῃ, χρῶτά τε μυδαλέον θείη. κατὰ θ' εἵματα
δεύσῃ Op. 553, 554. τρίχες means the hair and skin
Hom. Od. κ 239. Hesiod states that the North wind
can penetrate every kind of skin and hair except a
sheep's τρίχες, and, probably without knowing that Hes.
had said it 26 centuries before him, a writer in the
Times shortly before the army started for the Crimea
gave warning that no amount of woollen clothing, but
only sheep-skin with the wool, would avail against the
cold in that peninsula. Among the chiefs at Troy, Paris
and Menelaus wear leopard-skins Il. κ. 29: γ. 17, the
common soldiers probably wore sheep-skins in winter;
caps made of the skin of various animals are frequently
mentioned in the Iliad. Lastly Ibycus p. 218 Schneid.
speaks of στερφωτῆρα στρατὸν 'an army clothed in skins',
and Theogn. v. 55 ἀλλ' (οἱ πρόσθ') ἀμφὶ πλευρῇσι δορὰς
αἰγῶν κατέτριβον.

569. τὸ μήποτ' etc. gives the result or consequence of the statement made, exactly as v. 15 τὸ μὴ βεβαίως etc.

571. τὸν ζῶντα δ' ἀλγεῖν χρή. The dead have no further cause
for grief, but the living have, for they are still exposed
to the caprices of fortune. So Æsch. Fr. Ἀντίλοχ'
ἀποίμωξόν με τοῦ τεθνηκότος τὸν ζῶντα μᾶλλον.
Soph. Fr. 785 σὺ δ' ἄνδρα θνητὸν εἰ κατέφθιτο στένεις
εἰδὼς τὸ μέλλον οὐδὲν εἰ κέρδος φέρει.

572. See Critical note.

575. ποτωμένοις is a direct allusion to Theogn. 237 foll.

577. δήποτε in order to mean 'of yore' must be for ἤδη ποτέ.

584. Comp. Anth. 6. 111 κακοῦ δ' ἐπὶ γήραος ἡμῖν ἄλλυτος
ἡβάσκει γυιοτακὴς πενίη, Philost. V. S. s. v. Herodes
καλὸν καὶ γηράσκοντι τὸ μανθάνειν, Æsch. Supp. ἡβῶντα
δ' εὐγλώσσῳ φρενί. εὖ μαθεῖν is equal to εὐμαθέσιν εἶναι
'to be quick at learning'. just as δυσμαθεῖν Choeph·
225 is 'to be slow at learning (who I am)'.

590. Φρυκτωρὸς is 'a man who tends a signal-fire'. Paley accents
rightly with Schutz, but translates wrongly.

592. 'parvis mobili rebus muliebri animo' Livy 6. 34.

597. καινοῦντες is 'consecrating a thing when it is first used'.

607. δωμάτων κύνα is from Hes. Op. 602. The next line is from Sol. Fr. 5. 5 γλυκὺν ὧδε φίλοις ἐχθροῖσι δὲ πικρόν.

609. τὰ ταμεῖα σημηνάμενος κατέλειπεν Plut. Instt. Lac. 23.

611. 'mulier sine culpa, sine fabula'. Apul. De Magia 69.

612. The passage in Plutarch is the following: ἆρ' οὖν κρᾶσίς τις ἦν καὶ φάρμαξις τῶν πάλαι τεχνιτῶν περὶ τον χαλκὸν ὥσπερ ἡ λεγομένη τῶν ξιφῶν στόμωσις ἧς ἐκλιπούσης ἐκεχειρίαν ἔσχε πολεμικῶν ἔργων ὁ χαλκός; de Pyth. Or. p. 102 (C. Tauchn.), It is evident that he is not alluding to the existence of any 'dye' for bronze, but to some alloy which in time produced the bluish-green colour: for he goes on to speak of 'Corinthian brass' which neither he nor any one else, we may presume, ever supposed to be dyed. He also proves that there was a well-known tradition of some long lost mode of tempering copper to the strength of steel, as in the following: διὰ τοῦ χαλκοῦ δὲ τὰ γεωργικὰ ἔργα εἰργάζοντο, διὰ τινὸς βαφῆς στερρποιοῦντες αὐτόν Mosch. Hes. Op. 150. διὰ τινὸς βαφῆς τὸν χαλκὸν στερρποιοῦντες, ὄντα φύσει μαλακόν. ἐκλιπούσης δὲ τῆς βαφῆς ἐπὶ τὴν τοῦ σιδήρου χρῆσιν ἐλθεῖν, Procl. l. c. χαλκοῖς γὰρ το παλαιὸν καὶ ὅπλοις καὶ ξίφεσι καὶ γεωργικοῖς ἐργαλείοις ἐχρῶντο. βαφῇ τινὶ ταῦτα στομοῦντες· ἀπολλυμένης δὲ τῆς στομούσης βαφῆς τὸν χαλκόν. χρώμεθα τῷ σιδήρῳ J. Tz. l. c.

615. Lit. 'thus she told her tale to you a learner (who have much to learn about her conduct) cleverly in the opinion of sharp-witted interpreters (those who know the whole story) of her words. There is no reason for hesitation in the case of τοροῖσιν ἑρμηνεῦσιν. Cp. Soph. Fr. 305, Didot: καὶ τὸν θεὸν τοιοῦτον ἐξεπίσταμαι. σοφοῖς μὲν αἰνικτῆρα θεσφάτων ἀεί. σκαιοῖς δὲ φαῦλον κἂν βραχεῖ διδάσκαλον,

such, as I've learned, is god: he speaks his will
always in riddles to the wise; to fools
he is a poor and curt interpreter.

620, 1. ne me in breve conjicias tempus gaudio hoc falso frui' Ter. Hec. 5. 4. 2. λέξαιμι, because without οὐκ ἔσθ' ὅπως the form would be εἰ λέξαιμι οὐκ ἂν καρποῖντο.

623. σχισθέντα τάδε, i. e. τἀληθῆ and τὰ κεδνά, the other com-

binations being τὰ ἀληθῆ κακά, and τὰ ψευδῆ κεδνά. Si-
milarly Evenus Fr. 3 πρὸς σοφία μὲν ἔχειν τόλμαν μάλα
σύμφορόν ἔστι, χωρὶς δὲ βλαβερή. That is μωρία with
τόλμα, and σοφία with δειλία are not good.

626. ἀναχθεὶς ἐμφανῶς. This is the Homeric account, which
Æsch. does not follow; Hom. Od. 3. 151, 168. κοινὸν
is 'common to the whole fleet'.

641. The dead body is ἄγος. hence ἐξαγίζειν may be said of
carrying a corpse out of a house. But the 'callida
junctura' gives the word a new meaning as if it might
also come from ἐξάγειν to drive out. The latter is more
prominent, and is so rendered in the Trans.

645. τόνδ' is τόνδ' ἄγγελον.

649. θεομηνία τῶν θαλασσίων δαιμόνων Procl. Hes. Op. 664.

651. πῦρ ὕδατι μιγνύναι. τὸ παροιμιαζόμενον ἐν τοῖς ἀδυνάτοις
Plut. de Primo Frigore p. 410 (C. T.); see Theogn. 1245.

659. 'Tum mare velivolum florebat navibus' Lucr. 5. 1441. Ἀτ-
τικώτερον δὲ τὸ Αἴγαιον Suid. s. v. whom the Ed. was
unwilling to follow, in the absence of any confirmation.
Αἰγαῖον contains an allusion to αἶγες and so keeps up
the imagery in κεροτυπούμεναι, ποιμένος στρόβῳ and v.
670; for τὰ μεγάλα κύματα αἶγας ἐν τῇ συνηθείᾳ
λέγομεν Artimid. 2. 12. 'vagues' and 'Waegen, Wogen'
contain the same root as αἶγες acc. to Reiffius l. c. who
quotes the erroneous explanation of Varro de L. L. 4
'Ægæum dictum ab insulis — a similitudine caprarum'.
Compare also Αἰγαῖον πέλαγος· τὸ φοβερώτατον Suid.
s. v. so that it was a proverb, as in Hor. 'tutum per
Ægæos tumultus'.

660. νεκρῶν πέρι ἢ ναυαγίων οὐδὲ ἐπενόουν αἰτῆσαι ἀναίρεσιν Thuc.
7. 72; in which passage the νεκροὶ are the dead bodies
floating in the water, and the ναυάγια the wrecks as
containing many corpses in the lower decks; otherwise
ἀναίρεσις would not be either asked, or said of the latter.
So ναυάγιον to a Greek would mean nearly the same as
πολλοὶ νεκροί.

662. 'saved either by fraud or intercession'. Instances of similar rescues occur in Homer; but both verbs seem to
be taken from the law-courts at Athens.

664. ἀεὶ δὲ ἀγαθὴ ἡ καθεζομένη (Τύχη) Artemid. 2. 37. ἤ τιν' ἄλλον
ἐκ μηχανῆς θεὸν ἐπὶ τῷ καρχησίῳ καθεζόμενον Luc. de M. C. 1.

677. αὖον ἀπὸ χλωροῦ τάμνειν Hes. Op. 751. ζωόν τε καὶ ἀρτεμέα Hom. Il. 5. 515. καὶ ζῶντα καὶ θάλλοντα Soph. Trach. 235. χλωρόν· τὸ ἀκμάζον. Μένανδρος. Harp. s. v.

682. ἐς τὸ πᾶν occurs eight times in the Eumenides.

683. μή τις i. e. one of the dæmons 'quos licet sentire, non datur cernere' Apul. Flor. 2. 10. The only visible divinities are the sun, moon and stars Apul. de Deo. S. 1 and 2. προνοίαισι is the knowledge of the individual's μοῖρα possessed by the dæmons. Plutarch (after Plato, and Plato interpreting the Orphic doctrines) explains πρόνοια (1) ἡ τοῦ πρώτου θεοῦ (τοῦ πάντων πατρός τε καὶ δημιουργοῦ) νόησις εἴτε καὶ βούλησις. (2) ἡ δευτέρων θεῶν, τῶν κατ᾽ οὐρανὸν ἰόντων (sun, moon and the other ὄργανα χρόνου, 'hands of Time'), (3) πρόνοιά τε καὶ προμήθεια τῶν ὅσοι περὶ γῆν δαίμονες τεταγμένοι τῶν ἀνθρωπίνων πράξεων φύλακές τε καὶ ἐπίσκοποί εἰσι. De Fato 9.

686. ἀμφινεική Δηάνειραν Soph. Tr. 104.

689. 'Death-knell of navies etc.' This trans. is given as being slightly less odious than that which has hitherto been adopted by translators. The word 'hell' is so entirely theological, un-Attic, and in every way objectionable that it ought on no account to be admitted.

692. γίγας is the same as γηγενής. οὓς καλέουσι γίγαντας οὕνεκα Γῆς ἐγένοντο Orph. Fr. 50; so E. M. ὁ γηγενὴς στρατὸς Γιγάντων Soph. Trach. 1058. ἡ δὲ τῆς γενέσεως (τῶν ἀνέμων) ἀρχὴ δῆλον ὡς ἐκ γῆς ἐστιν Arist. Meteor. 2. 4. venti, qui facti e telluris halitu constent terrigenæ nuncupantur, Apul. de Mundo c. 10. τὸν γηγενῆ καὶ χερσαῖον ἀέρα is opposed to τὸν ἔναλον καὶ πελάγιον Plut. de Pr. Fr. 20. A wind blowing off the land, which Helen would require, is called ἀπογεία Arist. Probl. 26. 23, 25 τὸ ἐκ τῆς γῆς πρὸς τὴν θάλατταν πνεῦμα γενόμενον. Lastly γίγαντος has a side-meaning of ἀσεβοῦς καὶ θεομάχου Suid. s. v. γηγενεῖς, as in γηγενεῖ φυσήματι Ar. Ran. 825 and πρὸς τοὺς Γηγενεῖς Ar. Nub. 853. That the winds were believed to be earth-born in the Orphic Theogony is clear from Suid. and E. M. s. v. τριτοπάτορες. Thus we have the three meanings (1) earth-born, like all winds; (2) blowing off land, proper to this particular wind; (3) breathing the impious spirit of the Giants (Typhos, Kottos, Briareus, Gyges all wind-

gods). γίγαντος· μεγάλου, ἰσχυροῦ E. M. s. v. is a
wrong interpr. of this word.

698. ἀεξιφύλλους, the genuineness of which is beyond doubt, is
from Hes. Op. 392 ὥς τοι ἕκαστα ὥρι· ἀέξηται. Compare
Æsch. Supp. 856 ὕδωρ ἔνθεν ἀεξόμενον αἷμα βροτοῖσι βάλλει.

700. Pandora is κήδεα λυγρὰ Hes. Op. 49.

706. ἐκφάτως. δυσφάτῳ v. 1152. ἄφατός τε φατός τε Hes.
Op. 3.

707. From Hes. Sc. 273 foll. τοὶ δ᾽ ἄνδρες ἐν ἀγλαΐαις τε χοροῖς
τε τέρψιν ἔχον — πολὺς δ᾽ ὑμέναιος ὀρώρει. See on v. 737.

709. μεταμανθάνουσα is accurately explained in Suid. s. v. μάθημα.

711. μέγα στένει. From Hes. Sc. 90 foll. ἦ που πολλὰ με-
τεστοναχίζετ᾽ ὀπίσσω ἣν ἄτην ὀχέων. κικλήσκω is
especially used of a cognomen: Ἀφροδίτην κικλήσκουσιν
Hes. Th. 197 from ἀφρός. κορυνήτην ἄνδρες κικλήσκουσιν
Hom. Il. 7. 138; ἀφ᾽ οὗ δὴ Ῥήγιον κικλήσκεται Æsch.
Fr. 324, and often.

712. αἰνόλεκτρον. In the marriage-hymn he was εὔλεκτρος.

714. λαμπρῶς. λαμπρῶς ἰδεῖν Choëph. 810. λαμπρὰ μαρτύρια
Eum. 797. λαμπρῶς κοὐδὲν αἰνικτηρίως Prom. V. 833
which equals ἐναργῶς Sept. 139. λελυμένων λαμπρῶς
τῶν σπονδῶν Thuc. 2. 7 λαμπρῶς ἐλέγετο ibid. 8. 67
where the Schol. explains by φανερῶς, ἀναμφισβητήτως.
ταῦτ᾽ οὖν ἐπειδὴ λαμπρὰ συμβαίνει Soph. Trach. 1174
where the Sch. φανερά. σαφῆ, πρόδηλα. λαμπρῶς· τὸ
φανερῶς. οὐ τὸ ἐνδόξως Suid. s. v. The phrases in which
θην occurs are, in Homer οὔ θην, twice; οὐ μέν θην,
twice; Πηλεύς θην. λείψετέ θην. ἦ θην, twice; ἦ θήν που.
ἦ θην μὲν μάλα, οὐ θην οὐδ᾽, ὥς θην, καὶ γάρ θην. ἐπεί
θην, — in Theocritus, τύ θην, twice, καὶ γάρ θην. αἶνός
θην λέγεταί τις. λέγομες δὲ πρῷαν θην, πείρᾳ θην πάντα
τελεῖται. In δῆθεν (Prom. V. 202, 986 etc.) θην is
shortened to θεν, as μὴν to μέν.

717. The false notion that Paris is the subject of this allegory
of the lion's cub arose from the mention of him v. 713
But he is introduced there only for the purpose of showing the mistake which was made in calling him εὔλεκτρος, and Helen is the burden of all these four first
strophes and antistrophes.

718. ἀγάλακτον is 'weaned from his mother's milk', ἀπογεγα-
λακτισμένον.

720. προτελείοις contains a side-meaning of πρὶν ἐντελῆ γενέσθαι.

723. ἔσχ', 'hæsit' Herm. The meaning should rather be as Prof. Weil would have it like ἐκεῖνος δ' αὐτὸ (τὸ κυνίδιον) κατέχων ἐν τοῖς κόλποις Ps-Babr. App. 6. 6.

725. Compare πρηΰνειν ἐπὶ χεῖρα Hes. Op. 795. κνυζήσεται πρὸς τὴν χεῖρα καθάπερ κύων Philost. Apoll. 3. 4. The Ed. has followed Bamberger and others, in construing σαίνων τε φαιδρωπὸς-ποτὶ-χεῖρα.

728. ἦθος is very common in Hes. and Theognis. Nothing could be more complete and absolutely certain than Professor Conington's correction of this and the strophic line. The metre and the sense are alike thoroughly changed to that which is exactly right. For instance, no one would think of ἔθος in such a passage; and in all the precisely similar passages the word is ἦθος, Pind. Ol. 11. 21, Philost. Apoll. 4, 38, Plut. de Sera N. V. 20. τρόπος· ἦθος Suid. ἦθος ἀνθρώπου δαίμων a saying attributed to Heraclitus is either an Ionicism or we should read ἔθος Plut. Plat. Quæst. 1.

733. ἄμαχον. The meaning 'prodigious', which is so common in later writers, seems to be got by a confusion with ἀμαιμάκετος (ἱστός Hom. Od. ξ. 311); as to the derivation E. M. hesitates between μῆκος, μαιμάσσω, and μάχη. Æsch. uses it in that sense derived from μάχη.

737. 'εὐσσώτρου ἐπ' ἀπήνης ἤγοντ' ἀνδρὶ γυναῖκα and the rest of the passage Hes. Sc. 273; see Stesich. Fr. 27 Bgk. We must imagine Paris and Helen riding in a chariot from the ship to the city while the Trojan citizens sing songs of love and marriage, and scatter roses, myrtle, violets, quinces. Gower C. A. Book 5 tells the story remarkably well:

> Paris vnto the quene wente
> and hir in both his armes hente
> with hym, and with his felauship;
> and forth thei beare hir vnto ship.
> Up goth the saile, and forth thei wente:
692. and suche a wynde fortune hem sent
696. till thei the hauen of Troie caught,
> where out of ship anone thei straught,
> and gone hem forth towarde the towne:

706, 7, 8. the whiche came with procession
,,   ayene Paris, to sene his praie.
,,   And euery man began to saie
,,   to Paris and to his felauship
,,   all that they couthen of worship.
,,   Was none so littell man in Troie
,,   that he ne made mirthe and joye,
,,   of that Paris had wonnen Heleyne.
    But all that mirthe is sorow and peyne
    to Helenus and to Cassandre.
1156. For thei it tolden shame and sklandre
395, 6. and losse of all the common grace,
401. that Paris out of holy place
402. by stelth hath take a mans wife:
    whereof he shall lese his life
715, 1305. and many a worthy man thereto,
1171. and all the citee be fordo,
    whiche neuer shall be made ayene.
    And so it fell right as thei seyne:
70. the sacrilege whiche he wrought
    was cause why the grekes sought
    unto the town, and it belaie,
    and wolden neuer part awaie,
    till what by sleight and what by strength
    thei had it wonne in brede and length,
818. and brente and slayne that was within.

πάραντα is παρ' αὐτὰ along of this, i. e. 'like this'.

742. μαλθακόν. ἀλλ' ("Ερως) ἐξάπτεται μαλακῶς. καὶ σχεδὸν οἷον ἐκτήκων ἑαυτόν Plut. de Am. 4. He tries to describe the glance which, for all its softness, pierces the soul.

743. δηξίθυμον ἄνθος. The metaphor is as yet unexplained. Perhaps the allusion is only to the bewitching beauty of some flowers.

744. ἄλλῃ παρκλίνωσι Hes. Op. 260.

750. γέμων λόγος. See Iambl. V. Pyth. p. 65 ὀνομάξαιμι δὲ τὰς ματέρας ἀκρασίην τε καὶ πλεονεξίην· ἄμφω δὲ πολύγονοι πεφύκαντι. ib. 145 τὸ πρῶτον τῶν κακῶν — ἡ καλουμένη τρυφή, δεύτερον ὕβρις, τρίτον ὄλεθρος.

758. The impious i. e. the unjust deed.

760. ἐοικότα τέκνα γονεῦσιν Hes. Op. 233.

761. εὐθυδίκων is from Hes. Op. 228 ἰθυδίκην which Eustathius

explains by εὐθυδίκην. ἰθείῃσι δίκῃσι ibid. 36, 224, Th. 85 is opposed to σκολίῃσι δίκῃσι Op. 217, 248, 260 etc. The metaphor seems to be taken from the scales of a balance. For the meaning see Theogn. 197.

762. καλλίπαις, is explained by Hes. Op. 223—235 from which this passage is taken. Plato calls Phædrus καλλίπαις, that is, αἴτιος πολλῶν καὶ καλῶν λόγων. See Babr. 11 καὶ καλλίπαις ἀμητὸς ἐλπίδων πλήρης.

763. After enumerating the beautiful offspring of Justice Hes. l. c. goes on to contrast that of ὕβρις. There is no word either in Latin or English equivalent to ὕβρις. See Sall. Jug. 41 ea quæ res secundæ amant lascivia atque superbia.

765. νεάζουσαν ἐν κακοῖς is the ὕβριν ἀτάσθαλον of Hes. Op. 133, 239, opposed to θάλλουσιν δ᾽ ἀγαθοῖσι v. 234. Now ἀτάσθαλον is always explained by θάλλουσαν ἐν ἄτῃς (Scholl. and Gramm.) It is clear that this is what Hes· intended, and Æsch. accepted as the etymon.

771. Construe 'an avenging dæmon like her parents in unholy recklessness of (which works) black ruin to families'. θράσος εἰδομένη τοκεῦσιν is like Μέντορι εἰδομένη ἠμὲν δέμας ἠδὲ καὶ αὐδήν Hom. Od. last line, and often. For θράσος compare Hes. Op. 319 αἰδώς τοι πρὸς ἀνολβίῃ, θάρσος δ᾽ ἐπὶ πλούτῳ. μελαίνας ἄτας is after the model of μέλας θάνατος Op. 153.

773. δίκη δ᾽ ὑπὲρ ὕβριος ἴσχει ἐς τέλος ἐξελθοῦσα Hes. Op. 215 where Procl. explains by ἐκλάμπει. Electra's hut, Eur. El. 1140 is πολύκαπνον στέγος.

776. ἄφνειον ἔδεθλον (Rome) Dion. Per. O. D. 356. ἱερὸν ἔσκεν ἔδεθλον Ap. Rh. 4. 331. In each place the penult. is long. The word is also quoted from Antimachus Fr. 87 which the Ed. is unable to verify. σὺν πίνῳ χερῶν. κακότητί τε χεῖρας ἄνιπτος Hes. Op. 738.

779. προςβάλλει ἀρούρας ('Ἥλιος) Hom. Il. η. 421, Od. τ. 433.

782. εἰ μὴ μοῖρ᾽ ἐπὶ τέρμα βάλοι Theogn. 1188.

786. ὑπερῆραν· ὑπερέβησαν, not 'over' but 'past', Suid. s. v.

787. ἀλλὰ δόκει μὲν πᾶσιν ἀπὸ γλώσσης φίλος εἶναι Theogn. 63.

795. θυμὸν ἱππογνώμονα Æsch. Fr. 238.

803. ὄφρ᾽ ἀποτίσῃ δῆμος ἀτασθαλίας βασιλέων, οἳ λυγρὰ νοεῦντες κτλ. Hes. Op. 258, and the passage cited in the Cr. notes. There is no doubt of the correctness of Heimsoeth's emendation.

809. Lit. 'keeps the house of the city' as if they were stewards of the state in the absence of the king.

812. 'won': lit. 'exacted from'.

813. ἀπὸ γλώσσης is opposed to ἐκ φρενὸς Theogn. 63. and to διὰ γραμμάτων in Thuc. and so equal to ὑπὸ μνήμης, but here it is 'not according to the speeches of the two litigants' Comp. οὗτοι δικάζει ταῦτα μαρτύρων ὗπο Ἀρης Supp. 934.

814. ἀνδροθνῆτας is opposed to τὰς σωζούσας.

816, 817. See critical note. The literal translation would be something like 'Hope, impotent, went in to th' adverse unimpregnated womb-vase'. Here we may compare Soph. Ant. 615 which stands in need both of correction and interpretation: ἁ γὰρ δὴ πολύπλαγκτος ἐλπὶς παύροις μὲν ὄνασις ἀνδρῶν. πολλοῖς δ᾽ ἀπάτα κουφονόων ἐρώτων (παύροις Ed. πολλοῖς vulg.) 'wayward Hope is fruition (of love) for a few, for many she is a mockery of light-thoughted desires'.

819. The genuineness of θύελλαι is unquestionable, and Hermann's θυηλαὶ undeserving even of mention. The meaning is sufficiently given in the Trans. θύελλα δέ, πνεῦμα βέβαιον, καὶ ἔφνω προςαλλόμενον Arist. de Mundo c. 4. This is very fitly said of the smoke of a consumed city.

826. . 'quum fatalis equus saltu super ardua venit Pergama' Virg. Æn. 6. 515. It is needless to add that there is no allusion here to any wooden horse. — ἀμφὶ Πλειάδων δύσιν. This is aptly added as part of the description for the following reasons: the Sun (Δίκη of v. 774) is then in Libra; and at v. 815 we had οὐ διχορρόπως, 'with no even-weighted scales'; it accounts for the storm of retribution implied in θύελλαι v. 819; and for the physical storm which came upon the Greek fleet v. 649; there was a tradition that Electra the seventh Pleiad, mother of Dardanus by Zeus, fled from the sight of the destruction of Ilion; it was the time for turning up the soil and sharpening the coulter, v. 526, 528. δύσις δὲ ἐῴα ὅταν ὁ ἥλιος ᾖ ἐν Ζυγῷ Procl. Hes. Op. 384. εὖτ᾽ ἂν Πληϊάδες σθένος ὄβριμον Ὠρίωνος φεύγουσαι πίπτωσιν ἐς ἠεροειδέα πόντον δὴ τότε παντοίων ἀνέμων θύουσιν ἀῆται Hes. Op. 617. ἐν γὰρ τῷ εἰς Θεόπρομον ποιήματί φησι (Aratus) φυγεῖν τὴν Ἠλέκτραν καὶ μὴ ὑπομεῖναι ἰδεῖν

τὴν Ἴλιον ἁλισκομένην · τὸν γὰρ Δάρδανον παῖδα Διὸς καὶ
Ἠλέκτρας εἶναι Sch. Arat. Ph. 259. ἔρχεσθε ἀρότοιο
δυσομενάων (Πληϊάδων) Hes. Op. 382, where J. Tzetzes
τὰς βώλους τῆς γῆς ἀνάστρεφε τῇ δικέλλῃ. Add. Artemid. 2. 36 τὰ ἄστρα χειμῶνος αἴτια δυσθυμίας καὶ
ταραχὰς σημαίνουσι. J. Tzetzes Post-Hom. 761 to the
end will also repay for perusal.

829. Athenæus 13. 573 ἐκτείνας κατὰ τὸν Αἰσχύλον περὶ ἑταιρῶν
alludes to this use of the verb ἐκτείνειν here, to the
subject of this ῥῆσις i. e. ἑταιρεία, and there is an equi-
voque in ἑταιρῶν, wittily substituded for ἑταίρων.

833. For the idea see Stob. Fl. περὶ φθόνου 32, 43, 60.

834. φθόνος · νόσημα ψυχῆς. καὶ ἐσθίον ψυχήν, ὥσπερ ἰὸς τὸν
σίδηρον Suid. s. v.

839. δαιμόνων σκιάν Eum. 302 i. e. 'the shadow of an invisible
being' is a similar hyperbole. Compare Menand. Mein.
p. 205. περιττὸν οἴετ' ἐξευρηκέναι ἀγαθὸν ἕκαστος ἣν
ἔχῃ φίλου σκιάν.

841. Ulysses is the φρόνιμος ἀνήρ of Socrates, who alone does
not grieve at a friend's good fortune.

849. τὰ δὲ περὶ τὰς τομάς τε καὶ καύσεις ἥκιστα πάντων ἀποδέ-
χεσθαι · χρῆσθαι δὲ καὶ ταῖς ἐπῳδαῖς πρὸς ἔνια τῶν ἀρρωσ-
τημάτων Iambl. V. Pyth. p. 139. εὐφρόνως goes with
πειρασόμεσθα.

854. 'As Victory followed me when I went, so may she abide
with me where I stay'.

855. The original of this passage is Hes. Op. 371. μηδὲ γυνή
σε νόον πυγοστόλος ἐξαπατάτω αἱμύλα κωτίλλουσα.

865. τὸν μὲν — τὸν δ' depend on ἔκπαγλον κακόν, and λάσκοντας
is in apposition with them.

869. ἐπλήθυον. 'ran in a full stream'. See v. 1370. 'swoln',
without the metaphor, is 'exaggerated'.

870. λέγεται δὲ καὶ Γηρύων καὶ Γηρυόνης καὶ Γηρυονεύς Eust.
Dion. Per. 561, and E. M. s. v.

872. χλαῖνα τὸ ἐκτὸς καὶ παχύτερον, χιτὼν τὸ ἐνδοτέρω Mosch.
Hes. Op. 536. χλαῖνα τὸ παχὺ καὶ χειμερινὸν ἱμάτιον
Suid. s. v. That it was used for a blanket is clear from
Theoc. 18. 19 Ζανός τοι θυγάτηρ ὑπὸ τὰν μίαν ἵκετο
χλαῖναν. ib. 24. 61 τὸν ἄλλον ὑπ' ἀμνείαν θέτο χλαῖναν.

874. παλιγκότων. 'unassuaged' i. e. inflaming and festering
over again.

880. τὸν πρὸ τοῦ· φεύγων χρόνον Eum. 462 where Orestes is
speaking of himself as an absentee by force of circumstances; for Clyt. had sent him away at nine or ten years
of age. At that age, because the Watchman, both in
Hom. and Æsch., has been at his post only for a year;
and that she sent him away of her own will is proved
by Choëph. 913, 914. The story is handled differently
in Soph. El. and in the Editor's opinion far less skilfully. δορύξενος· δορυξένους ἐκάλουν καὶ τοὺς ὁπωσοῦν
ἐπιξενωθέντας. Suid. s. v.

881. 'of sorrows to be mentioned in each alternative'.

890. The light being λαμπτὴρ v. 22, the stack of wood is
λαμπτηρουχία.

891. ἀτημελήτους· λίαν ἠμελημένους Suid. s. v. οὐκ ἀτημέλητος
τοὺς κικίννους Alciphron 3. 55. 3. τημελές· ἐπιμελές.
τημελῆσαι· φροντίσαι Suid. s. vv.

893. ῥιπαῖσι. 'wing-strokes'. So Prom. V. 126 πτερύγων ῥιπαῖς.
From Hes. Op. 582 ἠχέτα τέττιξ λιγυρὴν ἐπιχεύετ'
ἀοιδὴν πυκνὸν ὑπὸ πτερύγων. φωνὴ belongs only to animals that have lungs. αἱ δὲ μυῖαι τοῖς πτεροῖς τρα-
χέσιν οὖσι πλήττουσι τὸν ἀέρα. καὶ ἠχοῦσιν· ἀμέλει στα-
θεῖσαι οὐκέτι βομβοῦσι Philop. ap. Suid. ἦχος.

896. From Theogn. 472 πᾶν γὰρ ἀναγκαῖον πρᾶγμ' ἀνιηρὸν ἔφυ.
So Alciph. 3. 37. 3 καλὸν μὲν γὰρ ἀπείρακτον εἶναι τῶν
ἀβουλήτων, ὅτῳ δὲ οὐχ ὑπάρχει τοῦτο, κρύπτειν τὴν
συμφορὰν ἀναγκαίαν.

898. μουνογενὴς παῖς Hes. Op. 374.

899. Klausen's interpretation of καὶ γῆν is very ingenious. 'The
preceding metaphors are taken from things which simply
give safety or comfort: καὶ introduces a new set, taken
from such as relieve from imminent danger or pain'.
But καὶ is proved to be wrong by the passage in the
Odyssey.

901. This is worked out by Catullus 68. 57.

904. That is, the envy which under ordinary circumstances would
be roused by the eulogies.

911. Justice leads him in, and Premeditation does the rest.

912. Lit 'not overcome by sleep'.

919. βαρβάρου φωτὸς δίκην is wrongly explained by Blomfield
and others; rightly by Enger and Paley: the latter
translates 'as if I were some Eastern king'. There are

not many examples of δίκην used in this way, but the
last line of Danae's lullaby to the infant Perseus affords
one; τεκνόφι δίκαν σύγγνωθί μοι 'forgive me as if I were
a child'. This, again, is wrongly rendered by Jortin in
Dr. Holden's Folia Silvulæ p. 125.

923. μὴ πρὸς ἐμὲ τὰ ποικίλα, ἀντὶ τοῦ τὰς τέχνας Greek Prov.
Suid. s. v. ποικίλα. ποικίλην δὲ ἐσθῆτα ἔχειν — κινδύνους
ἐπιφέρει — καὶ ἡ φοινικοφαὴς ἢ πορφυροβαφὴς τραύματα
ἐπιφέρει Artem. 2. 3.

924. καὶ πεφύλαξό γε ταῦτα ποιεῖν ὁπόσα φθόνον ἴσχει Golden
Verses 36.

927. Sed his (animi virtutibus) præstare prudentiam (σωφροσύνην)
Apul. de Dogm. Pl. 2. 1.

929. Δημόκριτος ὁ Ἀβδηρίτης τέλος τὴν εὐθυμίαν εἶναι λέγει —
καθ' ἣν γαληνῶς καὶ εὐσταθῶς ἡ ψυχὴ διάγει· καλεῖ δὲ
αὐτήν — εὐεστώ Diog. Laert. Democr. So truly spoke
the venerable precursor of the 'deus ille, deus' Epicurus.

930. εἶπον δὲ καὶ πρίν. οὐκ ἄνευ δήμου τάδε πράξαιμ' ἄν
Suppl. 398 is a strong corroboration of Prof. Weil's
correction.

933. Lit. 'if you had feared anything, you would have made a
vow to the gods to act thus'; she means that there is
no ground for fear, nor for acting as if there were.

943. 'None more' i. e. in fear of exciting the envy of the gods.

938. From Hes. Op. 761 as observed by others.

944. Compare Plutarch's anecdote of that precocious young lady
Gorgo, daughter of Cleomenes, τὸν δ' Ἀρισταγόραν ὑπό
τινος τῶν οἰκετῶν ὑποδούμενον (having his ἀρβύλας put on)
θεασαμένη. Πάτερ. ἔφη, ὁ ξένος χεῖρας οὐκ ἔχει. Lac. Apoph.

945. πρόδουλον ἔμβασιν. The shoe follows the foot like a slave
supplying it with a suitable stepping-place. An Eastern
prince might also, on occasion, make a slave lie down
to be trodden on. Hdt. 2. 107 is something like this,
αὐτοὺς δὲ ἐπ' ἐκείνων ἐπιβαίνοντας ἐκσώζεσθαι.

950. τοὐμὸν μὲν οὕτω is Emper's conjecture, adopted by Enger.
The Ed. has retained the Mss. reading, but no very in-
telligible explanation of it could be given. It is translated
as if it were περὶ τούτων οὕτω δοκεῖ μοι. The following
are similar expressions: τουτὶ μὲν οὕτως Babr. 116, 15;
ταῦτα μὲν οὕτως ἴσθι Theogn. 31; Golden Verses 9;
τοιαῦτα μὲν δὴ ταῦτ' Prom. V. 500; ταῦτα μὲν οὖν

14

ταύτῃ Plut. de Sera N. V. 7 and elsewhere. The passage is not yet emended.

960. παγκαίνιστον. Lit. 'all' or 'on every occasion, used for the first time', so that none need be used twice. The meaning of καινίζω, in Æsch., forbids the adoption of Paley's interpretation 'ever-renewable', which is objectionable on other grounds, and especially because such an allusion implies a lack of cloth to replace the old.

961. This and the following verse have a double meaning 'our house can claim to be rich in purple (blood) etc.' That idiomatic use of ὑπάρχει requires no illustration.

967. Σειρίου κυνός. Apposition; τὸν κύνα τὸν Σείριον Ælian Suid. s. v. Ἰαχήν. Σείριος· ὁ ἀστρῷος κύων ib. s. v. Σείριον· τον κύνα. ib. ὁ κύων ὁ Σείριος καλούμενος Sch. Arat. 327. Σείριος ἀστὴρ thrice in Hes.

970. i. e. 'ripens unripe grapes'; an expansion of θέρει ὅτ' ὄμφακες αἰόλλονται Hes. Sc. 399.

972. κατ᾽ οἶκον ἐστρωφᾶτο Archil. Fr. For τελείου compare Æsch. Fr. 31. It means 'with felicity complete as man, husband, father of a son and heir'.

974. Lit. 'let there be a care to thee for those things whatsoever they are which thou art about to fulfil'.

976. The degrees of φόβος are δεῖμα, ὄκνος, αἰσχύνη. ἔκπληξις. θόρυβος. ἀγωνία Diog. Laert. Zeno. The fear of the Chorus is a 'presentiment' without any material foundation, unless it be their knowledge of the queen's perfidy. The purple spread on the ground was a bad omen if you compare Hom. ll. σ. 538 εἷμα δαφοινεὸν αἵματι φωτῶν and similar passages. The Spartans wore φοινικίδες in battle, and were buried in them Plut. Instt. Lac. 18, 24; and Arist. in Suid. s. v. φοινικίδα. These and other omens might be found, but the Chorus speaks as if the presentiment was independent of omens.

976. προστατήριον is translated as if it were derived from προστάτης and προστατεῖν as in Eur. El. 932 αἰσχρὸν γυναῖκα προστατεῖν γε δωμάτων. But the other meaning is also intended as in προστατηρίας Ἀρτέμιδος Sept. 450 etc. The former, 'domineering over' like a προστάτης over a μέτοικος, is the more prominent.

977. μαντιπολεῖ is formed like ὀνειροπολῶ. ἔμισθος, alluding to the diviner's fee; see v. 1261.

984. προὔμνησ'. προύμνᾶτο 'advised beforehand' Xen. An. 7.
3. 18. προμνᾶταί τί μοι γνώμα 'forewarns me of' Soph.
O. C. 1075. ξυμβόλοις. ξύμβολον ὄρνιν φασιν· ἐπειδὴ
ξυμβόλους ἐποίουν τοὺς πρῶτα συναντῶντας, καὶ ἐξ
ἀπαντήσεώς τι σημαίνοντας Suid. s. v.

285. παρέβησεν. ἡ δ' ὥρη παραμείβηται Hes. Op. 407. παρη-
βῆσαι· παρακμάσαι Suid. s. v. The meaning is, that
the most dangerous crisis is past, since he has returned
in triumph from the expedition which was led forth by
those evil-boding eagles.

089. νόστος· ἡ οἴκαδε ἐπάνοδος Suid. s. v. 'home-return' as in
Shakspere.

990. ἄνευ λύρας. The phrase was πρὸς λύραν ᾄδειν, and ᾠδαῖς
χρῆσθαι πρὸς λύραν is one of the symbols of Pythagoras,
who recommended his disciples to practise only such
music as was of an inspiriting and cheering character.
μονωδεῖ. The passages referred to in the critical note
are Bacchæ 71 and Epich. Fr. ap. Hephæst. p. 15.
Herm. has also left a syllable short before μν at v.
1459 without giving the reader notice; and he has so
rendered it in his metrical translation 'hei memorique
etc.' In this palpable error he is followed by all editors
except Heimsoeth.

996. τελεσφόροις δίναις. An astronomical allusion: as the sun
and moon by repeated daily revolutions accomplish the
period of a year and a month, or any other comple-
ted cycle.

1008. πρὸ χρημάτων ὄκνον is 'a shrinking in defence of', that is
'from a desire to save the wealth'. The preposition
has this meaning both in Greek and Latin.

1011. πρόπας δόμος is from Hes. Op. 687 μηδ' ἐπὶ νηυσὶν ἅπαντα
βίον κοιλῇσι τίθεσθαι.

1014. 'Sinks', in the Translation, is an active verb.

1015. ἀμφιλαφῶς ἔχουσα τρυφημάτων Alciph. 3. 60. 3.

1016. ἐπετειᾶν. See v. 2. Lucretius 5. 1364 uses 'tempestiva'
with this meaning 't. examina pullorum' 'swarms of
young shoots in due season' Munro. There is a side-
meaning of ἐπηετανῶν 'plentiful'.

1021. ἐπαείδων. ἔστι δὲ καὶ — ὅπου καὶ πάθη καὶ νοσήματά τινα
ἀφυγίαζον. ὡς φασίν, ἐπᾴδοντες ὡς ἀληθῶς. καὶ εἰκὸς
ἐντεῦθέν ποθεν τοὔνομα τοῦτο εἰς μέσον παρεληλυθέναι

14*

τὸ τῆς ἐπωδῆς. Iambl. V. Pyth. p. 96. ἦν γὰρ αὐτῷ
μέλη καὶ πρὸς νόσους σωμάτων παιώνια, ἃ ἐπᾴδων ἀνίστη
τοὺς κάμνοντας. Porph. V. Pyth. p. 96. Kuster's Ed.

1023. τῶν Φθιμένων. ἃν θέμις εἴργει Æsch. Supp. 38.

1024. The story of the death of Asclepius by a thunder-stroke
from Zeus is told in a fragment of Hesiod, p. 319.
D. Heyne. In Philost. Her. p. 146 Boiss. Palamedes
says to Cheiron καὶ ἄλλως τὸ ὑπέρσοφόν σου τῆς τέχνης
ἀπήχθηται μὲν Διί. ἀπήχθηται δὲ Μοίραις. καὶ
λήγειν ἐν τὰ Ἀσκληπιοῦ εἰ μὴ κτλ. where the Schol.
ὡς τὸν ὁρισμὸν τῶν Μοιρῶν καταλύοντα ἀποθανεῖν
τὸν Ἀσκληπιόν.

1026. Μοῖρα μοῖραν. In the temple at Delphi there were statues
of only two Mœræ Plut. de Ei ap. Delph. 2; for
Εἱμαρμένη διττῶς καὶ λέγεται καὶ νοεῖται· ἡ μὲν γάρ
ἐστιν ἐνέργεια, ἡ δ' οὐσία. ἡ δὲ κατ' οὐσίαν ἔοικεν εἶναι
σύμπασα ἡ τοῦ κόσμου ψυχή κτλ. Plut. de Fato 1. 2.
i. e. one is the divine being who decides the lot of each
created thing, and the other the operation of her will
in each individual instance. This is θεολογικῶς or κατὰ
τὰ Ὀρφικά, and was adopted by Plato. The meaning of
this passage is "if ὁ τῆς φύσεως νόμος (Μοῖρα or Εἱμαρμένη τὰ καθόλου συμπεριλαμβάνουσα) did not deter-
mine that the fate, 'μοῖραν', of the individual, here
Agamemnon, should gain no advantage from any inter-
position". The first is προηγουμένως 'antecedently' as
containing that which operates universally τὸ καθόλου,
the second is ἑπομένως 'consequently', the application in
particular cases, τὸ καθ' ὑπόθεσιν, ibid. c. 4. Κὴρ also
has this double signification (1) Μοῖρα, and especially
as the Death-goddess; (2) μοῖρα, for in the Ψυχοστασία
of Æsch. the κῆρε of Memnon and Achilles are weighed
against one another. The Scholl. wrongly explained by
ψυχάς and censure Æsch. ὡς ἐδέξατο φαύλως Αἰσχύλος.
They did not understand him.

1027. πλέον φέρειν. Usually πλέον ἔχειν or ποιεῖν as in Plato
Apol. 2. end, and μεῖον ἔχειν.

1028. i. e. 'my heart would prompt words faster than my tongue
could speak them'.

1031. θυμαλγής: Hes. Th. 629, 635.

1032. ἐκτολυπεύσειν. χαλεπὸν πόνον ἐκτολυπεύσας Hes. Sc. 44.

This metaphor is suggested by the name κλωθώ, and perhaps τεταγμένα v. 1025 implies Ἄτροπος.

1033. ζωπυρῆσαι κυρίως ἐστὶ τὸ ἐκ μικροῦ σπινθῆρος Φυσῶντα μεγάλην φλόγα ἀνάψαι Suid. s. v.

1036. ἀμηνίτως. The latent meaning is 'independently of the μῆνις τεκνόποινος' of v. 155; so in χερνίβων there lies concealed 'the act by which Agamemnon's sin is to be purged away'.

1038. Ζεὺς Κτήσιος ἐν καὶ ἐν τοῖς ταμιείοις ἱδρύοντο ὡς πλουτο-δότην Suid. s. v. Her second meaning is Πλούτων a surname of Ἅιδης. βωμοῦ, as a victim to be slain.

1040. Heracles *also* went down to the chambers of Hades.

1041. Lit. 'being sold took heart to touch the slavish barley-dole'. μᾶζαν· τὸ ξηρὸν καὶ στερρὸν ἀρτίδιον J. Tz. Hes. Op. 588. It was black bread, as is evident from the proverb λευκὴν μᾶζαν Φυρῶ σοι· παροιμία ἐπὶ τῶν με-γάλα ὑπισχνουμένων. ἢ ὁ στρυφνὸς ἄρτος Suid. s. v.

1043. ἀλκὴν μὲν γὰρ ἔδωκεν Ὀλύμπιος Αἰακίδησι, νοῦν δ' Ἀμυ-θαονίδαις. πλοῦτον δέ περ Ἀτρείδησιν Hes. Fr. p. 317 D. Heyne.

1045. στάθμη, ἥτις ἐστὶ σχοῖνος τεκτονικὴ ἀποθλίψασα τὰ ξύλα Eustath. ad Dion. Per. 341. κατὰ στάθμην· ὀρθῶς, ἀκριβῶς. Sch. Theocr. 25. 194.

1047. Silence παρά γε τοῖς σοφισταῖς meant refusal, and not consent, Artemid. 3. 24. ὅτε κατεπαύσατο πολλὰ εἰπών. Plut. Apoph. Lac. Agis 9.

1068. i. e. not deemed worthy of a reply.

1075. See Plut. de Ei ap. Delph. who cites Pind., Eur., Soph., Stesich. in proof. 'The god of Gladness' Byron.

1081. Ἀγυιεὺς δέ ἐστι κίων εἰς ὀξὺ λήγων ὃν ἱστᾶσι πρὸ τῶν θυρῶν. τὸν Λοξίαν ὃν πρὸ τῶν θυρῶν ἕκαστος ἱδρύοντο Suid. s. v. ἀγυιαί. ἀγυιεύς· ὁ πρὸ τῶν θυρῶν ἱστάμενος ἐν σχήματι κίονος βωμός E. M. s. v.

1082. οὐ μόλις. 'non parum' Herm.

1090. συνίστορα is equivalent to συνειδυῖαν.

1091. ἀρτάνη ἡ ἐκ τῶν καλωδίων ἀγχόνη E. M. s. v.

1092. σφαγεῖον· τὸ τοῦ αἵματος δεκτικὸν ἀγγεῖον Suid. s. v. Paley compares ἀνδροκτονεῖον Bekk. Anecd. 1. p. 28. φονορραντήριον is aptly changed from περιρραντήριον 'a place sprinkled with lustral water' to 'a place sprinkled with the blood of murdered men'.

1294. Lit. 'she hunts those whosesoever blood-shed-by-murder she may discover'.

1103. ἄφερτον. Æsch. applies this word only to that which is superlatively bad; he knows no stronger word.

1105. δίζυος Ἴδριές εἶμεν Hes. Sc. 351.

1110. Lit. 'hand after hand (thrust after thrust) puts forth its outstretching'. By comparing Prom. 777 προτείνων κέρδος we see that the meaning is 'making an offer to strike'.

1115. The long broad mantle which Clytemnestra is about to *throw* over Agamemnon is δίκτυον, and she is ἄρκυς because she is like a stake holding up a net. δίκτυον, σαγήνη. βόλος are the same in Babr. 8. 4, 6, 8. ἄρκυς· τὸ θηρευτικὸν δίκτυον (in its abstract sign.). ἐκτείνεται ἡ ὑστέρα συλλαβὴ ἐπὶ τῆς ὀρθῆς Suid. s. v. It is short here, at any rate. ἀπὸ τοῦ εἵργω E. M. s. v.

1118. καταλεύσιμον· τὸν ἄξιον τοῦ καταλευσθῆναι εἶπε Δείναρχος ἐν τῷ κατὰ Λυκούργου Suid. s. v. 'ut cuncti conclamaverint lapidibus obrutum publicum malum publice vindicari' Apul. Met. 10. 6.

1121. τῶν γὰρ φοβουμένων τὰ ἄνω λειφαιμεῖ Arist. Probl. 4. 8. κροκοβαφὴς expresses no property of σταγών, but the effect of its action, δράμε, upon something else, viz. the colour of the face. With a transitive verb the proleptic case is of course the accusative, and with an intransitive, the nominative. So in Choëph. 185 δίψιοι πίπτουσι σταγόνες, the effect of the rush of tears is that the eyes are left dry.

1123. βίου δύντος. Translated by Lucret. 5. 987 'labentis lumina vitæ'.

1127. No translation is worthy of the name which does not preserve the obscurity of the oracular language. The dark-horned implement is the sword; compare such expressions as κελαινοῖς ξίφεσιν Soph. Ai. 231; but if she is a cow, v. 1125, the sword is her horn.

1130. Perhaps θεσφατογνώμων ἄκρος like προβατογνώμων ἀγαθός, v. 795.

1133. τὸ παρὸν οἱ ἄνθρωποι κακοδαιμονῶντες ὁρῶσι καὶ κακοὺς ὀνείρους σημαντικοὺς τῶν ἐνεστώτων κακῶν Artemid. 4. 21. A man in trouble went to a soothsayer with feelings like those of a person who goes to consult a physician, knowing that he is seriously ill, and in fear of what he may hear because of the nature of his pain. In the M. Schol. εἰςερχομένοις (on going in to the temple) is sound, (it is changed by Weil and Enger); but φανερὰ must be changed to φοβερὰ with Enger, a change anticipated by the Ed.

1138. 'thou' Clytemnestra, 'him', in the next v., Agamemnon.

1144. ἀμφιθαλῆ. The meaning in this passage is that given in the Trans.; 'fecunda poenis' is only a part of the meaning.

1145. She felicitates the bird upon its happy lot.

1149. ἀμφήκει δορὶ in the loose language of prophecy means 'a two-edged blade'. The oracle about Cleomenes, Hdt. 6. 77, has δουρὶ δαμασθείς, which neither Herodotus nor Pausanias, 2. 20. 7, seems to have understood. It means 'bound in wood' for Cleomenes died ἐν ξύλῳ, ib. c. 75.

1153. Suid. s. v. ὁμοῦ quotes Isæus for the signification 'simul'. but this is too tame for Æsch. ὄρθιος δὲ αὐλητικὸς νόμος, οὕτω καλούμενος. οἷον εὔτονος καὶ ἀνάτασιν ἔχων Suid. s. v. ἤϋσε μέγα τε δεινόν τε ὄρθια Hom. Il. λ. 10.

1156. This is Casandra's answer to the question 'whence etc.'

1158. ἀϊόνας. ἐπ' ἠϊόεντι Σκαμάνδρῳ Il. 5. 35 etc.

1159. τροφαῖς. Compare Æsch. Sept. 309; Supp. 856. Arist. Probl. 1. 13 ἢ ὅτι τὸ ὕδωρ γίνεται τροφή; Procl. Hes. Op. 735 οἱ παλαιοὶ καὶ πᾶσαν μὲν τὴν τῶν ὑδάτων φύσιν ὡς τρόφιμον καὶ αὐξητικὴν τῶν φύσεων ἱερὰν ἐνόμιζον εἶναι τῶν ζωογόνων θεῶν, μάλιστα δὲ τοὺς ἀενάους ποταμοὺς κτλ. So Sch. Hes. Th. 347.

1168. So Hecuba, Eur. Tro. 1242, μάτην δ' ἐβουθυτοῦμεν. In ἄκος, ἐπήρκεσαν, παθεῖν, θερμόνους there is the metaphor of a physician's unsuccessful treatment of a patient. χθονὶ πελῶ Prom. V. 282. As soon as the delirium of her fever subsides she too will sink to earth and die.

1178. ἐκ καλυμμάτων, that is with her face concealed by a veil. There is no allusion to the unveiling of the bride.

1180. The description is based on Solon Fr. 5. 17 foll., which may be translated:

"suddenly
as a wind instantly scatters clouds
in spring: having stirred the billowy unreaped sea's

deep water, and over the wheat-bearing earth
ravaged fair farms, it arrives at the gods' abode,
   high heaven, and makes us again behold clear sky;
and the sun's strength shines over the boundless earth,
   beautiful, and one can see a cloud no more:
such is the vengeance of Zeus; not in each case,
   like a mortal man, is he moved to wrath.
The oracle, χρησμός, contains the denunciation of the
vengeance, and, therefore, the same imagery is employed.
But Æsch., for whom no language is rich, grand, and
graphic enough, introduces a second simile, and the
wind becomes a monstrous wave which sweeps the deed
of vengeance into the sunlight, so as to be most clearly
seen. ὑπ᾿ αὐγάς· ὑπὸ τὸν πεφωτισμένον ἀέρα Suid. s. v.

1189. βρότειον αἷμα. The drink of the Erinnyes, Eum. 264 foll.

1193. ὅς τε κασιγνήτοιο ἑοῦ ἀνὰ δέμνια βαίνῃ Hes. Op. 326. 'tori
genialis calcato foedere Apul. Met. 9. 26.

1194. Another argument in favour of κυρῶ is the repetition of
the word by the Chorus v. 1201 κυρεῖν λέγουσαν 'hit
the mark in speaking'.

1196. ἐκμαρτυρεῖν φασὶ τὸ λέγειν οὐχ ἅπερ αὐτὸς εἶδεν ἀλλ᾿ ἅπερ
ἑτέρων ἤκουσε λεγόντων· ἐκμαρτυρία γὰρ γεγραμμένη
ἀναγιγνώσκεται, ὅταν τις ᾖ τελευτήσας ἢ ᾖ ὑπερόριος
Suid. s. v. and E. M. s. v. It means, therefore, to
read the affidavit, or deposition on oath, of an absent
person. So Eum. 461 λουτρῶν ἐξεμαρτύρει φόνον, 'bore
witness for Agamemnon in his absence'.

1198. The passages are Hes. Op. 802. Th. 232, 784, 792. There
is not the slightest excuse for adopting πῆγμα.

1205. or 'is more prim'.

1206. Lit. 'he was a wrestler'.

1218. Why should not an inspired person see something in the
appearance of the two children from which to infer
that they had been killed by a relative?

1228. μισητεία δὲ ἡ εἰς τὰ Ἀφροδίσια ἀκρασία Suid. s. v. μενετοὶ
θεοί. E. M. derives it either from μισεῖν or from
μίσγεσθαι.

1245. Lit. 'I run falling out of the course'.

1246. Observe the metaphor in ἐπόψεσθαι (autopsis, and a physician's visit), κοίμησον 'lull the pain', Παιὼν 'the god
who relieves pain', and λόγῳ, παρὰ προσδοκίαν for πάθει.

1251. πορσύνει· ἑτοιμάζει Suid. s. v.

1260. Φαρμακεία δέ. ὅταν διά τινος σκευασίας (cookery) θανατη-
φόρου δοθῇ τισι διὰ στόματος Suid. s. v. μαγεία.

1261. μισθόν. μίσθωμα· ὁ μισθὸς ὁ ἑταιρικός. καὶ ἑταιρικὸν Φά-
σκουσα εἶνα μίσθωμα Suid. s. v. πέλανος was ὁ τῷ
μάντει διδόμενος μισθὸς ὄβελος Suid. s. v. πέλανος. The
payment for the affront of bringing her, 'for her passage', does not come till v. 1263.

1263. i. e. 'what she had paid in mortification for my passage
here'.

1269. The Trans. shows that Enger's correction οὐκ δύων is not
required.

1272. Lit. 'not with even scales untruly' i. e. 'untruly, without
any doubt.'; construe 'mistakenly derided'.

1275. ἐκπράξας. This is much the same as ἐκδύων ἐμὲ v. 1269.
ἐκδιδάσκει is 'unteaches' Soph. Ant. 298.

1278. ἀποκτείνει (Clytemnestra Casaudram) θερμῷ τῷ πελέκει
Philostr. Imm. Κασάνδρα. πρόσφαγμα is the jet of blood
from a victim's throat.

1281. The Spartan mother killed her coward son and said οὐκ
ἐμὸν τὸ Φίτυμα Plut. Apoph. Lac. She meant that he
was his father's child and not hers. Φίτυμα in Æsch.
is the child of the father i. e. son. θρέμμα is the child
of the mother i. e. daughter, as in Æsch. Sept. 182,
and ibid. v. 792 παῖδες μητέρων τεθραμμέναι needs no
correction for it is equivalent to κόραι, as the Ed. has
already shown at Choëph. 502, οἴκτειρε θῆλυν ἄρσενός
θ' ὁμοῦ γόνον 'pity the female's offspring (the daughter)
and likewise that of the male (the son)'. θηλύσπορος
γέννα Prom. V. 855 is 'a brood begotten by the female,
the mother's children, i. e. daughters'; so the same
daughters call themselves θηλυγενῆ v. 29, but the sons
of Ægyptus are ἀρσενογενῆ v. 818, begotten by the
father. This is a great point in the Eumenides v. 606
where Orestes says that he is no more ὅμαιμος with
his mother than Agamemnon was. To Arist. G. A. 4. 1
cited by Klausen, and Apollod. 1. 7. 2, Plut. Pl. Phil.
5. 7 cited by the Ed. add Φιτύσαι· ἐπὶ τοῦ πατρὸς τίθησιν,
ἐπὶ δὲ μητρὸς οὐκέτι, ἀλλὰ γεννῆσαι Suid. s. v.

1284. θεῶν μέγαν ὅρκον Hes. Th. 784.

1285. ὑπτίασμα is 'a lifting up of the hands, with the palms

uppermost, in prayer'. See Prom. V. 1005 and χειρ-
οτόνους λιτάς Sept. 173. The meaning is that Agamemnon, as he lies expiring, will either lift or try
to lift his hands with a prayer that Orestes may
avenge him, or that the gods will so interpret his dying
thoughts.

1290. All attempts to explain πράξω are futile. It is rendered
in the Editor's translation as if it were a repetition
from πράξωσαν ὡς ἔπραξεν v. 1288. The best suggestion
is Enger's, but it is imperfect until the existence of
πράξω is explained, for that word could hardly be a
gloss on τλήσομαι, which would rather be ὑπομενῶ as
in Suid. s. v.

1293. ἀσφάδαστος. σφαδάζειν· δυσθανατεῖν Suid. s. v.

1297. βευλάτου βοός. τὸ δὲ ἱερεῖον αὐτόματον τῷ βωμῷ προςεισ-
τήκει Philost. Her. p. 254 Boiss. τῶν εὐγενῶν οἰκεῖον,
ὁ Φιλήμων λέγει, πρὸς τὸν πόλεμον καὶ θάνατον ὁρούειν,
ὡς ἱερεῖα Meineke's Men. et Phil. Rell. p. 531.

1299. ἄλυξις. Κύρν' ἔμπης δ' ὅτι μοῖρα παθεῖν, οὐκ ἔσθ' ὑπά-
λυξις· ὅ,ττι δε μοῖρα παθεῖν, οὔ τι δέδοικα παθεῖν.
Theogn. 817.

1300. τῶν ἡγουμένων πειθὼ πρεσβεύεται Plut. Apoph. Lac. Lyc.
20. 'obedience to rulers takes foremost rank'. (οἱ ἄλλοι)
Φιλοψυχοῦσι μέχρις ἐσχάτου. Suid. s. v. Φιλοψυχήσαντα.
A person condemned to die values most highly the latest
reprieve he can obtain.

1301. The day of sacrifice is come, and I, the appointed victim, shall gain little by flight from the altar.

1302. They wish to comfort her by expressing their sense of
her courage. Heath's transposition of the two next
verses was very perverse.

1305. τίς πατέρ' αἰνήσει εἰ μὴ κακοδαίμονα τέκνα; ἴσως ἐπὶ τῶν
προγονικὰ ἀνδραγαθήματα πρςφερόντων. Greek Proverb
in Suid. s. v.

1313. She sings her death-wail in the palace, v. 1445. She
here goes up to the door and starts back with a gesture
of loathing.

1311. τοσαύτην δυσωδίαν ἐξέπεμπεν ὡς οὐδὲν τῶν ἐν τάφοις
διαλυθέντων διαφέρειν. Suid. s. v. Μαξιμῖνος. 'ghostly'
because πρέπει implies that a thing is either actually
seen, or may be conceived as visible.

1316. θάμνον is sound, so that we need not think of θαμίν· ὅπως. θάμα occurs in Hes. Op. 350. The line is sufficiently explained in the critical note.

1320. ἐπιξενοῦμαι is exactly rendered in the Trans. κατεξ- ενωμένον Choëph. 706 is 'bound by my relation to him as ξένος'.

1322. θρῆνον λέγειν. λέγειν ἀοιδὰς πρὸ τοῦ θανεῖν Soph. Ant. 883. The word ῥῆσιν betrays the Grammarian; see Sch. Soph. Ai. v. 815.

1328. Prosperity is the outline of a picture; adversity is a wiping-out of that outline. Thus the state of man at its best is but the shadow of a semblance.

1331. ἀκόρεστον. Theognis says the same of wealth and wisdom, v. 1157.

1333. ἀπειπών. Crying 'hold, enough'.

1338. ἐὸν δόμον εἰςαφίκανε Hes. Sc. 45.

1340. ἐπικρᾶναι· τῆ κεφαλῆ κατανεῦσαι Suid. s. v., hinting at a root κάρα.

1354. ἐπειδὴ δρᾶν κατώρθωσαι φρενί Choëph. 512.

1355. ἀράσσοντες has a double meaning 'striking with the sword' and· 'striking notes on the lyre' from the phrase ἀράσσειν λύραν. So σημεῖα 'signs of tyranny', and, probably, 'musical notes in score'.

1364. Lit. 'death wins the day'. See note on v. 10.

1370. Lit. 'I flow with a full stream swoln by tributaries from all quarters'.

1374. εὖ κώτιλλε τὸν ἐχθρόν· ὅταν δ' ὑποχείριος ἔλθῃ τῖσαί νιν πρόφασιν μηδεμίαν θέμενος Theogn. 363.

1379. Lit. 'verily in time at least', but none the less surely because late.

1382. εἶχε δὲ χερσὶν ἰχθυσιν ἀμφίβληστρον Hes. Sc. 215.

1390. ἐρεμνὸς has the same root as ἔρεβος and this probably the same as ἐρεύθω and Latin 'rub-er', the red of the western sky; 'furvus' belongs to the same root 'ruf', the colour of the infernal regions. ·

1391. θεόςδοτα Hes. Op. 318.

1392. γάνος· ὕδωρ, χάρμα. E. M. s. v. γεγανωμένος. κάλυξ is the bud of a flower before it blows, or the sheath which contains the ear of wheat. σίτου ἐκβολήν, Θου- κυδίδης. ὅταν ὁ στάχυς τῆς κάλυκος ἐκφύηται Suid. s. v. σῖτος. From Hes. Sc. 398 ἦμος δὴ κέγχροισι περὶ

γλῶχες τελέθουσι, τούς τε θέρει σπείρουσιν. Lit. 'at
the bringing-to-bed of the wheat-sheath'.

1398. Tute hoc intristi: tibi omne est exedendum Ter. Ph. 2. 2. 5.

1406. κλυτὰ ἔργα περίφρονος Ἡφαίστοιο Hes. Sc. 313.

1407. 'what poisonous thing solid or fluid'. ἐξ ἁλὸς ὄρμενον is
an allusion to the old belief that rivers are formed by
the percolation of sea-water through the earth; as in
Homer Ocean is the father of rivers, and Lucret. 5.
269 partim quod subter per terras diditur omneis.

1409. She has *put on* the sacrificial incense in the form of frenzy,
a side-meaning of θύος, and has *thrown off* the curses
of the people. So she is like a victim ready to be
sacrificed in one respect, and unlike in the other.

1420. ἀγορῆς ἐπακουόν Hes. Op. 29. When applied to the gods
it means 'hearing propitiously'; in a forensic use,
'umpire', or, 'judge'; generally, 'a hearer'. Mosch.
Hes. p. 15 N. Heyne; Theocr. 8. 25; Choëph. 980;
Eum. 732. Callinus Fr. 236.

1430. Lit. 'pay for blow (given) with blow (received)'.

1434. The house of Fear is opposed to the house of Ægisthus.

1438. φονεὺς μητρὸς τῆςδε Eum. 122 'this mother's slayer' Clyt.,
speaking of herself.

1444. κύκνοι μεγάλ' ἤπυον Hes. Sc. 316. κύκνος οὐ πρότερον
φθέγγεται εἰ μὴ πρὸς τῷ ἀποθνήσκειν ᾖ Artemid. 2. 20,
where Reiffius quotes Paulinus Vidalinus in praise of
the musical and charming notes of the swans in Iceland;
but the story of their singing only when about to die
seems to be fabulous. See the passages cited by Blomfield.

1447. 'Brought an additional relish for the luxury of my triumph, as agreeable to me as the pleasure she was to
afford him in secret would have been to him'.

1452. As if he were τῶν σταθμῶν κύων as at v. 896.

1454. ἀπέφθισεν βιὸν. ἄνδρας ἀποφθίσειε θάλασσα Hes. Op. 664.
But ἀπέφθισεν βίον is an expression so strange as to
defy all explanation. It is usually translated as if
ἀπέφθισεν were the exact equivalent of ἀπώλεσεν, an
unscrupulous procedure which the Ed. has imitated
most unwillingly. For the metre forbids our ejecting
βίον with Karsten; rather a supplement must be obtained
for the antistrophic verse. No well-trained ear can

endure the trochaic monometer with monosyllabic clausula. It must be either an ithyphallic or a dimeter
catalectic. There is a corruption; and probably ἀπέφθισεν
is a gloss.

1459. ἄνιπτος Hes. Op. 728.
1460. Probably suggested by Hom. Il. 2. 137 αἱ δ' ἄλοχοι εἵατ'
ἐνὶ μεγάροις ποτιδέγμεναι.
1461. ἐριμνάστευτος. ἀμνήστευτα Metrod. Fr. v. 180. Such al-
lusions to the meaning of proper names are very
common, and many instances are given in Dilthey's
Cydippe pp. 36—41. Perhaps the first two lines of
the Iliad may be added, for Ἀχαιοῖς ἄλγεα is equivalent to ἄχη λαοῖς, just as Ὀδυσσεὺς is the hero
against whom Poseidon ὠδύσσατο, and the selection of
the names, like that of Helena and others would be
ascribed to the foreknowledge of the dæmons who suggested the names to the minds of the parents; as, in
the case of Ὀδυσσεὺς, to Autolycus by reminding him
of the ὀδύσσεια, or enmity, which he had himself in-
curred. Αἰγαίων', κυδεϊ γαίων Il. 1. 404 is another;
Virgil gives several etymologies, e. gr. 'cura *penum*
struere et flammis adolere *Penates*' Æn. 1. 704. There
are also cases like 'qua semita monstrat' which shows
that Virgil took semita to be connected with σῆμα,
σημαίνω, 'the road which points out the way'. Here
we may correct Soph. Ant. 990 which up to the present
time (Dind. Poet. Sc. Gr. 1868) has appeared as αὕτη
κέλευθος ἐκ προηγητοῦ πέλει, which no one can translate.
It should be αὐτὴ κέλευθος κτλ. 'a road, which is a
sufficient guide to others is itself travelled by a blind
man by means of a second guide'. It is plain that if
Virgil's notion of the primary meaning of semita has
been correctly pointed out, it is not of the smallest
importance to the reader of Virgil what philologists
may decree to be its root. It is of some importance
to them, but not to scholars. οἰζύς. φῦλα γυναικῶν.
πῆμα μέγα θνητοῖσι. μετ' ἀνδράσι ναιετάουσιν Hes. Th. 592.
1468. διφυίοισι is exactly equivalent to δυοῖν υἱέσι.
1470. 'Rule dispensed by a woman, and prompted by a spirit
like thine own; who, after throwing thine antagonist,
savagely fallest with all thy weight upon him'.

1473. μή τοι ἐφεζομένη κρώζῃ λακέρυζα κορώνη Hes. Op. 745. ὥςπερ οἱ κόρακες παρεδρεύοντες ἐξορύσσουσι τοὺς τῶν νεκρῶν ὀφθαλμούς Plut. Perd. Fr. 27.

1474. Predication by invocation, as often.

1480. ἰχώρ. ἰχῶρος· τὸ πεπηγὸς αἷμα Suid. s. v. Χειρώνειον ἕλκος· τραῦμα διηνεκῶς ἰχῶρας ἐκκρῖνον Suid. s. v.

1482, 3. αἰνεῖς. αἶνον (αἰνὸν wrongly, in Didot's Edition by E. A. Ahrens). αἶνος is 'an allegory' αἶνος· λόγος παροιμιώδης· αἶνος διαφέρει μύθου τῷ τὸν αἶνον μὴ πρὸς παῖδας ἀλλὰ ἄνδρας πεποιῆσθαι καὶ μὴ πρὸς ψυχαγωγίαν μόνον, ἀλλὰ καὶ παραίνεσιν ἔχει τινά Suid. s. v. Hesiod's lines about the hawk and nightingale are an αἶνος Op. 206.

1486. From Hes. Op. 667 ἐν τοῖς γὰρ τέλος ἐστὶν ὅμως ἀγαθῶν τε κακῶν τε, and Theognis 172 οὔ τι ἄτερ θεῶν γίγνεται ἀνθρώποις. οὔτ᾽ ἀγάθ᾽. οὔτε κακά. So Cleanthes, Hymn to Zeus, v. 15. But Pythagoras according to Iambl. 178 ἀπέδειξεν ὅτι οἱ θεοὶ τῶν κακῶν ἀναίτιοί εἰσιν. How he proved it is not told. There is a sentence in Seneca 'quidquid facimus mortale genus, quidquid patimur venit ex alto'.

1591. ἐπιλέγει· πρὸς τοῖς εἰρημένοις φησίν Suid. s. v.

1501. ἀλάστωρ. ἀλάστορας καὶ παλαμναίους ὀνομάζουσιν ὡς ἀλήστων τινῶν καὶ παλαιῶν μιασμάτων μνήμαις ἐπεξιόντας Plut. de Def. Or. 15.

1507. 'Whence, whence would he come? ἐστὶ τὸ μὲν πῶ Δώριον. τιθέμενον ἀντὶ τοῦ ποθεν Suid. s. v. πώμαλα.

1526. ἀνάξια. ἀπὸ τοῦ ἄγω ἄξω ἄξιος· ἀπὸ μεταφορᾶς τῶν σταθμῶν τὴν ἴσην ῥοπὴν ἐχόντων E. M. s. v.

1534. κὰδ᾽ δ᾽ ἄρ᾽ ἀπ᾽ οὐρανόθεν ψιάδας βάλεν αἱματοέσσας. σῆμα τιθείς Hes. Sc. 384.

1539. ἐν ἀρρήκτοισι δόμοισι of the vase in which Ἐλπὶς was confined Hes. Op. 96.

1544. ὁ ζῶντα βλάπτων μὴ νεκρόν με ὑρηνείτω Babr. 14.

1547. In prose ἔπαινος ἐπιτάφιος. ἰάψαι· ἐπιβαλεῖν Suid. s. v.

1550. πονήσει· 'perform its task of praise' as at v. 354.

1562. σὺ δὲ τρέφοντα τοῦτον τρέφεις Philost. Her. p. 12 B.

1566. ἀφάψαι· προσκολλῆσαι Suid. s. v. ἐκείνῳ ὁ δαίμων ἄτας προσῆψεν Dion. Hal. 7. in Suid., of Regulus.

1574. From Hes. Frag. p. 314 (D. Heyne) καὶ κτεάνων μοῖραν πόρεν.

1579. δαίμονες. Φύλακες θνητῶν ἀνθρώπων, οἵ ῥα φυλάσσουσίν τε δίκας καὶ σχέτλια ἔργα Hes. Op. 123; 252.

1586. Ἐρινύων ὑφαντὸν ἀμφίβληστρον Soph. Trach. 1051.

1585. Lit. 'being disputable in his rule' i. e. liable to have his claims to the throne disputed.

1588. εὕρετ' ἐν λιταῖς Æsch. Supp. 270.

1590. The following passage is ascribed to Hecatæus by Natal. Com. 9. 9, cited by Klausen, Hecat. Fr. p. 157; ὃν (Δία) αὐτοὶ (οἱ Λυκάονος παῖδες) καλέσαντες ἐπὶ ξένια, ἕνα τῶν ἐπιχωρίων παιδαρίων σφάττουσι καὶ τὰ σπλάγχνα συμμίξαντες παρέθεντο τῇ τραπέζῃ. τοῦτο δὲ Ζεὺς ἐγνωκὼς καὶ μυσαχθεὶς τὴν μὲν τράπεζαν ἀνέτρεψεν κτλ. If it is rightly ascribed to Hecatæus Æsch. imitated him in several particulars.

1591. The spurious verse was clearly made up of glosses. (πατὴρ v. 1590) Ἀτρεὺς (εὐθύμως v. 1592) προθύμως ἢ φίλως (τῷμῷ v. 1592) πατρί. So Enger and Schutz.

1594. ποδήρη are the joints attached to the feet i. e. the toes. χερῶν ἄκρους κτένας is in the style of Hesiod's πεντόζοιο 'the trunk with five branches' i. e. the hand.

1597. ἔσθειν occurs three times in Hes. Op. ἄσωτον. σωτός, E. M. s. v. ἔσωτος, in a transitive sense will mean 'saving' and ἄσωτος applied to things will be 'not saving' i. e: costing much, or, expensive.

1599. ὁ ἰατρὸς ἀπερᾶν ἀπηνάγκασεν Alciph. 3. 7. 2.

1601. ἐν ἀρᾶς ἔθηκε μέρει· συριττοίμην ὡς ἐκεῖνος Suid. s. v. ἀρᾶς.

1605, 6. ἐπεί μ' ἔτι τυτθὸν ἐόντα Hom. Il. 6. 222. παῖς ἔτ' ὢν ἐν σπαργάνοις Choëph. 755. παῖδ' ἔτ' οὖσα Soph. Trach. 557. τυτθὸν Hes. Op. 467. The notion that Atreus killed and cooked twelve children of all ages, and feasted a whole party of people with their flesh, is not only irresistibly ludicrous, but is absolutely without foundation in any tradition respecting this or any similar story.

1608. θυραῖος 'absent from the house at the time of the murder'. It means nothing more; perhaps only 'not in the room when he was killed'.

1612. Enger translates 'I do not think much of a coward's insolence'.

1613. σὺ δ' evidently follows ἐγὼ μὲν implied in σέβω.

1617. νέρτερος· κατώτερος Suid. s. v. who connects it with ἔνερθε νέρθε.

1618. ἄφρων δ' ὅς κ' ἐθέλῃ πρὸς κρείσσονας ἀντιφερίζειν Hes. Op. 208.

1626. ἀνδρὶ στρατηγῷ. 'a man and leader of men'.

1640. ζεύγλην δύσλοφον Theogn. 847.

1641. λιμὸν ἐχθρὸν συνοικητῆρα. δυσμενῆ θεόν Simonid. περὶ γυν. 101. ˙ τοῖςδε τὸν λιμὸν συνοικίζετε Alciph. 1. 20. 2.

1650. From Hes. Sc. 119 οὐκέτι τηλοῦ ὑσμίνη Hes. Sc. 119. λόχος˙ σύστημα ἐξ ἀνδρῶν ὀκτώ˙ οἱ δέ, ἐξ ἀνδρῶν ιβ'. οἱ δέ, ἐξ ις'. Suid. s. v.

1651. πρόκωπον ἔχων τὸ ξίφος˙ ἀντὶ τοῦ γυμνόν Suid. s. v.

1653. Chorus in Sept. 263 σὺν ἄλλοις πείσομαι τὸ μόρσιμον. to which Eteocles replies τοῦτ' ἀντ' ἐκείνου τοῦπος αἱροῦμαι σέθεν. τεφασκόπον σ' αἱροῦμαι Choëph. 551. In addition to the fact that εφ and αφ cannot be distinguished in the Medicean Ms., there is no doubt that αἱρούμεθα is right, were they ever so unlike.

1655. ἐξαμᾶ θέρος Pers. 222. The idea is taken from Hom. Il. 19. 222 αἶψά τε φυλόπιδος πέλεται κόρος ἀνθρώποισιν. ἧςτε πλείστην μὲν καλάμην χθονὶ χαλκὸς ἔχευεν. ἀμητὸς δ' ὀλίγιστος ἐπὴν κλίνῃσι τάλαντα Ζεύς. ἄμητος is commonly read, with an interpretation like that given in Liddell and Scott's Lexicon p. 667. But the meaning is: 'very soon doth a surfeit of fighting arise in men, for the swathe which the blade strews on the ground is thick, but the crop is scanty, when Zeus makes either scale to fall' i. e. there is plenty of straw in war, but little real good comes from war. Ulysses is the speaker, and he is always the interpreter of the poet's own sentiments.

1659. οὐδ' ἂν δεχοίμην ὥςτ' ἔχειν τιμὰς σέθεν Eum. 228.

1660. ὁπλὴ is a solid hoof like that of a horse; χηλὴ is a cloven hoof like that of a sheep, goat, or ox; or a foot with claws. See Scholl. on Hes. Op. 488 and Hes. Sc. 62.

1669. μιαίνων εὐσέβειαν Sept. 344.

1672. For the proper case with προτιμᾶν see Eum. 640, 739. The Œd. T. of Soph., and the Ion of Eur. also end with trochaic tetrameters.

EXPLANATION OF THE METRES.

Prologue: vv. 1—38, iambic trimeters.

According to Professor Weil iambic systems are composed of periods which correspond in number of lines, and consist of members also corresponding in number of lines, both periods (periodi) and members (cola, articuli) having for the most part a definite relation to one another in meaning. This symmetry arose, he says, from the correspondence of the choral odes; for tragedy was at first one chorus; and Æschylus who introduced the iambic and trochaic systems would naturally make them resemble the chorus in the responsion of their several periods. This theory has not yet been fairly tested, nor had Professor Weil discovered it when he edited his Agamemnon in the year 1858. His own account of it is to be found in his edition of the Choëphoræ page V foll., and its application to the Agamemnon in his Eumenides page 125 foll. The ordinary notation is adopted in the present edition, and no lacunæ are marked except in the dialogue. It is, therefore, inconvenient to give more than this one example of correspondence in the iambic systems. Thus, the Prologue consists of three periods:

6 lines; 14 (4, 8, 2); 14 (4, 8, 2); 4.

Introductory, intermediate, and concluding members (proodi, mesodi, epodi) are sometimes placed alone; so here the first 6 are a proodus and the last 4 an epodus. Interjections like φεῦ φεῦ count as a verse.

Parode: vv. 40—257. It consists of three parts,

(1) 10 anapæstic systems: 5 (6,6, 4½, 7½, 4½) = 28½ lines, relating to the past; the march from Argos, the sin of Paris, the certainty of vengeance: and 5 (10, 4, 3½,

$4\frac{1}{2}$, $6\frac{1}{2}$) $= 28\frac{1}{2}$ relating to the present, and the action of the drama. This requires Enger's text at vv. 42, 66.

(2) An ode consisting of strophe, antistrophe, epodus. The verses of the str. and antistr., vv. 104—139, are:

1. dactylic hexam. 2. dactylic pentam. 3. dactylic dim. 4. dactylic trim. 5. iambic dipodia, dactylic tetram. 6. dactylic dim. 7. dactylic hexam. 8. dactylic dim. 9. dactylic octam. 10. iambic dip., dactylic tetram. 11. dactylic trim. 12. dactylic hexam. 13. iambic dim. 14. dactylic tetram, ecbasis i. e. a base, in form, taking the place of a trochaic clausula. (All dact. orders are cat.)

The epodus vv. 140—159.

1. iambic dim. 2. iambic dip.; logaœdic order (dactyl, trochaic dip.) 3. dactylic tetram. 4. log. (base, dactyl, trochaic dip.) 5. dactylic tetram. 6. dactylic pentam. 7. anacrusis, base, dactylic trim. 8. dactylic hexam., dactylic dim. 9. dactylic hexam. 10. dactylic hexam., dactylic trim. 11, 12, 13. dactylic hexam. 14. dactylic dim. 15. dactylic tetram., ecbasis.

(3) An ode consisting of five strophes and antistrophes vv. 160—257.

Str. ά. 1. base, two trochaic dimeters cat. 2. trochaic dim. cat. 3. two trochaic dimeters cat. 4. dactylic pentam. 5. trochaic dim. cat.

Str. β'. 1. two trochaic dimeters cat. 2. trochaic dim. cat. 3. base, trochaic dim. cat. 4. cretic trim., trochaic dim. cat. 5. three trochaic orders: tripodia, dipodia, dim. cat.

Str. γ'. 1, 2. iambic dip., trochaic trip. 3. iambic dim., trochaic trip. 4. anacr., base, trochaic trip. 5. iambic dip., trochaic trip. cat., ecbasis. 6. iambic trip. 7, 8. log. (dactyl, trochaic dip.) 9. log. (choriambic hexapodia, dactyl, trochaic dip.)

Str. δ'. 1, 2. iambic dip., trochaic trip. 3. iambic dim. 4, 5. iambic dip., trochaic trip. 6. iambic trip., trochaic dip. 7. log. (iambus, trochaic trip. cat., dactyl, trochaic trip. cat., dactyl, trochaic dip.) 8. dactyl, trochaic dip.

Str. έ. 1. iambic dip., cretic dim. 2. iambic dip., trochaic trip. 3. iambic dip., cretic, trochaic trip., trochaic dip. 4. iambic dip., trochaic dim. cat. 5. iambic dip., cretic. 6. iambic dip., trochaic trip. 7. iambic dip., cretic trim. 8. log. (iambic dip., trochaic trip., dactyl, trochaic dip.)

First Episode: iambic trimeters, vv. 258—354.

First Stasimon, consisting of,

(1) three anapæstic systems: 2, 4½, 5. vv. 355—366:

(2) an ode of three strophes and antistrophes and an epodus, vv. 367—488.

Str. ά. 1, 2. anacr., base (or bacchius, or syncopated iambic dip.), troch. trip. 3. anacr., troch. dip., troch. trip. 4. iambic dip., cretic dim. 5, 6. iambic dip., cretic. 7, 8. anacr., base, cretic. 9, 10. anacr., base, trochaic trip. 11. iambic dip., cretic dim., trochaic trip. 12. log. (dactyl, trochaic dip. 13, 14. Pherecratic (base, dactylic dim.) 15. Glyconic (base, dactyl, cretic.), Pherecratic.

N.B. Cretic is only a convenient name for a trochaic dip. cat., and a trochaic trip. is called an Ithyphallic. In the same way a verse which consists of cretics having the arsis uniformly resolved is called Pœonic. This multiplication, however, of technical terms which are not absolutely necessary is unscientific, and bears the appearance of pedantry. Probably all metres could be fully explained by the use of about a score technical terms.

Str. β'. 1. iambic dip., cretic dim. 2. iambic dip., cretic, trochaic trip. 3. iambic hexapodia. 4. anacr., base, trochaic trip. cat. 5. iambic pentap. 6. iambic dip., trochaic trip. 7, 8. iambic dip., trochaic dim. cat. 9. iambic dip., cretic, trochaic trip. cat. 10. iambic dim. 11. iambic dip., cretic. 12. cretic, trochaic trip. 13, 14, 15. as in strophe ά.

Str. γ'. 1. iambic dip., cretic dim. 2. iambic dip., trochaic dim. cat. 3, 4. iambic dip., cretic. 5. trochaic order: three trochaic dimeters cat. 6 iambic order: two iambic dimeters. 7. log. (iambic dim., dactyl, trochaic trip. cat. dactyl, trochaic trip. cat., dactyl, trochaic trip. cat., dactyl, trochaic dip.) 8, 9, 10. as 13, 14, 15 in ά, β'.

Epodus. 1, 2. iambic dip., cretic. 3. trochaic dim. cat. 4, 5. iambic trim. 6. iambic dip., cretic. 7. iambic

dip., two trochaic dimeters cat. 8. iambic dip., cretic.
9. iambic dip., trochaic dim. cat. 10. iambic trim.
11. iambic dim. 12. iambic dip., trochaic dim. cat.
Second Episode: iambic trimeters vv. 489—680.
Second Stasimon: an ode of four strophes and antistrophes,
    vv. 681—782.
      Str. *d.* 1. two trochaic dimeters cat. 2. trochaic dim.
cat., cretic, trochaic dim. cat. 3. trochaic dim. cat.
4. log. (dactyl, trochee, cretic; dactyl, trochee, cretic;
dactyl, trochee, dactyl, choriambic dim., dactyl, trochee,
cretic; dactyl, trochee, cretic; choriambus, dactyl, trochee,
cretic; dactyl, trochaic trip.) 5. log. (base, dactyl, cre-
tic, dactyl, trochaic dip.) 6. Pherecratic (base $\widehat{\upsilon\upsilon}$;
dactylic dim.)
      Str. β′. 1. log. (iambus, dactyl, cretic, trochee, dac-
tylic dim.) 2. anacr., base, dactylic dim. 3, 4, 5. dactylic trim. 6, 7. trochaic dim. cat. 3. log. (base, dactyl,
cretic; trochee, dactylic dim.)
      Str. γ′. 1. iambic dip., trochaic dip., three trochaic
tripodias cat.; trochaic dip., trochaic trip. 2. dactyl,
trochaic trip. cat. 3. log. (base, dactyl, cretic; choriambic dim.; dactyl, trochaic trip. cat.; choriambic trim.,
dactylic dim.) 4. anacr., base, dactylic dim., (monosyllabic
catalexis). 5. pherecratic (base, dactylic dim.)
      Str. δ′. 1. iambic dip., cretic trim., trochaic dim. cat.
2. log. (anacr., base, dactyl, trochaic dim. cat.) 3. iambic
dip. 4. Cretic trim. 5. log. (trochaic dip., cretic, dactyl,
trochaic dip.) 6. dactyl, trochaic dip.
      N.B. In verse 4 the cretic order is either catalectic, or
      has the last syllable common.
Third Episode: vv. 783—974. (1) six anapæstic systems vv.
    783—809. (2) iambic trimeters vv. 810—974.
Third Stasimon: an ode of two strophes and antistrophes vv.
    975—1034.
      Str. *d.* 1, 2. trochaic dim. cat. 3. trochaic dip.,
trochaic trip. 4. dactylic pentam. 5, 6, trochaic dim.
cat. 7. cretic dim., trochaic dim. cat. 8. iambic trim.
9. cretic dim., trochaic dim. cat. 10. trochaic dim. cat.
      Str. β′. 1 pæonic trim. 2. ionic a minore (= anacr.
$\widehat{\upsilon\upsilon}$ and base $\div$ —), two dactylic trimeters cat. 3. log.
(dactyl, choriambic dim., dactyl, trochaic dip.) 4, 5, 6,

7, 8, 9. trochaic dim. cat.   10. base, dactylic heptam.
11. trochaic dim. cat.

Fourth Episode: vv. 1035—1330.   (1) iambic trimeters vv.
1035—1071.   (2) Commatica: seven strophes and antistrophes, vv. 1072—1177.

Str. *ά*. 1, 2. bacchiac dim.

Str. *β'*. 1. bacchiac dim.   2. bacchius, dochmius.
3. iambic trim.

Str. *γ'*. 1. dochmiac dim.   2. cretic, dochmius.   3. iambic trim.

Str. *δ'*. 1. iambic dip., dochmius.   2. trochaic dim. cat.
3. iambic trim.   4. dochmius, cretic tetram.

Str. *έ*. 1. dochmiac dim.   2. iambic dim. cat.   3. iambic trim.   4. iambic dip., dochmius.   5. dochmius, cretic
dim. Mesostrophe *ά*: 1, 2. iambic trim.   3, 4. dochmiac
dim.   5. dochmius, cretic dim., dochmius.

Str. *ϛ'*. 1. iambic dim. cat., dochmius.   2. dochmiac
dim.   3, 4. iambic trim. Mesostrophe *β'*: 1. dochmiac
trim.   2. cretic, dochmius.   3. dochmius, cretic dim.
4. dochmiac trim.

Str. *ζ'*. 1, 2. iambic trip., dochmius.   3. dochmiac
trim.   4, 5. iambic trim. Mesostrophe *γ'*: 1. dochmiac
dim.   2. iambic dim.   3. dochmiac dim.   4. dochmius,
cretic dim.   5. dochmius.

(3) vv. 1178—1330, iambic trimeters, except v. 1307 φεῦ φεῦ
an iambus. and vv. 1214. 1256, 1315 iambic dipodias.

Three anapæstic systems, vv. 1331—1342, occupy the place
of the Fourth Stasimon.

Fifth Episode: vv. 1343—1447, iambic trimeters, except vv.
1344, 6, 7, trochaic tetram. cat., and a strophe and antistrophe vv. 1407—1411; 1426—1430:
v. 1. dochmius.   2. iambic dim.   3, 4. dochmiac dim.
5. iambic trip. dochmius.   6. pherecratic (base, dactylic dim.)

Commatica: five strophes and antistrophes alternating with
ten anapæstic systems, vv. 1448—1577.

Str. *ά*. 1. log. (dactyl, cretic, dactyl, cretic, pherecratic.)   2. iambic dip., trochaic trip.   3. log. (dactylic
dim., trochaic dip.)   4. trochaic dim. cat.   5. cretic tetram.,
trochaic dim. cat.

Str. *β'*. 1. log. (dactylic trim., trochaic dip.)   2. log.
(dactyl, trochaic dip.)   3. anacr., base, trochaic trip.

Str. γ'. 1. dactylic trim. with monosyllabic catalexis. 2. log. (dactylic dim., trochaic dip.) 3. log. (anacr., dactyl, trochaic dip., pherecratic). 4, 5. two iambic dimeters. 6. iambic trim. cat. 7. log. (iambus, dactyl, trochaic dip.)

Str. δ'. 1. anacr., two bases, dactyl, cretic. 2. ionic a minore, cretic. 3. log. (dactylic dim., trochaic dip.)

Str. ε. 1. iambic dip., trochaic trip. 2. log. (dactyl, trochaic dip.) 3. iambic dip., trochaic trip. 4. iambic dip., trochaic dim. cat. 5. iambic dip., trochaic trip. 5. iambic trim. 7. anacr., base, trochaic trip.

Exode: vv. 1578—1673,

vv. 1578—1648, iambic trimeters: vv. 1649—1673 trochaic trimeters catalectic.

ADDITIONS.

V. 893, Commentary. The experiments of Professor Burmeister have proved that this is incorrect. Breathing is the true cause of the sound made by insects, which is in reality a whistle. Insects hum after their wings are cut off, but not when the air-holes of the thorax are closed up. Again, the common house-fly, for instance, does not always hum during its flight.

V. 1110. 'And then he adjusted it very carefully in his grasp, and made two or three experimental picks with it in the air'. The murderer in 'Uncle Silas' by J. S. Le Fanu, Vol. III. p. 302.

Having at length, August 7 th. 1868, obtained a copy of Canter's edition, after the final impression of all these sheets except the last, I am enabled to give a short description of that rare book. It is in 32mo., 3 inches broad by 4¼ long, and about ¾ of an inch thick. It contains 368 pages. The critical notes to the seven plays take up 12¼ of these little pages. Here is a translation of the Title-page: "The Seven Tragedies of Æschylus. In which besides the removal of an infinite number of blemishes, the structure of the odes, which was hitherto unknown, is now first explained; by William Canter of Utrecht. Published at Antwerp, from the press of Christopher Plantinus. 1580." It is dedicated in Greek to Peter Victorius, whose text Canter adopts without inserting his own corrections. At the end we have the Approbatio of 'Thomas Gozeus a Bellomonte, Professor of Theology and Inspector of Books': "I have read through a Sophocles and Æschylus and the observations made upon them by William

Canter, and have found nothing objectionable. Done at Louvain, April 1, 1570."

Canter prefaces his critical notes to the Choephoræ as follows: "Quemadmodum hæc tragœdia principio caret, sic etiam iis quæ insuper præponi debent, destituitur: quorum nos utrique, quantum poterimus adferemus remedii. Hæc igitur præponenda sunt.

'Υπόθεσις τῆς τοῦ Αἰσχύλου Τραγῳδίας, ἣ ἐπιγράφεται χοηφόροι. 'Η μὲν σκηνὴ τοῦ δράματος ἐν "Αργει ὑπόκειται· ὁ δὲ χορὸς ἐκ παρθένων ἐντοπίων συνέστηκεν, αἳ τὰς χοὰς πρὸς τὸν Ἀγαμέμνονος τάφον κομίζουσιν. ἡ δ' ὑπόθεσις, Ὀρέστης ἐκ φυγῆς ἐπανιών, καὶ τήν τε Κλυταιμνήστραν ἅμα καὶ τὸν Αἴγισθον κτείνων."

This Argument, it will be observed, is 'about four lines' as I have supposed above. παρθένων is wrong: it should be γυναικῶν. ἐντοπίων is right; as I have proved at p. XII of my Choephoræ, independently of Canter. With reference to the lacuna in the Prologue of the Choephoræ he says: "Jam quod ad principium tragœdiæ pertinet, id nobis *fere totum* conservavit in Ranis Aristophanes."

THE END.